LABOUR MOBILITY AND RURAL SOCIETY

Of Related Interest

ECONOMIC MOBILITY AND POVERTY DYNAMICS IN DEVELOPING
COUNTRIES
Edited by Bob Baulch and John Hoddinott

MEN AT WORK
Labour, Masculinities, Development
edited by Cecile Jackson

THE WORKERS' STATE MEETS THE MARKET
Labour in China's Transition
edited by Sarah Cook and Margaret Maurer-Fazio

DEVELOPMENT AND THE RURAL–URBAN DIVIDE
edited by John Harriss and Mick Moore

BEYOND URBAN BIAS
edited by Ashutosh Varshney

LABOUR MOBILITY AND RURAL SOCIETY

Editors

Arjan de Haan
and Ben Rogaly

LONDON AND NEW YORK

This group of studies first appeared in a Special Issue on 'Labour Mobility and Rural Society' of *The Journal of Development Studies* (ISSN 0022-0388) 38/5 (June 2002)

First published 2002 by
FRANK CASS PUBLISHERS

Published 2016 by Routledge
2 Park Square, Milton Park, Abingdon, Oxon OX14 4RN
605 Third Avenue, New York, NY 10017

Routledge is an imprint of the Taylor & Francis Group, an informa business

British Library Cataloguing in Publication Data

Labour mobility and rural society
1.Migration, Internal – Social aspects – Asia 2.Migration, Internal – Social aspects – Africa 3.Labour mobility – Asia 4.Labor mobility – Africa 5.Asia – Rural conditions 6.Africa – Rural conditions
I.Haan, Arjan de II.Rogaly, Ben III.Journal of development studies
307.2´12´095

Library of Congress Cataloging in Publication Data

Labour mobility and rural society / edited by Arjan de Haan and Ben Rogaly.
p. cm.
includes bibliographical references and index.
1. Migration, Internal –Developing countries–Case studies. 2. Labor mobility–Developing countries–Case studies. 3. Developing countries–Rural conditions–Case studies. I. Haan, Arjan de. II. Rogaly, Ben.
HB2160 .L32 2002
331.12´7–dc21
                2002005008

ISBN 13: 978-0-714-65334-1 (hbk)

This volume is dedicated to the memory of Greet and Remko de Haan

Contents

Introduction:
Migrant Workers and Their Role in Rural Change

ARJAN DE HAAN and BEN ROGALY

There is no dearth of literature on migration in and from Asia and Africa. Yet the literature insufficiently accounts for one of the most important forms of population mobility: migration of rural people for various forms of work elsewhere, often returning to the place they started from. Much migratory work, particularly for poorer migrants, is seasonal, temporary, and remains within rural areas. Employment in areas of origin may be scarce or even unavailable; yet the daily earnings for migrants at the destination may be only marginally higher. Migrants undertake this work to maintain or slightly improve their situation at home.

Too little is known about this type of migration, its contribution to the livelihoods of migrants and their households, and how it interacts with wider changes in rural societies. This collection provides a set of studies, based on recent empirical research, dealing with these themes, from South and South-east Asia (India, Indonesia) and Africa (Burkina Faso, Mali, Kenya, Lesotho). The contributions provide detailed analyses of labour migration as a social process, showing how it is structured by gender, class and ethnicity, and how migration in turn affects social relations and structures. It moves away from seeing migrants as helpless victims, and describes migration as a highly dynamic process. This view remains rooted in an understanding of the political economy of rural society, of the way in which migration is shaped by wider forces of economic change or development, and the way this complexity is influenced (intentionally or otherwise) by public policy.

The collection thus bridges a gap between two kinds of studies. On the one hand, studies of rural change tend to assume, sometimes driven by data availability, static populations, or ignore population movements and

This introduction draws on the authors' own research on the topic. Sections III and IV on migration as a social process and the political economy of labour mobility were first drafted by Rogaly based on work-in-progress with colleagues (for details of this ongoing research project, see Rogaly, Coppard, Rafique, Rana, Sengupta and Biswas, this collection; Rogaly, Biswas, Coppard, Rafique, Rana and Sengupta [2001]).

remittances. On the other hand, migration studies have paid too little attention to the interaction of migratory movements with broader changes in the areas of origin, in effect isolating migration as an exceptional phenomenon. In both cases, there is a tendency to see migration as a disjuncture. In contrast, the contributions to this collection taken together show this type of employment migration to be a central feature of most, if not all, rural societies – even though its role is context-specific and changes over time. The contributors examine the ways in which migration is structured by, and in turn structures, societal norms and relations.

The analyses provide detailed descriptions of a variety of migration streams. The first two are about the highly unpredictable environment of the Sahel, where labour mobility has historically been a predominant way of managing risk. But even within this environment, patterns of mobility are complex: Hampshire's study focuses on the mobility of young men in and out of agro-pastoral production; de Haan *et al.* show contrasting pictures of differently endowed areas, the role of various forms of seasonal migrations, and the unique pattern of migration to small plantations in Ivory Coast that villagers from Mali have cultivated for a number of decades.

Three studies focus on India. For western India, Mosse *et al.* analyse the seasonal labour migration among the Bhil community, mainly to urban areas, and differentiation within this, with slightly less poor migrants developing different patterns of migration. The subject of the study by Rogaly *et al.* is seasonal migration within rural areas of eastern India, involving a comparison of four streams with very different social compositions converging on the same destination for the same kind of work. Whereas these two contributions describe contemporary migration streams, de Haan's essay about Bihar, one of India's poorest states, suggests that labour mobility has been a common feature of rural South Asia for centuries, and has significantly influenced the social and economic structures of many areas.

While the analysis in all the contributions is gendered, describing the differences between the ratios of men and women involved in migration in different contexts and analysing how gender relations influence migration patterns and are changed by it, Elmhirst focuses explicitly on gender relations, on relatively recent female labour migration to Greater Jakarta and the way gender ideologies changed when migration became a more established and accepted strategy. The effect of predominantly male migration, and particularly return migration, on household power relations and bargaining, are explored in an analysis by Francis based on work in Lesotho and western Kenya.

The rest of this introduction briefly alludes to the central focus running through the collection, of the social structuration of migration and its interaction with the wider political economy, indicating how these are developed in the individual studies. After a short section on the quantitative importance of migration, we describe central issues relating to the link between migration, rural change and poverty. Section III then describes how and why employment migration should be seen as a social as well as an economic process and cannot be reduced to either one or the other, and the ways in which the pattern of migration is influenced by gender ideologies and vice versa. This is followed by a description of how these social factors interact with wider political and economic changes. The last section discusses public policies and their intended and actual outcomes for migrants and potential migrants.

I. DOES MIGRATION REALLY MATTER?

The contributions in this collection present a clear indication of the role migration can and does play in rural life. Although this is true of people from all social classes, the focus here is on manual wage workers, who are usually among the poorest in rural societies. In tribal districts in Gujarat, India, over 80 per cent of households had at least one member migrating for longer or shorter periods. Bihar in India has been known for its large numbers of out-migrants; the analysis in this collection indicates that in districts in western Bihar at the *beginning of this century* half the households may have depended on migrant income. Among the Fulani in northern Burkina Faso, sampled by Hampshire in 1996, 73 per cent of individuals were involved in some form of migration lasting at least two weeks. And 12 of the 16 households in Zaradougou in the Sudano-Sahelian cotton zone derive a large part of their income from and spend much of their active labour time on their cocoa and coffee farms in Ivory Coast.

Of course, such findings cannot be generalised across all rural societies. The research on sustainable livelihoods, summarised in the contribution by de Haan *et al.*, emphasises (though does not fully explain) differences in the incidence and effects of migration between the research sites in Mali and Ethiopia – where a past history of forced mobility may have reduced migration – and also between two sites in Bangladesh. Neither can the findings in India be generalised for the whole country. Even within the same region of a country there is diversity in terms of the propensity to migrate [*Srivastava, 1999; Racine, 1997*].

Neither are such patterns static. The study in Lesotho and western Kenya by Francis focuses on the effects of reducing migration (or increasing return migration); crises and adjustment in Africa have led to reduced migration opportunities over the last decade or two. The essay by Elmhirst on female migration to Great Jakarta describes rapid changes, from the newly emerging opportunities typical of the economic miracle in south-east Asia, until the sudden collapse of these opportunities in the crisis of 1997–98. And the study on Bihar in India suggests long-term trends, possibly of declining incidences of migration, and how the composition of migration may have changed over a period of one century.

Nevertheless, the collection as a whole indicates that migration is much more common than is often suggested. Within the literature on rural or agricultural development, more often than not the role of migration is ignored [de Haan, 1999]. Partly as a result of neglecting how communities derive their income from various sources, migration is seen as a disjuncture. The migration literature has tended to focus on the kinds of mobility that represent transitions, particularly in the context of urbanisation, articulated in the famous Harris-Todaro model [1970]. Further, in studies that do incorporate migration, the indicators used may do insufficient justice to the numbers of migrants – most notably in macro-studies using net-migration as measure (an example is discussed in the study on Bihar). Policies are aimed to reduce out-migration, and development strategies are often aimed at reducing migration pressures. However, such attempts fail to understand how migration can be a critical element in the livelihoods of households and communities, as Mosse et al. and Rogaly et al. argue in this volume.

Thus, the importance of migration is context specific, and the contributions in this collection provide cases of how migration matters in particular places at particular points of time. This does suggest, however, that a priori studies and policies need to start from an assumption of population mobility. As a rule, in most societies people are mobile, both rich and poor. In this collection we focus on labour migration, by manual workers, who are generally poor. Social stratification is a crucial dimension of migration, as the next section suggests.

II. MIGRATION, RURAL CHANGE AND POVERTY

The migration literature, unsurprisingly, indicates that relationships between migration and rural development are complex and context-specific. Macro-level studies suggest there is some consensus that migrants tend to help to increase welfare: migrants often contribute much to the economy of the host society, and have high rates of labour force participation. But there is little evidence that migration helps to reduce economic inequalities between areas of origin and of destination. For example, migration from Burkina Faso to Côte d'Ivoire during the 1950s and 1960s seems not to have reversed increasing inequality [Cordell et al., 1996].

Research on the effects of migration on areas of origin is relatively scarce, but generally it shows that, at the macro-level, remittances contribute relatively little, and out-migration usually does not radically transform poor areas. Many studies emphasise that migration may create dependency rather than generate development. However, such effects are context-dependent, as research on the contrasting consequences of (international) migration from two Punjabi districts, Jullundur in India and Mirpur in Pakistan showed [*Ballard, 1983*].

As access to opportunities is not equally distributed, migration may enhance inequality. Even if remittances are relatively less important for the rich, as indicated for example by research in Kenya [*Knowles and Anker, 1981*], they might still contribute to increasing inequality. A 1970s study of migration out of a large sample of villages across India [*Connell et al., 1976*] emphasised that better-off migrants are 'pulled' towards better job prospects, while the poor are 'pushed': '"push" and "pull" migration are twin children of inequality in the same sort of village; but they are also sources of new inequality' [*Lipton, 1980*]. Research in Pakistan [*Adams,1994*], Bangladesh [*Greeley, 1999*], and the Philippines [*Rodriguez, 1998*] suggests that in comparison international migration is more likely to increase inequality than internal migration; what this indicates is not that we can generalise about such differences, but that different forms of migration are likely to have different effects.

Even when the definition of migration is narrowed down to a specific type, as in the contributions to this issue, there can be no simple generalisations. Also, the micro-views presented do not always square with macro-level studies as quoted above, partly because returns are often hidden from macro analyses, as they may go straight into paying-off debts, or be spent during annual festivals. The studies show that migration reduces the uncertainty of a family income, provides investment funds, and contributes to livelihoods for those with small plots. The study on Bihar indicates that this has been the case for generations. Although poor households have less access to opportunities, income from migration may form a *more* important part of their income than that of the better-off. Rural-to-rural migration for wage work can help reduce poverty and insecurity, but the case of the migration from Mali to the small plantations in Côte d'Ivoire suggests that it can increase inequality too. Out-migration may negatively effect agricultural production, particularly, perhaps, in the much less densely populated areas such as West Africa; at the same time, migration allows the straddling of agricultural zones forming crucial livelihood strategies during lean seasons.

Also, the analyses emphasise that material gains are only a part of what migrants obtain and bring back, and only one of the reasons – though usually the main one – why people leave. Education is often a very common motive for migration, but many labour migrants come back with some newly acquired skills as well. Sometimes these amount to no more than speaking a little in a foreign language, for instance migrants from Mali who picked up a few words of French in cities in Côte d'Ivoire. Sometimes practical skills help returned migrants to set up trading or other activities and, occasionally, to improve productivity in agriculture. Migrants tend to invest in education, and help to build or teach in schools, through remittances or after their return. Like the material returns from migration, these educational gains may also increase differentiation and inequality, as was shown in Western Kenya [*Francis and Hoddinott, 1993*].

The contributions in this collection suggest various ways in which rural society changes under the impact of migration. This may involve changes in ideologies of work (see Elmhirst, this collection) or changes in class relations in migrant source areas (see Rogaly *et al.*, this collection). In other cases, as shown in the Mali and Burkina Faso studies, the changes that migration engenders are less striking, and migration is more integrated into existing household strategies and ideologies. In any case, migration is not just an economic process, and social analysis is important in understanding and explaining migration patterns, as discussed in the next section.

III. MIGRATION AS A SOCIAL PROCESS

The analyses in this collection indicate that in order to understand the perspectives of migrants on employment migration, migration needs to be seen as a social as well as an economic process. The specific way in which migration is arranged and what it means to particular people is bound up with social identities. Who the migrant thinks she or he is affects the type of migration – for example, as a younger or older person, as a woman or a man, a member of a particular ethnic group or social class. This is shown in the papers on Burkina Faso and Mali, where different groups have different migration patterns.

However, these are not fixed positions. They vary across both space and time, and are contested. Indeed migration is one way in which boundaries around social identities may be affirmed, broken down or otherwise changed, including, but not always, through the conscious agency of migrants. Rogaly *et al.'s* analysis provides an example of the countering of the arguments of an older man and woman about whether a young woman with a child should migrate for work. Through migrating, the woman may be asserting different ideas about what is proper work for her. Identity in this case is closely bound up with ideologies of work, related to gender, age and position in a family hierarchy. It is not merely a matter of following a script – but finding possibilities to change the rules even in incremental ways, including through migration.

While the migration of young women in Mali indicates accepted patterns of migration by women before they marry, Elmhirst's study provides ample evidence on changing gendered ideologies of work due to the action of young women seeking factory work away from home. The contribution by de Haan *et al.* describes how young women negotiate with their families over migration to cities, which is as much to experience city lives as for its economic returns. As Kapadia [*1999*] has shown in south India, and Sen [*1999*] in her historical study of labour in colonial Bengal, ideologies of work may change with the changing rewards to that work and how they are valued by people in positions of power in a household. Men may change the way they view their daughters or wives being employed in factory work if it means an increase in income.

The ways in which ideologies are deployed in negotiations and contests over who migrates and who does not is related to the way the household is organised. The contributions in this collection include a broad range of archetypal households, varying in structure and size within diverse social contexts. Ideas about the appropriateness, or otherwise, of migration by a particular household member, relate in part to what each member of the household – and indeed other connected kin outside that household – consider a proper relation to the labour market for that person. In the Indian context, a young woman with a child, in a household where she is the only earner, will be differently located in contests over migration decisions to a young woman with a child living with an earning spouse and earning parents-in-law. Differences in the overall size of a household are also likely to be important where there may be own account production, including livestock rearing, or homemaking work to be managed in the absence of the migrant.

The meaning of migration to different individuals within a household varies according to age as well as sex. Some young men view migration as a means of belonging to their peer group – proving that they can do it. Migration can also be a temporary escape out of the pressure of family responsibilities, a period of roaming around between leaving the parental household and setting up one's own. The analysis of Indonesia suggests that migration is a way of rebelling and demonstrating independence from parents, and the possibility was always there in the migration of young men from the tightly structured households in Mali.

Migration may also be an expression of collective identity. The examples of the Fulaani in the study by Hampshire and of Muslim workers in West Bengal in Rogaly *et al.*'s analysis provide detailed examples. In the latter case, Muslim men migrants maintain their identities as men, for example insisting on being paid in cooked food as well as cash – food which is cooked by women in employer households. In contrast, the Santal migrants working on the same fields migrate as whole family units and bring cooking utensils with them. Indeed many migrants in West Bengal 'choose' their employer on the basis of religious identity, and in several cases potential migrants refused to work for people of another religion.

The exposure to 'other' people, people who are foreign to the experience of living in migrants' source areas, can also reinforce a strong sense of identity among migrant workers. This is abundantly true in the UK, for example, among first-generation migrants from South Asia. The experience of living in a predominantly white British environment changes people's ideas of who they are. While identities based on race and country of origin may be heightened, others, based perhaps on locality of origin, for example, are likely to diminish [*Gardner, 1995*]. In Elmhirst's study a group of elders is found to have formed in the destination area to remind young women migrants of their duties and responsibilities as daughters of their area of origin. However, as Rogaly *et al.* show, they may not need reminding – the experience of living 'abroad' is enough to reinforce a sense of belonging to 'home'.

To understand migration from the perspective of migrants is therefore to understand how it fits into migrants' social world-view, and how this changes as a result of migration. The social world of the place of origin influences migration, but is also influenced by it. Rogaly *et al.* show how migrants can deploy collective social identities in labour market negotiations – we know who we are and will not compromise that, say, by accepting food in a way which we find an insult to our religion. The way identities are deployed in finding employment under particular terms and conditions feeds back into the social world of the place of origin, through the interaction that migrants, whether temporary or longer term, maintain with people in that place. This in turn can influence the future deployment of identities by migrants from that place and thus the pattern of future migration.

The ways in which migrants go about finding employment often revolve around social networks, based on some commonality, for example, on ethnicity or gender or place of origin, or a combination of these and others. The study on Mali shows that migration of young women occurs within large extended kinship networks, in turn reinforcing those, and the contribution on Indonesia shows how these networks rapidly evolve after initial migration by young women. Social networks are needed not only for information about where work is available, where other people from the same place are living and working, and on the likely terms and conditions that are to be found, but also in providing support in the process of migration. The trading of favours can be important as well. Networks are not limited to issues of identity but also include the construction of 'contacts' and of expectations of reciprocal action.

Networks may of course be regressive – they may be experienced as binds that tie, ways in which people back home can keep an eye on one and enforce conformity. Migration can be undertaken intentionally to break out of boundaries of expected and accepted behaviour as in the case of many women migrants (see Elmhirst, and Rogaly *et al.*, this volume). However, knowing the right people is likely to enable people to take more control over whether and how to migrate. Networks are particularly important for gang leaders (*sardars*) in the study by Rogaly *et al.* Knowing potential employers, and building and maintaining reputations for work through regular interaction, provide *sardars* with the opportunity to make extra money in addition to the wage. This also comes through reaching deals on transport costs with the operators of buses, for example, with whom networks have been developed.

Networks clearly influence the pattern and extent of migration from particular places [cf. *de Haan and Rogaly, 1996*]. Except to the most abstract economists, this is hardly surprising. What is important for social analysis, however, is to be able to identify which networks are important in specific contexts, how they influence patterns of migration, and how this in turn feeds back on the networks. Several of the contributions to this volume attempt to do this, for example in the papers on Mali and Indonesia.

Migration is thus bound up with contests and negotiations over one's place in society. For some, decisions of when to migrate and for which kinds of work reflect ascribed identities – not every act is an act of resistance. Moreover, migrants make use of social resources and networks – who they know – to access or avoid particular types of work and/or migration destinations. Collective identities contribute to the meanings of migration for individual migrants – as Rogaly *et al.* suggest, they may be deployed positively to decrease the loss of dignity in hiring out for wage work in a 'foreign' place. Migration also gives rise to changes in ideologies and identities and can increase the social resources at migrants' disposal. As the next section suggests, none of this changes the bigger picture within which migrant wage workers operate and which is bounded by the instrumental action of larger more powerful forces – but it provides a way of understanding migrant workers' actions within this.

IV. A POLITICAL ECONOMY OF LABOUR MOBILITY

Our discussion of migration as a social process emphasised the agency of migrant workers – the ways in which migrants themselves use their identities, as well as their networks, to create a degree of choice as regards who they would work for and on what terms. The structures in which people are located were referred to only in terms of ideologies of work – of what particular people should be and do according to ascribed identities and local forms of hegemonic power in source areas. Although we stress the capacity of migration to change social relations back at the source area, this is partly to balance an overdetermined understanding of structure. None of the contributors to this collection neglect the way in which political economy – local as well as at regional, national and international levels – is able to define the broader field within which migrant work is done.

Structuralist political economy has interpreted the patterns and extent of migration as determined by the actions of large-scale capital (financial and physical). Capital requires labour; it also sheds labour, as the seminal work on western India by Breman [*1985, 1994*] has shown, and as described in this collection in the study by Francis for eastern and southern Africa, and alluded to in the description of migration to Côte d'Ivoire where the unusually welcoming immigration policies are gradually being reversed. Employers hire a mixture of migrants and local labourers in order to create divisions of the workforce and the conditions for low-wage production. Ideology also operates in this bigger picture. The ways in which workers are hired – or immigration policies formulated or implemented – are also related to complex sets of motivations on the part of the owners of capital. These are likely to be ideological rather than for pecuniary gain alone, and may include desires to influence the social mix (or lack of it) in an area, to counter or to reinforce notions of who belongs where.

The power of capital relative to labour is not, however, absolute. Nor is it fixed. It changes over time and not necessarily in the same direction. It also varies across space. In Western Europe, for example, the second half of the twentieth century was the peak period for labour power in relation to capital, but by the turn of the century unskilled labour lost some of its bargaining power. Wage workers have less power than large-scale capital – but in many of the contexts discussed in this collection, the story is complex. Within western Africa (see the studies on Mali and Burkina Faso), the influence of capitalist forces seem much more limited than in eastern and southern Africa, and South and South-east Asia. In all contexts, migrant wage workers are often not proletarians, but 'polybians' (Kearney [*1996*] cited in Harriss [*2000*]): their multiple economic activities include the control of land and other physical and/or natural capital from which part of their livelihood is gained. Some are at certain times of year also employers of labour. Most of the employers of migrant labour in the study by Rogaly *et al.* are smallholders, themselves subject to relations with larger-scale capitalists in the form of rice traders, millers and fertiliser dealers.

In this collection we explicitly leave open the possibility that migration can change the nature of class relations in source areas, in favour of migrant workers [*Rogaly, 1998; Srivastava, 1999*]. Out-migration tightens local labour markets, with an increase in the relative market power of people hiring out labour in that locality. This may influence wages upward. The seasonal nature of migration and local production also matters. Migration may also influence the terms which employers and workers use to address each other. These shifts in language are likely to be highly significant for the livelihoods of workers in terms of the meanings of the work people do and their sense of themselves.

Much depends on the way in which different interest groups play their hand. Do employers unite or even act collusively to determine events from the demand side? Or are they divided atomistic individuals or clusters in intense competition with each other? If the latter is the case employers may use the labour market to harm their rival employers, perhaps, if they have the power, by buying up all available local labour (see Rogaly *et al.*). The struggle with their neighbours, with people of similar class background, may be of more immediate salience than the struggle between classes.

Relations among migrant wage workers (and between migrant workers and local workers) are also contingent. If local workers are relatively disempowered and there are ethnic, linguistic or other differences which can be exploited between local and migrant workers or between different groups of migrants, the workers may be more easily exploited. On the other hand, associations of migrant workers, or strong local unions may constrain the power of employers, and an accommodation may have to be reached to avoid local workers being undercut by migrants.

All this is a matter for empirical investigation rather than a priori assumptions. It is also subject to change. One of the agendas of this collection is to report on the extent to which migration has determined changes in the political economy of migrants' areas of origin. This is not a new subject – Lenin [*1964*] wrote on late nineteenth-century seasonal migration for agricultural work in Russia that, despite the very great hardships involved, returning migrants were conscious of a 'different order of things' [*1964: 240–54*]). This would, he implied, enable them to demand progressive change in their own interests. Part of a political economy of migration is understanding in which contexts migration implies a move away from oppressive social relations towards a greater degree of choice for migrants about whom to work for. Just as migration is often economically coerced by debt (see Mosse *et al.*), in some situations remittances may be used to buy one's way out of debt.

V. WHAT ROLE POLICIES?

The last section emphasised the interests and power struggles that are inherent in migration processes. Obviously, these inform public policies, and the way they in turn influence outcomes for migrants and potential migrants. Much migration literature is silent about the kinds of policies that may matter. This is no coincidence because for policy-makers migration tends to be an uncomfortable area. Few policies relate directly to migration, particularly at the national level: positive examples include employment bureaux in Bangladesh, the Ministry for Malians abroad, the West Africa ECOWAS protocol on the free movement of people, and labour-export agencies to manage and control recruitment, train potential migrants, explore new labour markets, and provide bilateral agreements on behalf of workers.

Studies and policies tend to assume immobile populations. Migration is seen as a disjuncture, and as undesirable. National policy-makers try to control cross-border migration. However, within national boundaries, policies often aim to restrict migration as well: governments often want to slow down or reverse rural–urban migration; policies in Zimbabwe after independence encouraged urban workers to choose between rural and urban areas; the Department of Land Affairs in the Northwest Province of South Africa insisted that applicants for land make a full-time commitment to the enterprise – despite land owners' dependence on multiple sources of livelihood [*Francis, 1999*]. China established strict controls, officially to ensure that peasants would not experience the effects of capitalism and flood into the cities; extreme controls have been abolished, but China still fears its 'floating population'. After periods of extreme forms of control on population mobility, Ethiopia's government still aims to limit urbanisation, and settle its nomadic population. In the literature, discussions of policies that can reduce 'migration pressures', including trade, investment and development aid, are common. Employment programmes in India, for example, often aim to prevent migration of labour.

The introduction to this collection is not the right place to analyse such policies, their pros and cons, but it is important to point out that many such policies affect the livelihoods of migrants, particularly those that do not have the means to pay bribes, illustrated for example in the huge disparities in well-being between rural and (registered) urban Chinese populations. Moreover, many policies that are not directly related to control over population movements affect migrants as well. The establishment of borders may crucially affect opportunities for migrants, as in the case of the India–Bangladesh border, or borders in West Africa. In a less direct way, agricultural policies, such as the West African *gestion de terroir* are explicit in the conceptualisation of the space of livelihoods, as being limited to a particular area, ignoring the mobility that is crucial for the livelihoods of many rural people.

The contributions in this collection show how important migration can be for the survival of poor households. Policies to restrict migration often do more harm than good. Policies should be realistic about the possibilities of providing alternatives to migration, of which patterns have often been long established, and been central to livelihoods, though at the same time exploitative, and shaped identities. The study by Mosse *et al.* suggests ways of supporting the contribution of migration to the livelihoods of poor Bhil farming communities, and reducing the cost of migration. These include de-linking migration from the vicious debt-cycle through savings and credit programmes, improving the bargaining power of migrants in relation to recruiting agents, enhancing migrant workers' awareness of labour legislation and rights, and also practical measures to improve conditions of employment, arrangements for child care, health and hygiene, and education. In a similar vein, Rogaly *et al.* examine ways in which combinations of actors, including agencies of the state and trade unions might realistically be persuaded to contribute to the security of migrants on the journey, and to health facilities and other protective services at destination area work-places.

The contributions to this collection indicate that there are no simple solutions. The existence of migration is bound up with the interplay of economic interests, as well as perceptions of who has the right of abode, who belongs and who does not. At the same time, the studies clearly show that migration is not an atomistic individual reaction to external forces, but that such movements are tightly structured by social institutions, households, kinship and other networks. Based on an understanding of the meanings of migration, economic as well as social and cultural, and the ways in which local institutions shape migration and are in turn shaped by it, there may be a case for genuine policies to support those involved in such movements, rather than focusing on hampering them. Policies could be designed to reduce the costs and stresses of migration to migrant workers, for example, via the provision of information about jobs, making it easier for remittances to be sent home, or providing support to the most vulnerable migrants, and facilities that enable parents to combine employment with child-care and other family responsibilities. In any case, understanding the complex economic, political and socio-cultural factors that structure migration – to which this collection is a contribution – should be the basis of policies that aim to (or have the potential to) facilitate migration and support migrant workers.

REFERENCES

Adams, R.H., 1994, 'Non-Farm Income and Inequality in Rural Pakistan', *The Journal of Development Studies*, Vol.31, No.1, pp.110–33.
Ballard, R., 1983, 'The Context and Consequences of Migration': Jullundur and Mirpur Compared', *New Community*, Vol.11, No.1/2, pp.117–36.
Breman, J., 1985, *Of Peasants, Migrants and Paupers: Rural Labour Circulation and Capitalist Production in West India*, Oxford: Oxford University Press.
Breman, J., 1994, *Wage Hunters and Gatherers. Search for Work in the Urban and Rural Economy of South Gujarat*, Delhi: Oxford University Press.
de Haan, A., 1999, 'Livelihoods and Poverty: The Role of Migration. A Critical Review of the Migration Literature', *The Journal of Development Studies*, Vol.36, No.2, pp.1–47.
de Haan, A. and B. Rogaly, 1996, 'Eastward Ho! Leapfrogging and Seasonal Migration in Eastern India', in G. Rodgers *et al.* (eds.), *The Institutional Approach to Labour and Development*, London: Frank Cass.
Connell, J., Dasgupta, B, Laishley, R. and M. Lipton, 1976, *Migration from Rural Areas: The Evidence from Village Studies*, Delhi: Oxford University Press.
Cordell, D.D., Gregory, J.W. and V. Piché, 1996, *Hoe and Wage. A Social History of a Circular Migration System in West Africa*, Boulder, CO: Westview Press.
Francis, E., 1999, *Rural Livelihoods in Madibogo*, Multiple Livelihoods and Social Change Working Paper No.6, University of Manchester: IDPM.
Francis, E. and J. Hoddinott, 1993, 'Migration and Differentiation in Western Kenya: A Tale of Two Sub-locations', *The Journal of Development Studies*, Vol.30, No.1, pp.115–45.
Gardner, K., 1995, *Global Migrants Local Lives: Travel and Transformation in Rural Bangladesh*, Oxford: Clarendon Press.
Greeley, M., 1999, 'Poverty and Well-Being in Rural Bangladesh: Impact of Economic Growth and Rural Development', Main Research Report produced for ESCOR, Brighton: IDS.
Harris, J. and M.P. Todaro, 1970, 'Migration, Unemployment and Development: A Two Sector Analysis, *American Economic Review*, Vol.60, pp.126–42.
Harriss, J., 2000, 'The Second "Great Transformation"?' in Tim Allen and Alan Thomas, 2000, *Poverty and Development into the 21st Century*, Oxford: Oxford University Press with the Open University.
Kapadia, K., 1999, 'Gender Ideologies and the Formation of Rural Industrial Classes in South India Today', in Jonathan P. Parry, Jan Breman and Karin Kapadia (eds.), *The Worlds of Indian Industrial Labour*, New Delhi and London: Sage, pp.329–52.
Kearney, M., 1996, *Reconceptualising the Peasantry*, Boulder, CO: Westview Press.
Knowles, A.C. and R. Anker, 1981, 'An Analysis of Income Transfers in a Developing Country', *Journal of Development Economics*, Vol.8, pp.205–26.
Lipton, M., 1980, 'Migration form Rural Areas of Poor Countries: The Impact on Rural Productivity and Income Distribution', *World Development*, Vol.8, No.1, pp.1–24.
Lenin, V.I., 1964, *The Development of Capitalism in Russia, Collected Works Vol 3* (Second Edition), Moscow: Progress Publishers.
Nadvi, K., 1999, 'Shifting Ties: Social Networks in the Surgical Instrument Cluster of Sialkot, Pakistan', *Development and Change*, Vol.30, No.1, pp.141–75.
Racine, J.L., 1997, *Peasant Moorings: Village Ties and Mobility Rationales in South India*, New Delhi and London: Sage.
Rodriguez, E.R., 1998, 'International Migration and Income Distribution in the Philippines', *Economic Development and Cultural Change*, Vol.48, No.2, pp.329–50.
Rogaly, B., 1998, 'Workers on the Move: Seasonal Migration and Changing Social Relations in Rural India', *Gender and Development*, Vol.6, No.1, pp21–9.
Rogaly, B., Biswas, J., Coppard, D., Rafique, A., Rana, K. and A. Sengupta, 2001, 'Seasonal Migration, Social Change and Migrants' Rights: Lessons from West Bengal', *Economic and Political Weekly*, Vol.36, No.49, pp.4547–59.
Sen, S., 1999, *Women and Labour in late Colonial India: The Bengal Jute Industry*, Cambridge: Cambridge University Press.
Srivastava, R.S., 1999, 'Rural Labour in Uttar Pradesh: Emerging Features of Subsistence, Contradiction and Resistance', *The Journal of Peasant Studies*, Vol.26, Nos.2–3, pp.263–315.

Fulani on the Move: Seasonal Economic Migration in the Sahel as a Social Process

KATE HAMPSHIRE

Rural-to-urban migration is a well-documented phenomenon in West Africa. While most earlier work has concentrated on long-term or permanent movements, the importance of short-term and seasonal migration is becoming increasingly recognised [*Maliki et al., 1984; Findley, 1989, 1994; Cleveland, 1991; Painter, 1992; David, 1995; de Bruijn and Van Dijk, 1995; Davies, 1996; Cordell et al., 1996; Guilmoto, 1998*].

Most analysis of rural-to-urban migration and its impacts is framed in economic terms, ranging from individual or household rational choice models, where migration is seen as a strategy of income maximisation [*Knerr, 1998*] or risk-spreading [*Stark and Levhari, 1982; Stark and Katz, 1986*], to Marxist analyses which emphasise the structural nature of migration as part of the capitalist penetration of rural areas [*Breman, 1985*].

Rural out-migration is often portrayed as being driven by poverty and the failure of rural livelihoods. Those in the rural sector who fail to eke out an existence from agro-pastoralism are seen to resort to supplementary activities during the long dry season, often leading to a vicious circle of increasing vulnerability as domestic production becomes compromised by such activities. Maliki *et al.* [*1984*], for example, found in Niger that only the most destitute *WoDaaBe* households sent seasonal labour migrants to cities and, in parts of Mali, that short-term rural-to-urban migration is found to be concentrated among the more vulnerable rural households [*de Bruijn and Van Dijk, 1995*] or to intensify following a major drought [*Pedersen, 1995*] or a poor harvest [*Findley, 1989, 1994*]. For such households, driven to migration through poverty, the returns are apparently small and do little to mitigate the loss of domestic production and undermining of social networks resulting from the migrants' absence [*Maliki et al., 1984; Cleveland, 1991; Ruthven and David, 1995; de Bruijn and Van Dijk, 1995*], leading to the conclusion that temporary out-migration results in under-development of sending areas [*Cordell et al., 1996*].

The research was funded under the EU DG XII STD3 Programme (ref 921028), under the direction of Katherine Homewood at University College, London. Parts of the fieldwork were also funded by the Nuffield Small Grants for Social Sciences and Boise Fund. The author is grateful to Sara Randall, also at UCL, for her supervision of this work.

While not all economic analysis is this bleak (Ruthven and Koné [*1995*] found, for example, that Malian Dogon migrants partially compensated for the temporary loss of their labour by sending ploughs back to their families), the 'under-development school' view of the 1970s has been extremely pervasive in the literature of migration, linking it directly and synergistically with rural poverty (Chirwa [*1997*], cited by de Haan [*1999*]). This paper challenges the simple, often static, economic analysis of temporary rural to urban migration in West Africa. Through examining the economic status of migrants, it questions the pessimistic view of temporary rural out-migration as having its roots firmly embedded in poverty and underdevelopment. The primacy of a purely economic model of migration is challenged through an exploration of issues of identity and social networks, not easily incorporated into such a model, but potentially very important in explaining who migrates and why.

METHODOLOGICAL ISSUES

This study uses a combination of quantitative and qualitative techniques to investigate the economic and social relations of migration among the Fulani of Northern Burkina Faso. In April–June 1995, a single round demographic survey was carried out in 40 villages[1] on a sample of 8834 Fulani (834 households[2]) in order to assess, among other things, the magnitude and predictors of different types of migration. This was followed by a bimonthly multiple round study on a subsample of migrants in six villages, over the year December 1995–December 1996, allowing in-depth qualitative research on people's understandings and motives regarding migration.

Study Area and People: The Fulani of Northern Burkina Faso

The study took place in two provinces of northern Burkina Faso: Oudalan and Séno. This area forms part of the Sahel: a semi-arid belt stretching across Africa East–West, south of the Sahara Desert. Rainfall in the study area is low (between the 300mm and 500mm isohyets) and highly seasonal. The main economic activities are extensive pastoralism and rainfed agriculture, which is only possible in the short rainy season July–September [*Barral, 1977; Claude et al., 1991*].

The Fulani constitute about a quarter of the population of the study area [*INSD, 1994*]. Although widely regarded by non-Fulani as a single ethnic category, there are important class and status divisions [*Stenning, 1959; Dupire, 1970*]. In northern Burkina Faso there are two major classes: the high status *FulBe* (sing. *Pullo*) and their erstwhile slaves, the *RiimaaiBe* (sing. *Diimaajo*). Traditionally, the *FulBe* are considered to be pastoralists and the *RiimaaiBe*, cultivators but, over the past 30 years, the economic distinctions between the two groups have become blurred, and both now practise a mixture of pastoralism and cultivation, often with other supplementary activities besides.

Ethnic subgroups (*lenyi*, sing. *Lenyol*[3]) cross-cut class groups. In the study area there are three major *lenyi* of Fulani: *DjelgoBe*, *GaoBe* and *Liptaako*, the names deriving from their perceived place of origin. Of the three, the *FulBe DjelgoBe* are the most pastorally mobile, living in tents which can be easily dismantled and moved. The *FulBe Liptaako* are the most sedentary, living mostly in mud-brick villages alongside the *RiimaaiBe Liptaako*, with the *FulBe GaoBe* occupying an intermediate position.

SPATIAL MOBILITY AND MIGRATION AMONG THE FULANI

The Fulani are a highly mobile population and spatial mobility is seen as the key to survival in the patchy and unpredictable environment of the Sahel [*Raynaut, 1997*]. In 1996, 73 per cent of all individuals sampled were involved with some form of temporary migration lasting at least two weeks. Around three-quarters of those were movements with the household herd and directly connected with domestic agro-pastoral production: mostly some form of transhumance. The second most common form of migration was of men travelling on a temporary to large cities to earn money. Other types of migration encountered in the study included short working visits to gold local mines, extended visits to kin and, rarely, permanent migration out of the area.

This study focuses exclusively on one major type of migration: that of dry season migration to cities outside of northern Burkina Faso, with the purpose of earning money. This type of migration is a relatively recent phenomenon among the Fulani in the area, although central and southern Burkina Faso has a much longer history of out-migration (mostly longer-term), among the Mossi population [*Russell et al., 1990; Cordell et al., 1996*]. Fulani oral histories indicate that, in the study area, temporary out-migration really began following the major drought of 1973, which resulted in great loss of agro-pastoral livelihoods.

At first, it was only a few rather exceptional individuals who went. It was possible to talk to the pioneering migrants in some villages, such as Abdoulaye,[4] who went to the Côte d'Ivoire for the first time in 1974, the year after the major drought. He and a friend went despite the disapproval of the rest of the village. Abdoulaye sold some of his inheritance animals to pay for his travel there, and began buying and selling small stock (sheep and goats) in the markets of Côte d'Ivoire. Ten years later, he had built up enough capital to begin buying cattle in the Sahel and transporting them for sale at a large profit in the Côte d'Ivoire. At that time, his younger brother, Ali, began trading animals too.

In 1984, when Ali also began trading, there was another drought, less severe than that of 1973, but devastating because it came before many people had fully recovered from the previous drought. Many more Fulani, mostly young men, began travelling to towns and cities, mainly in Côte d'Ivoire, to earn money. Most of the migration was during the dry season, a 'slack season' for many, when rain-fed agriculture is not possible in the Sahel. Today, seasonal economic migration out of the Sahel takes many forms, with different destinations, and economic activities at the destination ranging from the very lucrative trade in livestock, to temporary wage labour, informal sector self-employment, to begging.

Despite this variation, which will be explored in detail later, for the purposes of quantitative analysis, all of these forms of temporary economic migration will be considered together. They all fall outside of the agro-pastoral subsistence sphere and remove economically active people from it for all least part of the year. The Fulfulde term for this type of migration is simply *egugol* [the general word for migrating] plus the name of the destination. For example, *min egi Abidjan* [I have migrated to Abidjan] is usually understood in this context to mean short-term, economic migration to Abidjan (in the Côte d'Ivoire). The French term *exode* is often also used by Fulani to mean the same thing, and this will be the term used predominatly here. For quantitative analysis, it is important to define the term clearly, to distinguish it from all the other kinds of population movements found in the Sahel. Throughout this analysis, *exode* is defined as:

  (i) movement beyond the Sahel Region of Burkina Faso;
 (ii) for a duration of between one month and two years;
(iii) with the *intention* of earning money.

Exode is thus distinguished both from transhumance, and from local economic migration, which tends to be very short term, and not incompatible with continuing involvement with agropastoral production.

Using this definition, the single round survey revealed that 361 people (4.2 per cent of the *de jure* population) had been on *exode* during the 12 months preceding the survey. Of these, almost all (333) were men between the ages of 18 and 64. Of all men aged 18–64, 15.8 per cent had been on *exode* in the preceding year. Nine hundred and thirty-eight people (11.0 per cent of the whole de jure population) had participated in *exode* at some point in their lives, and of the male population aged between 18 and 64, 36.6 per cent had ever migrated for work. The median length of time spent away was five months. Typically, men leave following the harvest, are away for much of the dry season and return in time for the rains in order to cultivate. The vast majority of migrants go to Abidjan in the Côte d'Ivoire (79.5 per cent of migrants in 1994–95). Only 5.5 per cent and 5.8 per cent went to the Burkinabè cities of Ouagadougou and Bobo Dioulassou respectively.

DOES EXODE REPRESENT A RESPONSE TO POVERTY?

By definition, *exode* has an economic basis: it is migration with the intention of earning money. It also has its origins at a time when agro-pastoral livelihoods in the Burkinabè Sahel were under serious threat. This part of the analysis examines the extent to which *exode* can be understood within an economic framework and, particularly, whether it represents a response to poverty, as suggested by much of the literature cited in the introduction.

Defining and Measuring Wealth and Poverty

First, it is necessary to define and measure 'poverty' in this population. Conventional snapshot measures of consumption and production are less than useful in this Sahelian population, where change and crisis are regular features. It makes more sense to use a vulnerability model [*Blaikie and Brookfield, 1987; Bayliss Smith, 1991*] which looks at how sensitive or resilient livelihoods become in times of upset. Other researchers working in Sahelian settings have found access to assets and human capital to be more important predictors of sensitivity and resilience in the face of crisis than average daily flows of goods [*Swift, 1989; Adams, 1993*].

The Fulani view of wealth and poverty reflects very closely this view. By far the most important facet of wealth is livestock ownership, particularly cattle. This view was expressed, not only by *FulBe*, for whom the importance of cattle is well-documented [*Stenning, 1959; Dupire, 1970; Riesman, 1977*] but among the traditionally cultivating *RiimaaiBe*, and among women as well as men. While livestock certainly contribute to daily consumption, the contribution is typically small. Cattle are primarily an investment: the most important symbol of social status and a buffer against future crises. For all groups, livestock represent an asset that can be sold to purchase grain when necessary, and any surplus cash is usually invested in animals. The primary measure of assets used here is, therefore, cattle ownership. Approximate household cattle holdings (total *and* per capita) holdings were ascertained, and households were subsequently classified into three wealth categories[5]

The other aspect of wealth emphasised by the Fulani is wealth in people. A household with many (economically active) people has greater productive and reproductive potential, since agro-pastoral production is labour-intensive. Large households also have the potential to diversify economically, and to spread risks, which can be critical in reducing vulnerability to crises. Extra-household social networks are also an important way of spreading risk and coping with vulnerability. These will be discussed in detail later. For this analysis, wealth in people at a household level is estimated by total household size, since most members except the very young and old are economically active in some way. In addition, because it is almost exclusively adult men who engage in *exode*, and because of the strict gender division of labour among the Fulani, the number of adult men in the household is taken as another measure of wealth in people with regard to *exode*.

Wealth, Poverty and Exode

The hypothesis that *exode* represents a response to asset-poverty in a straightforward way is refuted by Table 1. In fact, migrants are much more likely to come from wealthier, rather than poorer households in terms of livestock assets. And a hypothesis linking *exode* with people-poverty is similarly refuted by Table 2, which shows that men from larger households *and* households with large numbers of adult men are relatively more likely to migrate than those from people-poor households. Note both Tables 1 and 2 show figures for adult men only, because the numbers of women and children engaging in *exode* were so small. This is discussed later.

Why is *exode* apparently not associated with poverty in a straightforward way? This question can be answered in two ways. First, within a wider economic framework, it becomes clear that *exode* is not a good option for the poorest households. This argument will be developed here. Secondly, and equally importantly, a straightforward economic model is not sufficient to understand why some people migrate and others do not, and the meaning and consequences of that migration for those people. This will be explored later.

TABLE 1

PARTICIPATION IN *EXODE* IN 1996 OF MEN AGED 18–64 BY HOUSEHOLD CATTLE HOLDINGS

HH Cattle Holdings	N Men Aged 18–64	Men on SEM in 1996	
0-5	90	8	(8.9%)
6-30	99	17	(17.2%)
31+	88	26	(29.5%)
Total	277	51	(18.4%)

$Chi^2 = 9.8$, p<.001

Note: Classification of households based on total cattle holdings and weighted *per capita* cattle holdings came out almost identical, so here just the simpler measure, total cattle holdings, is used.

TABLE 2
LOGISTIC REGRESSION MODEL OF PARTICIPATION IN *EXODE* OF MEN AGED
18–64 IN 1994–95 BY HOUSEHOLD SIZE AND STRUCTURE (N=2149)

Variable	Odds Ratio (e^B)	sig
Household Size (Total)		**
1-9	REF	
10-16	1.4	NS
17+	2.1	**
Adults Men in Household		***
1-3	REF	
4+	1.9	***

statistical significance: *<0.05; **<0.01; ***<0.001

Notes: i) Other relevant variables (ethnic subgroup, age, subsistence system) have been
controlled for by multiple logistic regression, which minimises the risks of finding
spurious associations due to auto-correlation of explanatory variables.
ii) The odds ratio (e^B) for each variable (household size and adult men) represents the
odds of a positive outcome (in this case, migrating) compared with a reference group
(indicated REF). For example in this case, a man from a household with 4+ adults men
was more likely to migrate than a man from a household with 1–3 adult men, and the
ratio of the odds of their migrating was 1.9.

In order to understand why it is men from the wealthiest, not the poorest,
households who engage most in *exode*, it is necessary to place *exode* within
the wider context of coping options available. If a household is unable or
unwilling to survive from agro-pastoralism alone, a variety of options is
theoretically available. In addition to *exode*, people may elect to take on
local wage labour (mostly associated with local gold mines[6]) or to engage in
local commerce as a means of supplementing income. Pastoralists have the
additional option of taking on contract herding. Other alternatives
compatible with continuing within the agro-pastoral economy include
gathering wild foods, gleaning after harvests, soliciting gifts of millet from
kin and artisan work. Finally, households may elect simply to accept the
situation and suffer hardship, or to leave the Sahel and agropastoral
economy altogether on a long-term or permanent basis.

However, various constraints operate to limit this range considerably for
many households. Two important constraints are people and assets, which
operate particularly strongly on *exode* as a coping option. *Exode* demands
substantial initial investments: for transport costs, for lodging while away
and, if any trading is involved, for purchase of merchandise (anything from
tea and coffee to large numbers of livestock). It also exerts substantial
labour demands, in that it removes men entirely from domestic agro-
pastoral production for several months at a time. Although migrants tend to
be absent during the slack season for agriculture, pastoral labour demands

are high at this time. *Exode* is therefore an expensive option, both in terms of assets and people. To participate in *exode*, a household must have enough people of the right category (adult men) to spare without critically undermining domestic production. Time constraints were an often-cited reason for adopting alternative strategies, such as local gold-mining, which only involves much shorter visits.

In comparison, other diversification strategies may be less burdensome for some asset-or people-poor households. For example, a cow-poor pastoralist household may be able to take on contract herding extra animals with few additional labour demands. Gathering wild foods is very labour-intensive, but is almost exclusively women's and children's work, and, since men are primarily responsible for most agro-pastoral productive tasks, the implications for domestic subsistence are very different from options involving men's labour. Most local diversification strategies are less costly in terms of assets than *exode*.

Exode is, therefore, much more accessible to households with reasonably high levels of resources and labour, with the labour constraint being particularly pressing for the more pastoralist households. Such households are able to engage in *exode* without compromising domestic production.

Not only are wealthier households better able to engage in *exode per se* without undermining domestic production, they are also, generally speaking, able to reap larger rewards, making it a more appealing option than it might be for poorer households. The returns for migrants who go to beg or to engage in informal wage labour are generally low. Among older men who go begging, most bring back some 30.000–40.000 FCFA (around US$60) after six months or so. Younger men involved in begging, butchery, low paid employment or self employment in the informal sector often brought back considerably less, succumbing instead to the temptations of the big city.

Such returns are not unimportant: even small surpluses can make a useful contribution to livelihood security. Migrants usually return at the end of the dry season, when stocks of grain are running low. Using returns to buy even small amounts of millet means can avert the need to sell productive assets, livestock, at a time of year when terms of trade between grain and livestock are tipped against pastoralists. For poor households, reduced pressure on the household granary during the migrant's absence is another small, although potentially important contribution to livelihood security. However, these small gains must be weighed against the costs of migration: direct (costs of travel, accommodation, etc.) and indirect (loss of domestic labour) – a delicately balanced equation which could easily tip the wrong way.

Returns from activities such as livestock commerce are of a different order of magnitude. Large-scale livestock traders, who may take more than a hundred head of cattle at a time from the Sahel to the Côte d'Ivoire, might easily make several hundred thousand FCFA on each trip: enough to make a substantial contribution to their own agro-pastoral production. However, these more lucrative activities are the most demanding in terms of resources. To begin trading livestock, requires sufficient capital outlay to buy and transport the livestock and enough assets to be able to weather large losses at times, since the outcome depends very much on macroeconomic forces driving market relations over which the individual trader has no control. Begging, on the other hand, entails relatively small outgoings: just the transport costs plus accommodation which is usually provided at low cost through social networks (discussed later).

In other words, wealthier households are not only better able to sent migrants *per se*, they are in a better position to access the most profitable forms of *exode* which can make a substantial contribution to livelihood security, but which are not available to those from poorer households. This is shown clearly in Table 3. And there is little possibility, through *exode*, of upward economic mobility. Of 78 men who had been going on *exode* for more than ten years, only ten had ever changed activity, and the only significant graduation was from small-to large-scale livestock trading, a route from which poorer migrants are excluded altogether.

TABLE 3

EXODE ACTIVITIES UNDERTAKEN IN 1987–96 BY HOUSEHOLD CATTLE HOLDINGS OF MIGRANTS

SEM Activity		Total HH Cattle Holdings			
(Most Recent)		0-5	6-30	31+	TOTALS
No Work		1	2	1	4
Low Input,	Begging	5	3		8
Risk and	Wage Labour	1	3	3	7
Return	Contract Herding	7	1	2	10
	Petty Animal Market Work	5	0	3	8
Medium	Self Employment	5	12	5	22
Risk and	Butcher	4	16	3	23
Return	Marabout	1		1	2
High Input,	Small-Scale Animal	2	4	14	20
Risk and	Trading				
Return	Large-Scale Animal	0	2	12	14
	Trading				
TOTAL		31	43	44	118

Chi² Test: on collapsed 3x3 contingency table: Chi²=47.7, 4df, p<0.000005

As well as engaging in more profitable *exode* activities, migrants from wealthier households are also able to travel further. Abidjan in the Côte d'Ivoire is generally the preferred destination, offering greater economic opportunities than elsewhere. Because of the higher fares, fewer than half (47 per cent) of the migrants from poorer households (fewer than six cattle) went to Abidjan, compared with 77 per cent of those from households with six or more cattle. Moreover, people-rich households could afford to send migrants for longer, again allowing the flexibility to pursue more optimal *exode* strategies (linear regression of *exode* duration against adult men in household: $B=0.114$, $p<0.001$).

So, from a purely economic point of view, it is hardly surprising that it is the wealthier households, rather than the poorer ones, that are more likely to send seasonal economic migrants. Wealthy households can bear the costs of *exode* most easily and can engage in the more profitable forms of. For poorer households, *exode* is a far less appealing option. The costs in terms of labour and resources are high, and the returns are likely to be low: the cost-benefit equation is finely balanced and might easily be tipped the wrong way. For many such households, it makes more sense to turn to alternative coping strategies to supplement agro-pastoral production, which are less costly or risky.

IDENTITY, SOCIAL NETWORKS AND MIGRATION

An economic model of *exode* can, then, explain at least some of the reason why some Fulani migrate seasonally to cities. Contrary to the predictions arising from the literature, though, temporary economic out-migration, far from being associated with extreme poverty and destitution, seems to be more a way in which agropastoral households that are already reasonably well-off, can further increase their livelihood security. I now turn to the second part of the argument: that there are many other considerations encompassed in the decision of whether or not to migrate, where to go and why, which are less easily incorporated into a standard economic model of poverty-driven migration. This part of the paper considers various forms of identity that influence migration behaviour.

Gender

By far the most important single determinant of migration behaviour is gender. Of 346 adult migrants surveyed in 1994–95, all but 13 were men. The 13 women recorded as going on *exode* in that period were all accompanying husbands, who were away for longer than usual.

Gender divisions of labour, power and resources among the Fulani is very rigid (see also Stenning [*1959*]). These divisions, and the identities thus constructed, are also important in understanding the meanings attached to migration among different categories of people. Men are responsible primarily for all productive agro-pastoral work: herding, sowing, harvesting and so on, and women have a very limited role in that work. Men are responsible for providing the household with basic foodstuffs (although women contribute condiments). Women's responsibility lies largely in the domestic and reproductive spheres: preparing food, fetching water and childcare. Only widowed or divorced women with no male kin prepared to help are forced to engage in productive work, which is considered highly demeaning for them, and many prefer to suffer considerable physical hardship and shortage rather than risk shaming themselves in this way.

It is, therefore, not socially acceptable for women to become involved in *exode*, a productive economic activity, in their own right. For one thing, the domestic duties of women, particularly childcare, preclude their absence for extended periods. Moreover, younger women often have restrictions placed on their movements by husbands or fathers, associated with controlling their sexuality. Even older women, with no dependent children and those less immediately subject to male control, do not go on *exode*, although they may go on other journeys deemed more appropriate to their gender. In particular, many older *GaoBe* women leave for a month or two in the cold dry season to purchase grass on the Mossi Plateau for weaving into grass mats to make tents: a domestic/reproductive task, therefore considered acceptable. None of the women accompanying husbands on *exode* in 1994 were economically active themselves: they were all going to perform the same domestic and reproductive tasks that they would at home.

For any women who does try to go alone, the costs are high and the opportunities for gain, low. Because economic migration lies beyond the female sphere, women have very poor access to destination networks upon which men rely to make *exode* successful. Moreover, local support networks may be threatened by unacceptable behaviour. One *Gaojo* woman in the sample had been on *exode* alone a few years previously. She had little to lose: she was already regarded as something of an outcast by her community and figured in many witchcraft accusations, and her economic position was very bad as a result of a completely useless husband and son. After a few months away, involved in undisclosed economic activities (probably prostitution) she returned with a little money among much criticism from other villagers.

Village Identity and Social Networks

The importance of social networks in the *exode* has already been mentioned. Extra-household networks in sending villages can be called upon to plug labour deficits left by migrants and to provide small amounts of credit for

TABLE 4
HOW HOUSEHOLD LABOUR DEFICITS LEFT BY MIGRANTS IN 1996 WERE MET

Labour Covered	No. of Households
within the household	18
kin networks within the village	12
kin networks outside the village	1
paid contract herders	13
no animals	7
no data available	1
TOTAL	42

migrants to meet travel costs. A third of all households with one or more men away on *exode* relied on local, extra-household kin networks to plug labour deficits, particularly herding work, the major dry season agropastoral activity (Table 4). The main alternative to this, for labour-poor but resource-rich households, was paying contract herders.

Migrants also rely on networks at the destination to help them get established and find work and to provide cheap accommodation, particularly for new migrants. Good destination networks can also replace domestic credit networks by paying the travel costs for first-time migrants. This is well illustrated by the case of Salou and Boureima, young first-time *Pullo Gaojo* migrants to the Côte d'Ivoire. The two cousins travelled together, with other young men from their village, on the 'pay on arrival' bus from Ouagadougou to Abidjan. They were met by Boureima's older brother, longer established in *exode* to Abidjan, who paid their bus fares. Salou's cousins managed to find him work, transporting goods by donkey cart. Boureima's brother helped him to buy a donkey cart of his own, to begin a similar business. He also bought and sold tea. Accommodation in Abidjan was also provided through kin networks. Without these contacts, even the low investment forms of *exode* like begging would be much more expensive and risky, and few would-be migrants, except for the pioneers in the 1970s, set off with no contact at all.

Destination networks are fairly loosely organised, and tend to operate on a village, rather than an individual basis. All the migrants from a particular village, or group of villages, back home use the same system of networks and a village 'culture' of a particular type and location of *exode* becomes established. Guilmoto [*1998*] describes a similar situation in Senegal, which he calls an 'institution of migration'. This then, along with wealth, is highly influential in determining the *exode* possibilities open to new migrants from the same village: in the case of Salou and Boureima, for example, both new migrants began doing donkey cart work because of the nature of the networks they had at their destination. Migrants from other villages may

TABLE 5
EXODE ACTIVITIES OF *FULBE GAOBE* MIGRANTS FROM TWO DIFFERENT
VILLAGES

Exode Activity	Village A Migrants	Village BMigrants	TOTALS
No Work	0	1	1
Begging	0	6	6
Self-Employment	0	11	11
Wage Labour	0	5	5
Contract Herding	4	0	4
Petty Animal Market Work	4	0	4
Small-Scale Animal Trading	14	0	14
Large-Scale Animal Trading	7	0	7
Maraboutage	0	1	1
TOTALS	29	24	53

have very different sets of social networks, offering different kinds of opportunities. Table 5 shows substantial differences in the *exode* activities between migrants from two *GaoBe* villages, reasonably well matched for household size, wealth (cattle holdings) and economic activity. Extra-household networks do not exist within a social vacuum. As well as operating along kinship and village lines, the networks open to an individual are intimately connected with issues of ethnic identity, discussed in the following paragraphs, which also play a crucial role in understanding the patterns of migration among the Fulani.

Ethnic Identity

Although this study focuses on one broad ethnic category, the Fulani, subgroups within this category are central to ethnic identity in this area. People consider themselves to be, not just Fulani, but *FulBe DjelgoBe, RiimaaiBe Liptaako,* etc. Over several generations, ethnic boundaries, particularly the *FulBe*/non-*FulBe* one, can be ambiguous with shifts occurring. The process of '*FulBeisation*', or adoption of *FulBe* identity, well documented elsewhere [*Dupire, 1962; Burnham, 1996*], has been observed in the study area among some Sonrai groups in particular. However, over the short-term (since the start of Fulani labour migration in around 1973), ethnic subgroup is stable and can be unambiguously assigned. Marriage is endogamous within subgroups, almost without exception.

When asking men why they do or do not migrate, the answers are almost always framed initially in terms of this ethnic identity: 'we are *FulBe DjelgoBe* – of course we don't go to Abidjan!' This is also borne out by the quantitative analysis. Table 6 shows the complete logistic regression model for individual correlates of *exode*: ethnic subgroup accounts for more of the variation than any other single variable.

TABLE 6
COMPLETE LOGISTIC REGRESSION MODEL OF INDIVIDUAL PARTICIPATION IN
EXODE IN 1994–95. MEN AGED 18–64 (N=2149)

Variable	Odds Ratio (*eB*)	sig
Household Size (Total)		**
1-9	REF	
10-16	1.4	NS
17+	2.1	**
Adults Males in Household		***
1-3	REF	
4+	1.9	***
Ethnic Subgroup		***
RiimaaiBe Liptaako	REF	
FulBe Liptaako	0.84	NS
FulBe GaoBe	2.16	***
FulBe DjelgoBe	0.25	***
Economic Activity		***
Pastoralist	REF	
Agropastoralist	1.1	NS
Cultivator	2.8	***
Age Group		**
18-27	REF	
28-40	1.6	**
41-64	0.64	*

statistical significance: *0.05; **0.01; ***0.001
Source: SRDS.

See also notes to Table 2.

Most ethnographies of *FulBe* populations document the centrality of cattle and herding to *Pulaaku*, *FulBe* identity [*Hopen, 1958; Stenning, 1959; Bonfiglioli, 1988*], and similar views were expressed by all groups of *FulBe* in the sample. However, many Fulani groups in West Africa have supplemented pastoralism with other forms of livelihood, particularly agriculture, at various times, and there is considerable evidence to suggest this is not a new phenomenon [*Hopen, 1958; Dupire, 1962, 1970; Raynaut, 1997*].

Among the Burkinabè *FulBe*, the social and economic situation has altered considerably over recent decades. Under French colonial rule, the system of slavery was dismantled. Previously, not just a few wealthy individuals, but the whole *FulBe* class had slaves (*RiimaaiBe* or *MaccuBe*) who cultivated land owned by their *FulBe* masters, and gave them a substantial proportion of their harvested grain. Under these circumstances, many *FulBe* were able to pursue largely pastoral activities themselves. When this system broke down (something which happened very gradually in many areas) most *FulBe* found themselves in a position whereby they could no longer rely purely on herding but had to become involved directly in agriculture. Their economic position worsened as a result of the two major droughts in 1973 and 1984. Many people, *FulBe* and *RiimaaiBe* alike, found themselves obliged to diversify into non-agro-pastoral activities. Thus there was a move from a system where diversification happened at the level of society with specialisation between households and class groups to a situation of diversification within households.

Both *RiimaaiBe* and *FulBe* acknowledge that, for the *RiimaaiBe*, the transition was rather less problematic. For a long time, *RiimaaiBe* had been the under-class and were accustomed to coping with hardship. For the *FulBe*, however, even engaging in agriculture challenged the *Pulaaku* ideal of pure pastoralism. Having to diversity further economically was a further threat to the increasingly fragile sense of *FulBe* identity. Among each sub-group of *FulBe* in the Burkinabè Sahel, a different hierarchy emerged of acceptability of diversification options.

Among the *FulBe GaoBe*, *exode* emerged as one of the least bad options. Although, according to accounts of early migrants from that group, most *GaoBe* did not like the fact they had to migrate, it was preferable to the alternatives of engaging locally in alternative activities. At least by going far away the shameful activities were hidden from those back home, and there was a chance of earning enough money to buy animals and move towards the pastoral ideal again. Since its beginnings after 1973, labour migration has become more common and widespread and no longer carries the social stigma it once did, although most migrants still express the hope that one day they will be able to be full pastoralists again.

For the *FulBe DjelgoBe*, on the other hand, *exode* came to be seen as highly degrading. To leave the Sahel and the pastoral way of life, even for short periods, implies extreme poverty and destitution: few *DjelgoBe* would risk the humiliation involved in *exode* while other options still exist. *FulBe DjelgoBe* have long been widely known for their herding skills and, where possible, prefer to supplement agropastoralism through taking on contract herding. (This is not always possible since the demand for herding work exceeds the supply.) It is better to herd someone else's cattle than none at all. Thus, among the *FulBe DjelgoBe*, the few economic migrants are those who have few other options and little to lose.

The occupation undertaken on *exode* and the destination are also important. For example, most young *RiimaaiBe* who go to Abidjan are self-employed butchers. Butchery is seen by the Fulani to be an exclusively *RiimaaiBe* occupation, and for high status groups to engage in such activities is highly demeaning. However, sometimes, options are limited and *FulBe* are obliged to undertake demeaning forms of employment, as the following case study illustrates.

The older of two *RiimaaiBe* brothers goes each year to Abidjan to work as a butcher. He bought animals in the market there and sold mainly cooked meat. He always hoped to earn enough money to invest in livestock back home, but usually only manages to bring back enough money to buy millet and some small gifts. A *Pullo* man from the same village also went to the Côte d'Ivoire hoping to become an animal trader but, on arrival, he found he did not have enough money. With few other options available to him, he ended up working as a butcher too, which he regarded as being extremely shameful, as it was the work of *RiimaaiBe*. The ultimate ignominy was that he was forced to go and ask 'his' *Diimaajo* for help to get started. He hopes this will only be a temporary arrangement and his intention is to make enough money to start doing animal trading but, after four years, he has not yet managed to achieve this. *FulBe Liptaako* who engage in such work risk becoming the objects of ridicule, albeit jokingly, in their home villages. For such migrants, it is a case of hoping that the end (eventually earning enough to return to a more pastorally-based economic system) justifies the means.

Another advantage of going to Abidjan becomes apparent here. As well as offering more economic opportunities than other destinations, it also has the advantage of conferring some distance and anonymity. It is preferable to engage in a shameful activity far away, even if this is common knowledge, than under the gaze of those at home.

Interestingly, of the *FulBe DjelgoBe* who had ever migrated for work, nearly half (five out of 11) ended up doing contract herding while away. The usual reason given for this by *DjelgoBe* migrants is that they are born herders and are incapable of doing anything else. However, it may also be that, by doing contract herding, migrants are attempting to redefine something which is unacceptable to them (that is, *exode*) as something which is highly acceptable (that is, herding animals, albeit someone else's). This way of adapting cultural models to fit a situation is described by de Bruijn and Van Dijk [*1995*] in the context of Malian Fulani in times of crisis.

The costs of breaking ethnic norms and going on *exode* when it is not acceptable, or doing the wrong sort of *exode*, can be high. Such migrants are unlikely to receive the sort of support they require, either from their home village or in the destination. Networks in destination areas are limited or non-existent if there is no tradition of *exode*, and networks at home are threatened by unacceptable, shameful behaviour. This is well illustrated by the case of Issa, a young *Pullo Djelgojo* man who had spent three years in the Côte d'Ivoire. Because he knew his father would disapprove and forbid him from going, he pretended he was just going to the local market. Once at the market, he sold his only goat and borrowed extra money to pay for his travel and went off to Abidjan. Issa's only contact in Abidjan was his father's half-brother, another failed migrant, who was little help in finding profitable work. Issa worked firstly as a night watchman and later selling frozen fish. During his stay he was effectively unable to return home through lack of money. Not only was travel unaffordable, but the shame associated in returning empty-handed was too great. He ended up being 'trapped' in the Côte d'Ivoire for three years.

Because he migrated in circumstances where this was not regarded as an acceptable option, he placed his family in a difficult position, both economically, because they had to repay the loan he had taken under false pretences, and socially, because of the shame (*semteende*[7]) brought on them. When he finally returned, penniless, he was extremely unpopular with everyone and was ostracised by his family for some time. In an environment like the Sahel, where long-term livelihood security is very dependent on social networks, which can be drawn upon in times of crisis, to threaten such networks by behaving in such an unacceptable manner can be disastrous.

Generation

Finally, generation is an important consideration with regard to who migrates and what they do while away. Of adult men, the middle-age group (28–40) were the most likely to go, and the oldest men (41–64), the least likely (Table 6). This may be partly a function of life-cycle differences in opportunities and resources to travel. However, interviews with migrants indicated that a generational dimension to the acceptability of *exode* was important.

Men from the two younger age groups (under 40) have grown up during a time when *exode* was becoming increasingly widespread, particularly among *FulBe GaoBe*, and *FulBe* and *RiimaaiBe* Liptaako. Many younger men are torn between the competing ideals of wanting to be 'modern' and taste the city life, and the enduring *pulaaku* ideal of being a pastoralist. For them, however, going on *exode* does not carry the same stigma that it does among the older generations, for whom any departure from a pastoralist way of life is seen as a greater source of shame.

Age also influences which type of *exode* is acceptable. For young, able-bodied men, begging is a highly shameful activity, wherever it is done. This does not mean no young men beg. In one village, a large proportion of young, male migrants were primarily involved in begging, although this was not disclosed to me for some months, because of the shame attached. For older men, who are no longer expected to be economically active, begging in mosques can be more acceptable than engaging in physical labour. Several elderly men from a *GaoBe* village travel to Ouagadougou to beg in mosques for a few months each year. Although the begging closer by might be more dubious, there is no great stigma attached to this. It is regarded as being part a proper part of Islam. Again, it may be that people are juggling aspects of identities, so that an activity unacceptable to a Fulani becomes redefined as an activity acceptable to a Muslim.

The generational aspect underlines the dynamic nature of seasonal economic migration and the way it has changed since 1973. New generations of migrants are different from previous ones. Among the most recent cohort of new *GaoBe* migrants in their late teens, the stigma is more of a joke than of real concern and there is evidence of what Cleveland [*1991:230*] describes as 'an increasing desire on the part of young men to "see a bit of the world ..."'. Among some groups, *exode* might even be becoming a sort of *rite de passage* necessary for boys to become men. New generations have different ways of making labour migration compatible with *pulaaku* ideals and the construction of ethnic identity. As Burnham [*1996:54*] points out: ' ... despite the essentialist nature of this Fulani discourse on their culture, it is plain that the notion of *pulaaku* does not in fact refer to a primordial source of Fulani tradition but reveals instead, in its recognition of the many microscopic variations of Fulani custom, the processes of change and adjustment constantly at work in Fulani societies.'

CONCLUSIONS: SEASONAL ECONOMIC MIGRATION AS A
DYNAMIC SOCIAL PROCESS

By definition, *exode* has at its core an economic motive: people leave the Sahel to work in cities in order to make money, usually with the hope that one day they will have sufficient herds to live comfortably from (agro)pastoralism alone. However, simple economic analysis falls a long way short of explaining the processes involved and understanding who goes, why, and with what consequences.

First, the expected relationship of rural out-migration being a product of the failure of rural livelihoods, driven by poverty and resulting in rural underdevelopment, was not borne out by the data. Other recent studies are also beginning to challenge this over-pessimistic view [*de Haan, 1999*]. The Burkinabe Fulani are using *exode* selectively, as part of a range of strategies designed, not just to cope with livelihood failure, but to optimise livelihood security. *Exode* is used most by those households that stand to gain the most from it, usually the wealthiest in terms of the locally defined criteria of cattle and people. Poorer households, for whom migration might excessively compromise domestic production for relatively small rewards, turn to alternative strategies, like gold-mining locally, which carry fewer costs. Only when these sorts of households, through destitution and a real lack of alternatives, are forced into labour migration, does *exode* represent part of the downward spiral described by researchers such as Maliki *et al.* [*1984*] in Niger.

In other words, it is time to start seeing Sahelians, not as helpless victims, pushed into economic diversification through destitution, but as strategic actors, using diversification to enhance long term livelihood security. However, it is also important to recognise the circumstances under which *exode* can turn from an optimising strategy to part of a downward spiral of destitution: where it is associated with poverty, and where there is a serious lack of viable alternatives.

Secondly, a range of factors not easily incorporated into simple economic analysis, such as village-level social networks and identity, emerge as being essential to the understanding of migration in this population. The meaning and acceptability of migration to different groups is influenced heavily by identity, based on ethnic group, gender and generation. In this sense, *exode* should be seen as part of a social process and not simply an economic one, although the two interact in interesting ways. Where *exode* is defined as being socially unacceptable, for whatever reason, the balance of costs and benefits tips firmly the wrong way, and costs to network formation are likely to outweigh any benefits gained.

Thirdly, *exode* emerges as a highly dynamic process, which an ahistorical, static framework of analysis fails to capture. Since the Fulani started going to work in cities, in around 1973, the meanings of migration to different sectors of the population have been constantly renegotiated, as ideologies adapt to changing circumstances. Ethnic and generation identity, which are so important in shaping the migration process, are undergoing rapid change, with new generations of migrants having very different perceptions of migration and how it fits in with Fulani identity. The impact of gender identity on migration seems more resistant to change, although the time-scale in question (less than 30 years) is quite small, and evidence from other studies suggests that male out-migration in itself might be a trigger for changing gender roles and division of labour and power [*Monimart, 1989; Timaeus and Graham, 1989*].

How generalisable are the findings in this paper? In one sense, they are highly specific to the Fulani in Northern Burkina Faso. Even within a small area and broad ethnic category, there is great diversity in the range and meaning of migration, making any attempt at simple extrapolation fruitless. However, this study and other similar work (Mosse *et al.*, Rogaly *et al.*, de Haan, all in this collection) have wider implications in their suggestion that it is time to move away from simple, static, and often pessimistic, economic models of temporary migration, towards a more dynamic and historical analysis, which sees migration as a social process, and not simply as an economic fact.

NOTES

1. Villages ranged from temporary nomadic camps of one or two households to large permanent villages of 50 or more compounds.
2. It is recognised that the term 'household' is not straightforward and cannot be translated easily into different contexts, particularly where units of consumption, production, reproduction and socialisation do not necessarily coincide. For the purposes of this analysis and discussion, a broad, local definition is used: *baade* or *wuro* (depending on the ethnic sub-group), equivalent to the largest unit at which regular economic co-operation (herding, cultivating, cooking, etc.) occurs on a day to day basis.
3. The Fulfulde term *lenyol* can be used in two senses. Here it is used to mean broad ethnic subgroups. It can also be used in a much narrower sense to refer to clans and lineages traceable to a recent common ancestor.
4. Names of informants have been changed to protect identity.
5. Data on cattle holdings among Fulani are notoriously difficult to collect [*Hampshire and Randall, 1999*]. It was, therefore, only possible to collect data on *approximate* cattle numbers, and for the smaller sub-sample only.
6. A number of gold mining sites exist in the Sahel, run by the mining company CEMOB (*Compagnie d'Exploitation de Mines d'Or au Burkina*). Plots of land are leased by the company to individuals. The leaseholders, in turn, employ men on a casual basis to perform the difficult and very dangerous tasks of digging mines and extracting gold. The gold is sold to CEMOB at a fixed rate and the miners are given a (very small) share of the profit. It is rarely a lucrative business: while stories of those who have gone and struck it lucky proliferate, these appear to be largely apocryphal: most return with little or nothing.
7. *Semteende*, a strong sense of shame, is intimately linked with the restraint needed to conform to the *Pulaaku* ideal [*Riesman, 1977*].

REFERENCES

Adams, A., 1993, 'Food Insecurity in Mali: Exploring the Role of the Moral Economy', *IDS Bulletin,* Vol.24, No.4, pp.41–51.
Barral H., 1977, *Les Populations Nomades de l'Oudalan et leur Espace Pastoral,* Paris: ORSTOM.
Bayliss Smith, T., 1991 'Food Security and Agricultural Sustainability in the New Guinea Highlands: Vulnerable People, Vulnerable Places', *IDS Bulletin,* Vol.22, No.3, pp.5–11.
Blaikie, P. and H. Brookfield, 1987, *Land Degradation and Society,* London: Methuen.
Bonfiglioli, A.M., 1988, *Dudal: Histoire de Famille et Historique de Tropeaux chez un*

Groupe WoDaaBe du Niger, Cambridge: Cambridge University Press/Editions de la Maison des Sciences de l'Homme.

Breman, J., 1985, *Of Peasants, Migrants and Paupers: Rural Labour Circulation and Capitalist Production in West India*, Oxford: Oxford University Press.

Burnham, P., 1996 *The Politics of Cultural Difference in Northern Cameroon*, Edinburgh: Edinburgh University Press for the International African Institute.

Chiraw W. C., 1997, '"No TEBA ... Forget TEBA": The Plight of Malawian Ex-Migrant Workers to South Africa, 1988–1994', *International Migration Review*, Vol.31, No.3, pp. 628–54.

Claude J., Grouzis, M. and P. Millville, 1991, *Un Espace Sahelien: La Mare d'Oursi, Burkina Faso*, Paris: ORSTOM.

Cleveland D.A., 1991, 'Migration in West Africa: A Savanna Village Perspective', *Africa*, Vol.61, No.2, pp.222–46.

Cordell, D.D., Gregrory, J.W. and V. Piché, 1996, *Hoe and Wage: A Social History of a Circular Migration System in West Africa*, London: Westview Press.

Davies, S., 1996, *Adaptable Livelihoods: Coping with Food Insecurity in the Malian Sahel*, London: Macmillan Press.

David, R. (ed.), 1995, *Changing Places? Women, Resource Management and Migration in the Sahel*, London: SOS Sahel.

de Bruijn M. and H. Van Dijk, 1995, *Arid ways*, Amterdam: Thesis Publishers.

de Haan, A., 1999, 'Livelihoods and Poverty – the Role of Migration: A Critical Review of the Migration Literature', *The Journal of Development Studies*, Vol.36, No.2, pp1–47.

Dupire, M., 1962, *Peuls Nomades: Etudes Descriptives des Wodaabe su Sahel Nigérien*, Paris: Institut d'Ethnologie.

Dupire M., 1970, *Organisation Sociale des Peul*, Paris: Edition Plon.

Findley, S.E., 1989, 'Choosing Between African and French Destinations; The Role of Family and Community Factors in Migration in the Senegal River Valley', Bamako: CERPOD Working Paper.

Findley, S.E., 1994, 'Does Drought Increase Migration? A Study of Migration from Rural Mali During the 1983–1985 Drought', *International Migration Review*, Vol.28, No.3, pp.539–53.

Guilmoto, C.Z., 1998, 'Institutions and Migrations: Short-Term versus Long-Term Moves in Rural West Africa., *Population Studies*, Vol.52, No.1, pp.85–103.

Hampshire, K.R. and S.C. Randall, 1999, 'Seasonal Labour Migration Strategies in the Sahel: Coping with Poverty or Optimising Security?' *International Journal or Population Geography*, Vol.5, No.5, pp.367–85.

Hopen, C., 1958, *The Pastoral FulBe Family in Gwandu*, Oxford: Oxford University Press.

Iliffe, J., 1987, *The African Poor: A Comparative History*, Cambridge: Cambridge University Press.

INSD, 1994, *Analyse des Resultats de l'Enquête Démographique* 1991, Ouagadougou: INSD.

Knerr, B., 1998, 'The Impacts of Labour Migration on the Sustainability of Agricultural Development in Arid Regions', in J. Clarke and D. Noin, *Population and Environment in Arid Regions*, Paris and New York: UNESCO / Parthenon Publishing.

Maliki, A.B., White, C. Loutan L. and J.J. Swift, 1984, 'The WoDaaBe', in J.J. Swift (ed.), *Pastoral Development in Central Niger: Report of the Niger Range and Livestock Project*, Niamey: Ministère du Developpement Rural and USAID.

Monimart M., 1989, *Femmes du Sahel: La Désertification au Quotidien*, Paris: Karthala.

Painter T.A., 1992, *Migration and AIDS in West Africa*, New York: CARE.

Pedersen J., 1995, 'Drought, Migration and Population Growth in the Sahel: The Case of the Malian Gourma 1900–1991', *Population Studies*, Vol.49, No.1, pp.111–26.

Raynaut C., 1997, *Societies and Nature in the Sahel*, London: Routledge.

Riesman P., 1977, *Freedom in Fulani Social Life*, Chicago, IL: University of Chicago Press.

Russell S.S., Jacobsen, K. and W.D. Stanley, 1990, 'International Migration and Development in Africa. Volume II: Country Analyses', *World Bank Discussion Papers, African Technical Department Series*, No.102.

Ruthven, O. and M. Koné, 1995, 'Case Study: The Dogon, Cercle de Bankass, Mali', in David [*1995*].

Ruthven, O. and R. David, 1995, 'Benefits and Burdens: Researching the Consequences of Migration in the Sahel, *IDS Bulletin*, Vol.26, No.1, pp.47–53.

Stark O. and D. Levhari, 1982, 'On Migration and Risk in Less Developed Countries', *Economic Development and Cultural Change*, Vol.31, No.1, pp.191–6.

Stark, O. and E. Katz, 1986, 'Labour Migration and Risk Aversion in Less Developed Countries', *Journal of Labor Economics*, Vol.4, No.1, pp.134–49.

Stennings D., 1959, *Savannah Nomads*, Oxford: Oxford University Press.

Swift J., 1989, 'Why are Rural People Vulnerable to Famine?' *IDS Bulletin*, Vol.20, No.2.

Timaeus I. and W. Graham, 1989, 'Labour Circulation, Marriage and Fertility in Southern Africa', in R.J. Lesthaeghe (ed.), *Reproduction and Social Organisation in Sub-Saharan Africa*, Berkeley, CA: University of California Press, pp.365–400.

Migration, Livelihoods and Institutions: Contrasting Patterns of Migration in Mali

ARJAN DE HAAN, KAREN BROCK
and NGOLO COULIBALY

I. INTRODUCTION

Migration is often explained through narratives in which rural inhabitants, mostly men, migrate in response to negative factors such as environmental change, population growth or increasing economic pressure. In the case of Mali, vagaries of weather, mismanagement of land, agricultural stagnation and high population pressure on cultivated land, for example, are often quoted as major causes of emigration. Also, migration has often been seen as a cause of a decline in social cohesion. For example, Adepoju and Mbugua [*1997*], in the introduction to a volume on family, population and development in Africa, state that migration is eroding day-to-day mutual support among family members. This study challenges such visions of migration, in the context of West Africa. Like Hampshire in this volume, it challenges the view of Sahelians as passive victims of external forces. While placing labour migration squarely in the context of the extremely risk-prone environment of the region, we try to reinstate a notion of agency, by examining the role of migration in the livelihoods of two villages in Mali.

Research in the two villages provided surprising and strongly contrasting pictures – though in both areas migration was crucial to the villagers' livelihoods [*Brock and Coulibaly, 1999*]. Migration from Dalonguebougou in the Sahelian dryland was complex and dynamic, with different patterns for various ethnic groups, and marked differences between men and women. In contrast, the livelihoods system in the village Zaradougou in the Sudano-Sahelian cotton region was inextricably

---

Arjan de Haan is currently social development adviser at the Department for International Development, based in New Delhi; Karen Brock is a researcher in the Participation Group at the Institute for Development Studies, Sussex, UK; and Ngolo Coulibaly is at the Institut de L'Économie Rural, Bamako, Mali. Research was carried out from the Institute for Development Studies, and funded by ESCOR, Department for International Development.

intertwined with extensive migration to small cocoa and coffee plantations, occupied by the households for a long time, in Côte d'Ivoire – that for decades has had the strongest economy in the region and has relied heavily on immigrant labour from neighbouring countries.

Migration in both villages was a central feature not only of their local economies, but also of social networks and relations. Social networks mediated access to resources, locally but also away from the villages. In Dalonguebougou migration of young women was strongly embedded in wide kinship networks, and their notions of obligation and reciprocity. In Zaradougou, migration to Côte d'Ivoire was a central element not only of the economics of the large extended households, but also of the way in which their heads managed the social relations within the households. In both villages, the households were characterised as much by the separation of their members over hundreds of kilometres as by their common residence, and the migration of young men and women formed a *rite de passage* as well as being driven by economic necessity.

The research on which this analysis is based was part of a cross-country study using a framework of 'sustainable livelihoods' – which in our view provides a language through which economic and anthropological views can be integrated. The framework is described in the next section, followed by a description of some of the characteristics of the two sites, and the history and current incidences of migration. The livelihoods analysis emphasises the institutional (formal and informal) arrangements through which people gain access to resources. Section IV therefore describes the institutions that determined forms of migration in the two villages. Female migration, and the way this was embedded in kinship networks, is described in section V. Section VI describes the contribution migration made to the livelihoods of villages, and section VII concludes.

II. THE LIVELIHOODS FRAMEWORK

The research on which this study is based was part of a multi-country, comparative research programme based at the Institute of Development Studies (IDS), Sussex, funded by ESCOR, DFID, on sustainable livelihoods. This studied villages in different agro-ecological zones in Bangladesh and Ethiopia as well as Mali. Fieldwork was undertaken during 1997/98.

The concept 'sustainable livelihoods' relates to households' and communities' conditions of poverty, well-being and capabilities, resilience, and their natural resource base. Households attempt to improve these aspects of their livelihoods, or at least try to avoid their deterioration.[1] In improving their livelihoods, households do not rely on agriculture alone –

though this has been emphasised in past research. Throughout history, in varying degrees, rural households have undertaken a variety of strategies, local non-farm activities, and migration, often to distant places. In the research in Mali, rural livelihoods were conceptualised as composed of a combination of three strategies: agro-pastoral activities, livelihood diversification and migration.

The focus here is the contribution of migration to the sustainable livelihoods of poor rural households.[2] In the region labour migration has been an integral part of the livelihoods of the majority of households for at least two generations (section III below describes some of the macro-factors that shaped the migration patterns). Populations have been highly mobile for centuries, which underlines the necessity to conceptualise these movements – their various forms, and their roles for different socio-economic groups – as integral parts of peoples' and households' livelihoods, rather than as mere survival strategies in times of adversity.

Our approach to understanding livelihoods has an institutional focus. Societies are not unstructured groupings of free individuals. Neither is a society a homogeneous unity, in which all elements conform to a general set of agreed rules. Societies consist of individuals living *in* groups. Their living together is made possible by rules, written and informal, which have widespread use in society. These rules are not fixed and uncontested, but they do 'structure' the ways people behave in society.

This framework corresponds well with recent directions in migration research, that have emphasised the importance of the structuration of migration streams, how people migrate using their networks, and how their migration movements are determined by rules of their 'home society'. Migration is not an atomistic reaction to economic or environmental pressure, but is embedded in societal rules and norms. Two kinds of institutions have been identified as having a particularly strong impact on migration – and in turn are structured by migration: the networks through which migrants obtain access to resources, and households' structure and management. These institutions determine the contribution migration can make to improving livelihoods, but this link is by no means direct or simple, as section VI describes.

III. MIGRATION FROM THE TWO VILLAGES: BACKGROUND

Mali is a landlocked country with three principal agricultural systems: cotton, irrigated rice, and rain-fed food grains. Livestock play an important role in all three systems, while further north pastoralists are more numerous and rain-fed agriculture becomes less viable. Two villages were selected to illustrate different agro-ecosystems: Zaradougou in the cotton-growing

MAP
LOCATIONS OF RESEARCH IN MALI

region of Mali Sud; and Dalonguebougou in the rain-fed millet region on the North bank of the Niger river, where Toulmin carried out field research during the early 1980s.[3]

Zaradougou is a small village located in the Sudano-Sahelian cotton region, 27 kilometres from the major town of Sikasso. Cotton, cereals and sedentary livestock were the main local sources of livelihoods. Compared to Dalonguebougou, Zaradougou was more commercialised, with Sikasso as an outlet for products and services, and had experienced more relatively capital-led agricultural intensification. The majority of villagers were Sénoufo and could trace their lineage to one of three households of early settlers. Apart from two households who lived on the periphery of the village, no strangers had immigrated since it was founded in the late nineteenth century. The majority of households were large and extended.

Dalonguebougou is situated in the risk-prone Sahelian dryland. It had experienced little formal agricultural extension, though some agricultural intensification in the form of fertilisers had taken place through farmer innovation. Farming and grazing remained the principal uses of land, and millet and both sedentary and transhumant livestock the predominant local livelihood sources. The village's sandy soil was valued for agriculture, making it a popular choice for in-migrants seeking to establish themselves as farmers in the area. The village was relatively isolated, and integration into the cash economy was ongoing. There was an efficient system of marketing millet, but few opportunities for marketing anything else. The village was ethnically diverse, with four distinct social groups: the largest group of 'village Bambara', 'visiting Bambara', Fulani and Maure. Large extended households predominated, and there was one female-headed household at the time of the research.

West Africa has historically been marked by a dense network of migration.[4] At the beginning of the century, migration of individuals was not common, but travelling caravans were (Sikasso was a significant trading centre). French colonial policies led to improved infrastructure, and the introduction of taxes, forced labour on 'administrative fields' and in construction, and military conscription. This widened the sphere of economic responsibility of households, and increased amounts of work outside the household to fill forced labour quotas and to earn cash to pay taxes. In Dalonguebougou, for example, young men started to migrate in the dry season migrations during the 1930s, walking to Senegal to work on the groundnut harvest to raise money to pay household taxes.

High rates of migration have continued,[5] though patterns have changed under the influence of altering policies and environmental circumstances. During the 1930s, for example, falling cotton prices, extremely poor harvests and plagues of crickets and grasshoppers led to high out-migration from Sikasso *cercle*. During the 1960s and 1970s, low prices for cereal farmers and stagnating production contributed to out-migration: young men recalled wanting to escape from the repressive atmosphere and lack of opportunity at home. The Sahelian droughts of the 1970s and 1980s had a strong impact on migration patterns [*Pederson, 1995; Findley, 1994*]. But the period 1962–84 was also a golden period for migration across the border, because of the relative over-valuation of the currency in Côte d'Ivoire after Mali's withdrawal from the CEFA, and because migrants were welcome in Côte d'Ivoire.

The two villages had high incidences of migration, but with very different patterns. In both sites, migration was predominantly circular.[6] Permanent migration was rare, and usually restricted to very poor households, or large complex households that were not functioning well. The benefits of the security that the household offered, and the promise of a marriage partner, seemed to outweigh the risk of striking out alone and the restrictions within the household structure.

From Zaradougou migration to Côte d'Ivoire over a distance of 800 kilometres was the pre-dominant strategy. This cross-border migration was of a fairly unique type. Most of the long-established Senoufo households had developed a livelihood strategy based on cultivation of cotton and grains around the village, combined with plantations in different parts of Côte d'Ivoire. Twelve out of the 16 households in Zaradougou farm (not necessarily own) one or more cocoa and coffee farms in a different agro-ecological zone, effectively straddling the two and reducing risks. Family labour was predominant on the farms; agricultural labourers were nearly always other Malians or Burkinabè (and short in supply).[7] The number of plantations had increased slowly over time, and expanded to a number of different locations. Recently, obtaining a plantation had become increasingly risky and expensive. Not only was less land available than a few decades ago, the relative security of tenure experienced by the settlers had been shaken, illustrating the less welcoming atmosphere for migrants in Côte d'Ivoire as compared to earlier decades.

Migration was also a very common strategy in Dalonguebougou, with seasonal circular migration to rural and urban areas, and to Côte d'Ivoire. Some permanent out-migration had occurred. Patterns were very different for each of the four ethnic groups. The principal sources of income for Fulani and Maure – who both define themselves as herders though agriculture is central to their base livelihood activities – was sale of livestock and salaries from herding. Migration had long been a feature of the Bambara livelihood system. Young men worked as forced labour on the colonial public works projects. During the poor harvests in the 1930s men left the village to search for work in Senegal, to find the necessary funds to pay taxes. For the 'village Bambara' migration was the second most important source of income, after the sale of agricultural surplus. Many 'visiting Bambara' also migrated every year, to work in towns and in Côte d'Ivoire during the dry season.

The research provided detailed information about the activities of the migrants. Zaradougou households owned on average 18 hectares of plantation in Côte d'Ivoire – an average of 0.5 hectare per person – but with large variations. During the agricultural season 1997/98, households dedicated on average 34 per cent of their active labour force to these plantations, and 31 per cent of households defined the plantations as their most important source of income.

Activities of female and male migrants from Dalonguebougou are presented in Table 1. During the early 1980s, Toulmin's research showed that young men from Dalonguebougou spent several months of the dry

TABLE 1

DIVERSIFIED LIVELIHOODS AMONG VILLAGE BAMBARA, DALONGUEBOUGOU

Unmarried women	Seasonal urban circular migration, domestic work *Namadé:* waged agricultural labour in local area Cotton spinning
Married women	Individual field production Smallstock rearing Commerce Cotton spinning
Unmarried men	Seasonal circular migration to urban centres and distant rural areas (weaving, well digging, factory work) Waged agricultural labour in local rural area Waged agricultural labour in village Cotton weaving
Married men still active in household labour team	Seasonal circular migration Waged agricultural labour in village Artisanal/skilled activities (weaving, sewing, fortune telling, woodwork) Smallstock rearing Commerce Waged agricultural labour in local area
'Retired' married men	Individual field production Smallstock rearing Commerce Artisanal/skilled activities (granary and basket making, fortune telling)

Source: Brock and Coulibaly [*1999*].

season away from the village, and in weaving jobs at Ségou, harvesting rice, or digging wells in Côte d'Ivoire, returning for the first sowing. Patterns of migration changed; weaving declined, and new job opportunities were found in the irrigated agricultural economy in the canal town of Niono and its surrounding rural hinterland, in irrigated rice and vegetable production, both of which offer a longer growing season and in some cases a double-cropping cycle. Some men went to Bamako, to work in occupations ranging from brick-laying to loading and unloading cargo lorries. Several young men went to Guinea, where they worked as diamond miners during the 1980s. This was extremely lucrative but did not last. Men continued to prefer the established networks of support in Côte d'Ivoire, and well-digging became the most important activity.

In both sites, it was predominantly young men who migrated. Their moves were closely related to household management and demographic cycles. Migration from Zaradougou to Côte d'Ivoire plantations resembled a *rite de passage*. Heads of extended households decided about migration strategies and for young men to stay at the plantations for three years or so. A young man ceased to be an adolescent – a *bilakoro,* traditionally tasked with activities judged too tiresome for adults, like catching escaped animals, searching for termites to feed chickens and chasing away crop predators – after he returned from migration as well as when he married.

Each group of men from Zaradougou was accompanied by at least one young woman, to do domestic work.[8] But, as we describe extensively in section V, women migrated individually as well. Saving for marriage was a main motivation of female migrants from Dalonguebougou. Traditionally, they had migrated for seasonal rural work; recently, they had also taken up migration to urban areas, though this was hardly profitable.

IV. INFORMAL INSTITUTIONS AND MIGRATION

The research was centrally concerned with how institutions influence the way households tried to achieve a sustainable livelihood: institutions, both formal and informal, determined whether and how households could obtain access to the resources available. We focus here on the importance of personal contacts and kinship networks, the way household form and gender structured migration processes, and how in turn migration played a role in reproducing local informal institutions and norms.

In the case of migration from Zaradougou, after the journey of a first migrant to Côte d'Ivoire – reportedly with a friend – personal networks between origin and destination had been exceptionally close. Village-wide networks had played an important role in initial and subsequent access to the coffee and cacao plantations in various parts of Côte d'Ivoire, so much so that one could describe the areas of origin and destination as a single integrated economic and social space.

Dalonguebougou's migration patterns were strongly determined by ethnic identity. Seasonal circular migration was carried out mostly by Bambara, whereas activities involving migration by Fulani and Maure were restricted to herding and animal-related activities. In-migration of visiting Bambara to Dalonguebougou followed extended kinship networks. Young female migration also was within close kinship networks – this is described in detail in the next section. In Dalonguebougou, work was found through kinship networks, but also through public announcements for factory work on the radio and informal labour exchanges in towns like Ségou. First-time out-migration of young men (often relatively local) was usually funded by the household, whereas subsequent more distant departures tended to be funded by the migrant himself. It was not unusual to see the migrant undertaking a short period of local agricultural work to fund his journey. Many men left in pairs, often comprising one first-time migrant and one more experienced migrant. Returned migrants from Côte d'Ivoire were carefully questioned. They provided information and contacts to those about to depart.

Migration patterns from both villages have been dominated by the existence of large extended households. Participatory sustainability ranking at the start of the research – which documented people's own perceptions of the elements of a household's sustainable livelihood [*Brock and Coulibaly, 1999*] – brought out the crucial importance of household (demographic) structure and management; other important criteria included ownership of a range of assets. People defined household as a group of people farming the same common field and eating from a single granary. Its members were related by patrilineal kinship, and headed by the oldest male member. Within households sub-groups existed, and women often cultivated individual fields.[9]

In Zaradougou, extended households remained the norm among Senoufou, but various large households had broken up during the last decade. More long-term data would be required to establish whether this implies a trend of declining practice. In Dalonguebougou, the traditional structure was maintained: the research showed an increase in the percentage of the population living in complex extended households. Most Bambara households were complex structures incorporating several generations of one family (the largest household in the village had 86 members). Every member of a household had obligations in terms of labour; in return, the household met their basic needs in terms of food, the payment of taxes and the funding of marriages.[10]

Within household management, migration played a crucial role. In Dalonguebougou, heads of households decided about the migration of their sons or nephews – and their wives. Migration served an important social function in maintaining the prevailing system of labour management. It helped to balance household and individual interests. It allowed a young man some independence in a labour management system with high level of control over the activities of individuals. Out-migration offered a chance to acquire status without withdrawing his labour permanently from the household. It also offered household heads the chance to reward young men for their continued work. The following case, of a relatively rich household, illustrates how household heads tried to manage the migration process, attempting to turn the leaving of members into a function of maintaining the household's unity.

> The head of one of the richest households in Dalonguebougou, which ran a shop and a mill and owned a comfortably large herd of cattle, forbade his children to migrate, with the argument that the household was capable of meeting all its needs – his sons were indeed visibly well provided for. Several years earlier, one of the sons repeatedly asked to be allowed to travel to Côte d'Ivoire, which he was permitted to do after much persuasion. He worked for three months of the dry season and returned. His father did not require him to remit any of his income to the household, and afterwards observed 'he found that it was the same thing there, and afterwards he was happy here'.

Generally, households remain unified, while strategies depended, in Zaradougou, on plantations in Côte d'Ivoire. Interestingly, in the context of reflections on the role of migration for social cohesion, some regarded migration as less threatening for household unity than livelihood diversification at home. But there was always the possibility that the young men used the opportunity, when they migrated, to establish their own household. In discussions about the contribution of plantations to livelihoods in Zaradougou, the issue of trust and distrust between those at home and at the plantation was central. Some people who were away were thought to be cheating, and preparing for breakaway from the household.

> Family L owned two plantations in Côte d'Ivoire. After the head of the household died, his brother took over the role of managing the household. Differences of opinion that existed before became accentuated. Within the household – that recently experienced the deaths of various children – much was managed at the level of the nuclear sub-household. The son of the original head of the household managed the first of the family's plantation, and seemed unwilling to accept orders from his uncle, the new chef of the

family. He felt that he was the settler of the plantation and therefore in a way the owner.

Migration decisions often depended on composition, size and wealth of the household. In very large households in Dalonguebougou, when there were many single young men, the household head could enforce a strict rotation for people wanting to migrate. This could cause resentment, and continued equilibrium then depended on the management skills of the head of household. In households which were short of labour, or where the young man in question had a particular skill, the household head could refuse to let the man depart. For example:

> A respondent in Dalonguebougou wanted to return to Côte d'Ivoire for a second season digging wells, but was told by his household head that his presence was needed to weave cloth for a family wedding taking place that year. Another wanting to leave to earn money for clothes for himself and his fiancée was ordered to stay to carry out essential tasks for the household, but given money by his father. And the head of a household forbade all young men to migrate after they had been forced to sell two oxen and another one died, and concentrated human labour on deepening the well to increase its capacity to attract herds.

Despite the difficulties of managing large households, and constantly underlying tensions, overall, larger households – in Dalonguebougou in any case – tended to be better able to diversify livelihoods successfully, and incorporate extensive labour migration in household strategies, than members of smaller ones.

The discussion so far has been mainly about male migrants, and how their patterns of movement were structured by the still dominant household structures and norms. But women migrated as well, not only to accompany men to the plantations, but also 'independently', as discussed next.

V. FEMALE MIGRATION

Most migration is by men, but among the Bambara in Dalonguebougou there was significant female migration as well. This was mostly within rural areas though relatively recently women had gone to urban areas as well. Women's circular migration served a different purpose from men's, but was equally embedded in the prevailing system of household management. It seems that this challenged the system less than, for example, the recent female migration in Indonesia as described by Elmhirst in this volume.

The basic motivation for wage earning activities amongst unmarried women was to buy goods for her *trousseau*, the astonishing collection of household goods that was taken when she married.[11] The women's mothers generally decided at what age they started migrating, and thereafter they departed almost every year. Some women did this for six or seven years, and in some cases also in the first two years of their marriage.

The movement of these young Bambara women, called *namadé*, was based on kinship networks. It formed part of the complex institutions surrounding marriage. For generations, households had been joined together, over a wide area, by long-standing links created by earlier marriages between two families. Strong links were maintained between a woman and her natal household, and the women would turn first to her father and brother when food was short in her husband's household.

Women left late in the agricultural season, before the harvest began, and sought lodging with a related family in another village. The host family took the young woman in and provided her with food and housing. The women carried out domestic work and some field work for their hosts, but the bulk of their time was spent working for a few days at a time with other households in the village, for which they were rewarded with the standard rate of pay. Host families arranged this work with neighbours. Some *namadé* undertook paid work for Fulani and Maure households. Many stayed in the village working until the end of the season. If it finished early, they could move on to another village for winnowing work.

There was an inflow and outflow of *namadé* in each village. This seldom balanced exactly, but villagers said that over the years there was an equilibrium which did not leave them at a disadvantage. Household heads could not turn a *namadé* away: asked what he did in difficult years, a household head said he simply hoped that no woman would arrive and left the rest up to God. The only acceptable ground for refusal was if there were already two or three *namadé* working for the household that day.

Urban migration by Bambara women from Dalonguebougou was a relatively recent phenomenon. In 1980/81 there were only a few instances where women left to work in towns. Throughout the late 1980s and early 1990s, increasing numbers of women persuaded their parents to allow them to migrate further afield. Many young women took the opportunity to seek cash wages and different working conditions, mostly as domestic servants in Bamako. They used kinship relationships to find work. Some built up relationships with their employers, and returned year after year.

Not all parents were convinced that young women should be allowed to migrate to town, and they could have a long struggle to depart. A mother of several teenage daughters said she felt it was only a matter of time before a young woman would find a husband in another place and fail to return, reflecting trends that she had heard of in other areas of the country.

Women's urban migration was not undertaken solely for lucrative wages. In fact, wages were extremely low. One woman emphasised that curiosity was an important motive for her. After an initial wave of women departing for Bamako in the early 1990s, the number reportedly diminished when women realised that they had a higher earning potential working as *namadé* when the millet price was good. Some women during 1997/98 worked as *namadé* until the harvest ended, before departing to spend the rest of the dry season in Bamako.

Thus the migration of young women, while being an essential part of the long-term livelihoods strategy – for women particularly to secure assets for marriage – remained within the confines of the kinship networks and existing norms. Like the migration of young men, women's movement was not without tensions. Yet, in general, the ties to the household remained strong, and usually even the potential long-term attractions of the towns did not separate the households.

VI. HOW DOES MIGRATION INTERACT WITH OTHER ELEMENTS OF LIVELIHOODS?

So far we have focused on the general background and institutions that influence migration patterns. This section describes the way migration interacted with the other elements of households' livelihoods. We do not ask the more commonly used question regarding effect of migration on poverty or other social factors. Particularly in Zaradougou, with its exceptional migration pattern, migration was so closely intertwined with the socio-economic position of the household that it is impossible to distinguish cause and effect. As found elsewhere, however, access to migration opportunities can contribute significantly to improving livelihoods, and hence to differentiation within or between communities.

The link between migration and livelihoods in general differed between the two villages. Data on village Bambara in Dalonguebougou allows us to explain migration in relation to three factors: household management, household structure, as well as households' ownership of assets (which, as described above, in the sustainability ranking came out as the most important elements of livelihoods). This suggests that migration in Dalonguebougou was most common in the households that were ranked in the *middle group*. The less well-off households had fewer migrants, probably because of a lack of available labour. The livelihood strategies of better-off households, by contrast, meant that migration was one of a range of options in which available labour could be invested.

By contrast, in Zaradougou better-off households clearly had profited from extensive migration to Côte d'Ivoire.[12] There was a clear relationship between those households that invested early and successfully in plantations in Côte d'Ivoire and the size of cattle holdings. In 1997, 93 per cent of the cattle in the village were owned by the first six households to invest in plantations. Also, households which successfully integrated crops and livestock were those that invested successfully in migration.

> The household of Bougou Sanogo, with 95 members (but expected to break up), was a clear example of how migration and improved livelihoods were inter-linked. It was the third to settle in Cote d'Ivoire – at which point the household was already well-off – owned no less than six plantations, and had many assets in the home village.

However, as the chapter on Bihar in India in this volume emphasises, such patterns are likely to change over time. Though migration for many of Zaradougou's households was related to improved livelihoods at the time of research, the first migration for example had not been by a better-off household. Aly Traore – whose household *became* one of the better-off in the village – was the first to set up a plantation in Côte d'Ivoire. He left, with the help of his cousin, and initial success with the help of such networks and sustained migration contributed to building up the household's position to what it was at the end of the 1990s.

The research did not quantify financial flows between households and their migrants, but case histories document their central importance. The people who had gone to the plantations returned with the profits, which were given to the head of the household, or kept individually or at the sub-household level. The exact form and quantity of remittances depended heavily on the cohesion of relationships within the household. The complexity of flows – financial, human and otherwise – between Zaradougou and Côte d'Ivoire over a longer period is illustrated below with a case study of one household.

Migration by village Bambara women might not provide a direct contribution to household agricultural expenses. However, by assisting the household in meeting its obligations in terms of marriage expenses, young women's earnings contributed greatly to the continued successful reproduction of the household, and thus to the sustainability of the livelihoods which it supported. Only women in the poorest households used any of their *namadé* earnings to make direct cash contributions to the household in the form of remittances to the household head.

Remittances by young men from Dalonguebougou were usually divided between the migrant and the household head. Part of the money kept by the migrant – very often the major part – was spent on clothes. Money remitted

CASE STUDY OF FLOWS BETWEEN ZARADOUGOU AND CÔTE D'IVOIRE
(ONE HOUSEHOLD, WITH LONG-ESTABLISHED MIGRANTS)

Type of Capital	Zaradougou to Côte d'Ivoire	Côte d'Ivoire to Zaradougou
Financial	Investments for the purchase of land in 1963 (100,000), 1985 (350,000) and 1988 (300,000*). At the same times, investments to establish three permanent work teams.	A variable annual contribution to the household *caisse*. Very low in 1976–78 and 1984–86 (drought); very high in 1981–82 (high coffee prices), and in 1984 (devaluation CFA franc). In 1994 and 1995 specific sums to pay for oxen, in addition to the annual remittance.
Human	Eleven working adults are generally based at the three plantations. In 1991 the household head visited one of the plantations when it was burned in an act of vandalism	Two workers returned to the village on the death of an active member of the household
Natural	A certain quantity of maize sent each year for consumption	
Social	Transfer of knowledge: one of the plantations now cultivates cotton	

* Estimates by household head, and may be exaggerated.

to the household head was spent at his discretion on the needs of the household. A visible impact of migration was in the material goods brought back – radios, mopeds, wooden beds and manufactured clothes – which contributed to changing demand for consumer goods.

But the returns were not only in 'consumer goods'. As noted by Toulmin, the first ploughs in the village in the 1950s were paid for directly with migration earnings and livestock sales. Most migrants returned speaking a few words of French, some young men had acquired basic literacy or other practical skills, and two migrants who received a brief training ran a class for a short period. But few skills were acquired that were directly relevant for livelihoods in the villages. As most dry-season migration was not for work in either livestock or agriculture, little knowledge directly related to work in the village was gained. Also, most worked in very different agro-ecological zones, rendering skills irrelevant to their home agro-ecosystem, though they could be used to start up non-agricultural activities.

The substantial and varied impact of migration is illustrated in the following case.

N'ganiba from Dalonguebougou made his first migration at the age of 25 in 1963, for agricultural work near Ségou. He paid for clothes for himself and remitted a sum to his father, specifically to assist in the payment of taxes. His migrations continued for four years until the death of his father, when he became head of the small household.

His place as provider of cash for household needs was taken by his younger brother, who worked first on the Niono rice harvest in 1968, and then established a prosperous dry-season weaving business in Ségou, where he lived for between four and seven months for seventeen years. Apart from clothes for himself and own wife and children, during these 17 years he paid all the household taxes, and allowed the household to purchase a donkey cart, a pair of oxen and the marriage costs for two wives. He retired from weaving in 1987.

Makono, the youngest brother, began to travel to the Côte d'Ivoire in 1977 after working with his older brother in Ségou, and undertook this journey almost every year for the last twenty, with breaks only for a hand injury in the mid-1980s, building a house for himself and his wives in the late 1980s, and a period in the early 1990s when he undertook a short administrative course in making out birth, marriage and death records. As one of only two literate French speakers in the village, his skills are much in demand. Makono made a mean annual remittance in cash of 41.000FCFA to N'ganiba, ranging from 10.000FCFA in a bad year to 90.000FCFA during the diamond-mining boom. In addition, he brought several bicycles, a mobylette, clothes, beds, spare parts for agricultural equipment and goods for trade. In early 1998, he departed for Côte d'Ivoire with his oldest nephew Modibo, N'ganiba's son.

This household became one of the most prosperous in the village, and remittances played a central role in this prosperity. Initially they allowed the small household to pay tax, then funded the acquisition of the necessary equipment and assets to assure its own reproduction, and finally helped the acquisition of a wider range of assets which insure against future shocks and stresses. The basic factor enabling this accumulation of wealth through diversification was the constant availability of at least three able-bodied adult men amongst whom the necessary tasks of household labour could be divided.

By contrast, in households where labour was very short and need great, migration could be a strategy to cope with adversity.[13]

Saba, being the only man of working age in his household, took the decision to spend most of the 1996/7 agricultural season away from the village earning the necessary money to buy a donkey cart. The women and children in the household did their best to cultivate a field in his absence, but by the middle of the 1997/8 agricultural season their granary was empty, and they spent the remainder of the season living off loans, and millet donated by family and neighbours.

At the household level demand for local labour usually was balanced against desire to migrate – though this was more difficult the less-endowed the household was. Nevertheless, the continued existence of uncultivated land in Zaradougou, in a context of increasing land shortage, could in part be attributed to the fact that most households employed a large proportion of their active labour force to work on their second farms in Cote d'Ivoire.[14] According to an extension officer in Zaradougou, the relatively low area under cotton, compared to immediate neighbouring villages, was related to the relatively high levels of out-migration in the village. Our research could not determine the exact effect of this.

Thus the descriptions of cases show that in many cases migration was clearly closely related to households livelihoods and well-being. They also indicate that the dynamics differed between the two villages – not surprisingly given the exceptional pattern of migration from Zaradougou – and that migration can enhance inequality. The next section suggests some of the reasons that determine success in migration.

VII. WHAT DETERMINES SUCCESS?

The research in Mali has not been able to quantify in a comparable way the impact of migration on livelihoods. But the research suggested a number of factors that determine whether migration is likely to make a positive contribution to household's livelihoods, also possibly enhancing inequalities between households.

First, of course conditions at the destination side of the migration streams mattered. For example, bad working conditions seemed crucial to the unpopularity of migration and lack of impact on livelihoods at home. In the case of the plantations run by the Zaradougou households, security of tenure was very important: the households that invested early in plantations tended to be the most sustainable (and they may emerge from the changing legal tenure situation with some of their assets intact).

Second, the research showed that a positive and sustainable outcome of migration usually cannot be evaluated outside its relationship with the other livelihood strategies, or the portfolio of household activities. In Zaradougou, the most sustainable households in the village all had at least two sources of income in addition to their plantations. The case of N'ganiba from Dalonguebougou described above indicates how migration could help to stimulate activities in the village. In other words, migration helped households to improve or maintain their livelihoods particularly if they were able to support migrants when necessary, and when income from migration could feed into local productive activities.

Third, as described in section IV, household structure mattered a great deal. In small households with an unfavourable demographic structure, migration opportunities were restricted, for example,[15] by the availability of immediate kin to take care of elderly parents.[15] In Zaradougou, a secure supply of labour to run farming enterprises at home as well as in Côte d'Ivoire, initially from within the household, influenced household heads' decisions to let young men move, and the success of the migration strategy.

Such attempts to orchestrate movements in the best interests of the joint household could create tensions, but if successful helped the households to use the – scarce – opportunities provided at both ends. Thus the cohesiveness of the household structure was also relevant. Perhaps paradoxically, in Zaradougou, cohesive household structures allowed independence to those running plantations in Côte d'Ivoire – thus also assuring regular financial remittances to the household.

Finally, networks – and what is now often termed social capital – were important for the success of migration. The limited development of physical infrastructure in the region did not restrict, and historically has not restricted, the existence of very close personal networks over long distances. The migration by young Bambara women was along long-established networks, and the research in Zaradougou indicated that social capital in Côte d'Ivoire allowed investments to be maximised by improving efficiency.

VIII. CONCLUSION

In West Africa, population mobility has been the rule rather than the exception. In the area of research on which this contribution is based, populations have been mobile for centuries, and labour migration has been central to livelihoods for at least two generations. The factors that have determined mobility have been complex and variable. Extreme insecurity and vulnerability in the Sahelian environment has been, of course, one of the dominant reasons for population mobility. The Sahelian droughts of the 1970s and 1980s had a strong impact on migration patterns. On the 'pull' side, economic opportunities in Côte d'Ivoire and the relative ease of cross-border movement altered patterns of labour migration, and to a great extent integrated economies over hundreds of kilometres.

This study, like Hampshire's in this volume, has challenged a common view of West African migrants as victims of vagaries of weather, mismanagement of land, population pressure, economic crises etc. Instead, by using a livelihoods framework, we have tried to describe how rural households integrate migration of their members into their overall strategies of survival and risk management. Patterns of migration are influenced, of course, by demand for labour, but also by local institutions determining access to opportunities and resources. Household structure and management are crucial in determining who migrates, and when – though such processes are by no means without friction. As other papers in this volume also show, migration is strongly gendered: most of the labour migration is by men, but women often migrate – within the boundaries of kinship networks – before they get married.

The migration patterns described challenge our notions of space, and of isolated villages. The history of migration in West Africa shows that mobility, including across current borders, has been the norm rather than the exception. The movement of young women, *namadé*, indicates that villages, and villagers, are part of social networks with wide geographical spread. The case of Zaradougou in particular, where for decades migration to Côte d'Ivoire has been a central part of household strategies, prompts us to reconsider our concept of village economies, and to think about integrated economies that spread over hundreds of kilometres, across political borders, straddling different agro-ecological zones.

For historical reasons, the patterns of migrations differ radically between the two villages, and between households within the villages. Nevertheless, as the anthropological perspective of the research in both villages showed, migration is integral to the livelihoods of households, and these livelihoods are as much 'social' as 'economic'. Though migration is clearly a strategy to cope with the insecurity of the environment, social norms determine who migrates, and hence who benefits. Household and kinship networks structure the movement of individuals, by providing them with some independence while at the same time retaining them within these networks.

NOTES

1. The livelihoods framework is described in Scoones [*1998*], and adapted in Carney [*1998*]. The framework followed Chambers and Conway [*1992*], who defined livelihoods as 'the capabilities, assets (stores, resources, claims, and access) and activities required for a means of living', emphasising the need for research to go beyond a focus on income alone.

2. See de Haan *et al.* [*2000*], summarising findings of research in the three countries. The role of diversification in rural livelihoods emerging from the livelihoods project at IDS is discussed in Toulmin *et al.* [*2000*]. The importance of non-agricultural employment has been emphasised, *inter alia*, by Reardon [*1997*], Ellis [*1998*], and Bryceson [*1999, 2000*]

who emphasises that at the end of the twentieth century sub-Saharan Africa's rural population, under the influence of liberalisation and adjustment, has become more occupationally flexible and spatially mobile.

3. Toulmin [*1992*]. Our study was not set up as a longitudinal one, though changes have been described where appropriate (and relatively straightforward), for example regarding changes in household composition, the price of the *trousseau* for women when they got married, and broad changes in migration patterns.

4. Before the current borders were created, population mobility may well have been higher in the region. With the creation of the borders, for example, Senoufo were divided between Mali, Côte d'Ivoire, Burkina Faso. International migration may have been more important for the livelihoods in these areas in the decades immediately after Independence. Descriptions of the importance of labour migration can be found, in, for example, Toulmin [*1992*], Painter, Sumberg and Price [*1994*], Ruthven and David [*1995*], Christiaensen and Boisvert [*2000*].

5. The West African Long-Term Perspective Study (in Winter [*1997*]) estimated that 30 to 40 per cent of West Africans live outside their district or village of birth, and that 11 per cent of West Africans (excluding Nigerians) live outside their country of birth. An estimated 3.3 million immigrants live in Cote d'Ivoire, or about a quarter of its population, mainly from Burkina Faso and Mali: numbers from Mali increased from 350,000 in 1975 to 735,000 in 1993 and about one million by 1994.

6. Cordell *et al.* [*1996*] is a fascinating study of circular migration in West Africa, showing how migrants effectively link village and town, origin and destination, and continue to circulate between 'hoe and wage'.

7. In rare cases, Malian children were recruited to work on plantations, on the promise of future wages. They work in conditions of virtual slavery, often for many years. In June 1998 a network of people trafficking child labourers between Mali and Côte d'Ivoire was uncovered, resulting in the return of 20 children between the ages of 12 and 18 to Mali.

8. One woman expressed negative feelings about life on the plantation: she felt herself hostage on the plantations, life was boring, she was isolated and lived far away from markets. Gender roles did not differ substantially at the plantations, but the manual tasks of women were harder, and shared between fewer women than in the large household at home.

9. Women usually left their household of origin when they married and became incorporated into another household, whereas men either stayed within their household of origin or left to establish an independent unit.

10. Fulani households were generally the smallest of the three groups, nuclear in structure, though often incorporating an elderly mother or other female relative. Though divided geographically, social and economic links between parents and sons, and between brothers, remained strong. Maure fathers, like Fulani, were obliged to find wives for their sons, but unlike among Fulani sons stayed in the father's household until their children reached maturity, at which point they established their own household.

11. The cost of a trousseau had multiplied alongside expectations of the manufactured goods it should contain: cost was approximately seven times that in 1980/81. The family, in particular the mother, contributed.

12. This is similar to Hampshire's conclusion in this volume regarding Fulani's temporary migration to cities being positively linked with wealth

13. An issue about which we do not have information is the reduction of household consumption – and thus reducing the likelihood of having to sell assets in dry seasons – due to the absence of the migrant. In some studies this has been shown to be the single most important contribution of migration to the household economy [*Swift, 1984*].

14. Other reasons for this include the relatively large village territory, and the success of

villagers in preventing in-migration
15. In the comparative sustainable livelihoods research, this was found to be an issue particularly in Ethiopia (in highland Wolayta), where nuclear households dominated. The research suggested that this was less of an issue in Bangladesh, perhaps partly because of the more closely-knit migration networks, partly because generally nuclear households were grouped together in larger units.

REFERENCES

Adepoju, A. and W. Mbugua, 1997, 'The African Family: An Overview of Changing Forms', in A. Adepoju, *Family, Population and Development in Africa*, London: Zed Books.

Brock, K., 1999, 'Implementing a Sustainable Livelihoods Framework for Policy-Directed Research: Reflections from Practice in Mali', IDS Working Paper 90, Brighton.

Brock, K. and N. Coulibaly, 1999, 'Sustainable Rural Livelihoods in Mali', IDS Research Report 35, Brighton.

Bryceson, D.F., 1999, *Sub-Saharan Africa Betwixt and Between: Rural Livelihoods Practices and Policies*, ASC Working Paper 43/1999, Afrika-Studiecentrum, Leiden.

Bryceson, D., 2000, 'Rural Africa at the Crossroads: Livelihood Practices and Policies', *Natural Resources Perspectives,* No.52, London: ODI.

Carney, D., 1998, *Sustainable Rural Livelihoods: What Contribution Can We Make?* London: DFID.

Chambers, R. and G. Conway, 1992, 'Sustainable Rural Livelihoods: Practical Concepts for the 21st Century', IDS Discussion Paper No. 296, Brighton: IDS.

Christiaensen, L.J. and R.N. Boisvert, 2000, *On Measuring Household Food Vulnerability: Case Evidence from Northern Mali*, Cornell University, Department of Agricultural, Resource, and Managerial Economics, WP2000-05, March 2000.

Cliggett, L. (n.d.), 'Economic and Social Components of Migration in Two Regions of Southern Province', Draft, Internet.

Cordell, D.D., Gregory, J.W. and V. Piché, 1996, *Hoe and Wage. A Social History of a Circular Migration System in West Africa*, Boulder, CO: Westview Press.

David, R., 1995, *Changing Places: Women, Resource Management and Migration in the Sahel,* London: SOS Sahel.

Davies, S., 1996, *Adaptable Livelihoods: Coping with Food Insecurity in the Malian Sahel,* London: Macmillan Press.

de Haan, A., Brock, K., Carswell, G., Coulibaly, N., Seba, H. and K.A. Toufique, 2000, 'Migration and Livelihoods: Case Studies in Bangladesh, Ethiopia and Mali', IDS Research Report 46, Brighton.

Ellis, F., 1998, 'Household Strategies and Rural Livelihood Diversification', *The Journal of Development Studies*, Vol.35, No.1, pp.1–38.

Findley, S.E., 1994, 'Does Drought Increase Migration? A Study of Migration from Rural Mali During the 1983–1985 Drought', *International Migration Review*, Vol.28, No.3, pp.539–53.

Painter, T., Sumberg, J. and T. Price, 1994, 'Your *Terroir* and My "Action Space": Implications of Differentiation, Mobility, and Diversification for the *Approche Terroir* in Sahelian West Africa', *Africa,* Vol.64, No.4, pp.447–64.

Pedersen, J., 1995, 'Drought, Migration and Population Growth in the Sahel: The Case of the Malian Gourma 1900–1991', *Population Studies*, Vol.49, pp.111–26.

Reardon, T., 1997, 'Using Evidence of Household Income Diversification to Inform Study of the Rural Nonfarm Labor Market in Africa', *World Development,* Vol.25 No.5: pp.735–47.

Ruthven, A. and R. David, 1995, 'Benefits and Burdens: Researching the Consequences of Migration in the Sahel', *IDS Bulletin*, Vol.26, No.1, pp.47–60.

Scoones, I, 1998, 'Sustainable Rural Livelihoods: A Framework for Analysis', IDS Working Paper 72, Brighton.

Swift, J., (ed.), 1984, *Pastoral Development in Central Niger: Report of the Niger Range and Livestock Project*, Niamey: USAID.

Toulmin, C., 1992, *Cattle, Women and Wells: Managing Household Survival in the Sahel*, Oxford: Oxford University Press.

Toulmin, C., Brock, K., Carswell, G., Toufique, K.A. and M. Greeley, 2000, 'Diversification of Livelihoods: Evidence from Mali, Ethiopia and Bangladesh', mimeo, IDS, University of Sussex.

Winter, M., 1997, 'Migration in the Central Sub-region of West Africa: Trends and Reflections', *Research Report*, London: Overseas Development Association.

Brokered Livelihoods:
Debt, Labour Migration and Development in Tribal Western India

DAVID MOSSE, SANJEEV GUPTA,
MONA MEHTA, VIDYA SHAH, JULIA REES
and the KRIBP PROJECT TEAM

I. INTRODUCTION

With a few notable exceptions [e.g., *Breman, 1996*], seasonal labour migration in India is a little studied subject. For one thing, being absent from routine and official data sources such as the National Sample Survey or local labour records it evades the attention of mainstream economics research. For another, the complex experiences and meanings of labour migration have been obscured by standard models. Following Gidwani and Sivaramakrishnan [*n.d.*] we can see these models as being broadly of two types.

The first is a 'dual economy' type model in which rational maximising labourers move from a lower paid agricultural (rural/traditional) sector to a higher paid industrial (urban/modern) one. The emphasis – albeit modified by imperfections of information and market competition – is on voluntary choice and individual response to an 'urban pull'.

The second is a Marxist model in which the stress is on structural factors rather than migrant agency, and on the efforts of dominant classes to 'expand surplus extraction by exploiting uneven patterns of proletarianisation and depeasantisation' [*ibid.*]. Migrants, 'pushed' out of peripheral areas, contribute to underpaid surplus labour in urban centres. It is a neo-Malthusian variant of the 'push factor' model which pervades development and environmentalist narratives [*Roe, 1991*]. Migrants are viewed as 'ecological refugees' [*Gadgil and Guha, 1995*] compelled to move by demographic pressure, declining agricultural production, de-forestation, water scarcity or soil erosion.

The authors would like gratefully to acknowledge support from the UK Department for International Development, and assistance and co-operation from Kribhco Indo-British Rainfed Farming Project for this study, although neither organisation is responsible for the views and analysis presented here. They also would like to thank Ben Rogaly and Arjan de Haan for useful comments on an earlier draft.

These models fail to capture seasonal labour migration as a dynamic aspect of rural livelihoods. Migration and rural livelihoods are falsely opposed, and rural *development* invariably is taken to imply the reaffirmation of a disrupted sedentary agricultural community; the measure of its success being the reduction of seasonal migration [*de Haan, 1999*].

In this study, we look for an approach to labour migration (or labour circulation) which moves away from a single model to allow an exploration of the relationship between structure and agency, urban work and rural society. We show that for some, labour migration is indeed a forced livelihood response, although it arises from a complex set of social relations (including relations of debt and dependency) rather than simply ecological crisis and subsistence failure. For others, however, migration provides a positive opportunity to save, accumulate capital or invest in assets.

While some migrants have surplus incomes to invest in agriculture or economically productive assets at home, others find their earnings already committed in relations of debt and dependency. Far from being uniform, the opportunities and social experience of migration within the communities of Bhil tribals who are our subjects here, are shaped by class, gender and existing relations of reciprocity, obligation or dependency, both within tribal communities and between them and non-tribal traders, moneylenders and labour contractors. Even the relationship between migration and livelihood security is by no means straightforward. Our case histories show that migration may not in fact improve income or security (may indeed undermine it by perpetuating debt and dependency) and yet it continues as a strategy of survival.

Our stories of migration involve both push and pull, structure and agency (indeed structurally embedded agency). They also collapse rather than evoke the binaries of urban–rural, or tradition and modernity. We will argue that the social phenomenon of urban migration is deeply embedded in rural social networks. The analysis explores the ways in which success in job hunting, the kind of working conditions, and levels of income earned are all shaped by the social position of households in their villages – their wealth and standing, prestige and position in village-based networks. It also examines the ways in which migration itself changes relations between and within households. Urban–rural connections are undoubtedly complex. Successful migrants invest in the forms of social and symbolic capital which ensure continued access to urban labour markets. But they prioritise investment in land and agriculture, assuring the continuity of peasant identities, even though the demands of cultivation often weaken their bargaining power with urban employers. In short, a perspective on migration is needed which goes beyond dichotomous models of push or pull, structure or agency, urban or rural, and allows labour migration to be seen as part of local and diverse livelihood strategies.

Engaging with the social experience of migration also requires that we move beyond a narrow economistic viewpoint. In ways that we can only hint at here, migration makes villages more cosmopolitan, introduces new types of consumption (of images as well as of goods or clothing) and challenges existing social relationships [*Gidwani and Sivaramakrishnan, n.d.*]. 'Migration is mostly about survival, but also a bit about adventure' (Farley, cited in Gidwani and Sivaramakrishnan [*n.d.: 13*]). Moreover, the experience of migration feeds into broader social and political aspirations, and ambivalent perceptions of identity culture and change among *adivasis* (tribals)in the western India region.

This study summarises the conclusions of team-based rapid research, arising from fieldwork undertaken between December 1996 and April 1997 [*Mosse et al., 1997*]. It focuses on Bhil tribal villages in the contiguous western Indian districts of Jhabua (W. Madhya Pradesh), Banswara (S. Rajasthan) and Panchmahals (E. Gujarat). The villages concerned are included in a DFID-funded participatory agricultural development project, the western India Kribhco Indo-British Rainfed Farming Project (KRIBP). Aiming to improve the livelihoods of poor farming families, this project involves an extended process of participatory planning in order to generate location-specific natural resources development plans [cf. *Mosse, 1994, 1996*].

Programme activities cover a range of farming system areas: crop trials and community seed multiplication, agro-forestry and 'wasteland' development, horticulture, soil and water conservation, minor irrigation, livestock development, and credit management for input supply. As far as possible these interventions are low cost, involve minimal subsidies and/or encourage cost-recovery. The sustainability of benefits beyond the life of the project depends upon continued involvement of communities in resource management, often through village-based groups (for example, irrigation groups, credit management groups). The project aims to achieve sustainable farming system improvements through enhancing the capabilities of women and men in tribal villagers to manage local resources and gain access to external resources and government programmes.[1]

From the start, migration was understood as an important coping mechanism of the poor in the project area. But the project's firm orientation towards a land resources view of livelihoods, meant that migration was viewed as a problem to be overcome rather than as a central part of livelihood strategies. Over the past five to six years, however, the project has deepened its analysis of Bhil livelihoods and the impact of its own actions through field-based participatory research, of which this study of seasonal migration is a part. The study involved four elements.

The first was a rapid survey covering 2,588 households in 42 project villages. Survey data were gathered by project 'Community Organisers' with the help of village volunteers. Secondly, more detailed qualitative work was undertaken in four villages to look at livelihood strategies and inter-household differences. Thirdly there was focused work with selected families carried out both in their home villages and at their sites of migration to give texture to the account of migration experiences and to identify issues concerning intra-household dynamics. Finally, work at recruitment centres in two urban sites (Kota and Baroda) involved contacts with industrial units, contractors, government labour officers, worker unions, and NGOs. As far as possible this research overlapped with other elements of the project's on-going impact assessment work and drew on existing data held in the project.

II. THE SOCIAL CONTEXT

The research focused on upland tribal districts in which almost all (89 per cent) of the Scheduled Tribe population are Bhils. Despite subtle socio-cultural variations between the districts, Bhil villages share institutions of kinship in relation to land. This is an area of dispersed non-nucleated settlement in which scattered homesteads are situated among their cultivated fields. Villages, as units of social and territorial organisation are, in theory and ideally, composed of a single male lineage – the core institution of Bhil social organisation which formerly defined rights over land and trees. Today, however, the association of lineage with territory is weak, and villages are more commonly composed of hamlets, which comprise sections of a dominant (founding) lineage or separate (perhaps inferior) lineages of recent settlers, or affinal relations. It is the hamlet (or *falia*) which is the unit of day-to-day social exchange (for example, goods and labour).

Livelihoods of Bhil households depend upon the cultivation of maize and upland rice staples on small plots (½ – 2 hectares) of sloping unirrigated land. Participatory research by the project suggests that 76 per cent of families are unable to meet their food requirements for more than six months a year, and many produce enough grain for only two or three months' subsistence. There is heavy dependence upon fast declining common property resources for fodder, fuel, fruits and other produce. Below subsistence production leads to seasonal and long-term borrowing for consumption and production and a majority of households in project villages have large outstanding loans. Limited access to institutional credit means that borrowing is largely at high interest from private money lenders. Deficit-induced debt gives rise to the mortgage and sale of assets among poorer families. However, the uniformly poor appearance of Bhil villages disguises significant differences in wealth, status and power within them, which, as discussed below, have an important bearing on the organisation and outcome of seasonal labour migration.

Despite the pervasiveness of the narrative of declining agricultural production, deforestation and migration, Bhil tribals have for long depended upon off-farm cash incomes to compensate for low agricultural output or to meet external cash revenue demands. Sources of income include those from employment as casual labour by forest departments and contractors and the collection and sale of forest produce such as *tendu* leaves, fodder, and fuel wood.

According to some surveys as few as 12 per cent of households are able to meet their needs through agriculture alone.[2] In the late 1940s one study of Bhils in eastern Panchmahals District (Gujarat) found that households were dependent on forest work (*kabadu*, felling and transporting logs for contractors) for 30–40 per cent of their income [*Naik, 1956*]. The ban on commercial logging reduced this source of local employment. Some alternative employment was available locally on public works such as canal and railway construction, or drought relief works.

However, by the late 1970s and 1980s Bhil farmers had to go further and further afield to secure employment. Initially much of this migration was to relatively nearby areas of commercial agriculture for harvest work. As will become clear, however, today tribal migration is predominantly to urban rather than rural areas. Indeed, casual labour in distant urban centres has largely replaced forest labour, local public works or migration to nearby rural areas as the main source of cash income.

III. THE EXTENT AND PATTERN OF MIGRATION AMONG BHILS

There have been few attempts to estimate the extent of seasonal labour migration from this Bhil area. Surveys in the 1970s done in the tribal taluks of Panchmahals district (Gujarat) indicated that 83 to 93 per cent of households had at least one member migrating for a longer or shorter period in the reference year [*Bureau of Economics and Statistics, 1974; Bhamania, 1976*]. Correspondingly, these studies indicated that between 27 and 40 per cent of the total working population were migratory at some time in the year. Studies in the 1980s showed a continuing increase in labour migration from tribal areas of the western region, in terms of numbers of migrants, duration of migration and the distances involved [*Breman, 1985; Mehta, 1982; Patel, 1987*].

The present research indicates a continuation of this upward trend. We found that 65 per cent of households and 48 per cent of the adult[3] population were involved in seasonal migration in 1995–96. On average two to three household members migrated for five to five-and-a-half months each in the year. A conservative estimate of earnings suggests gross annual earning from migration of about Rs 8,000 per family.[4] Today, earnings from migration are the primary source of cash income for the majority of households surveyed, contributing on average over 86 per cent of cash income. Labour migration, its networks and transactions are repeated year after year, and have become an integral part of Bhil social life.

By any reckoning, the movement of nearly half the adult population away from their homes and farms for nearly half of the year is a massive event in rural life. While the data we have are only for one year, they are broadly consistent with information from other studies.[5] However, taking migration in any one year almost certainly underestimates the proportion of households dependent on migration for their livelihood. We estimate that less than 15 per cent of households are non-migratory and non-dependent on migration earnings.

Although the pattern of migration is broadly similar across the area (Table 1), the extent of migration varies between villages (in 1995–96 anywhere between 21 and 95 per cent of families had migrant members) depending, among other things, on the extent of irrigation and *rabi* (winter) cropping, the availability of employment locally (for example, in mines, on public works), the proximity and accessibility of urban centres, the operating networks of contractor-recruiters, and the activities of the project.

More significantly, there is considerable variation between households in the number of migrants and period of work. The intensity of migration (taken as the reported total number of migration-months per family in

TABLE 1
SURVEY OF MIGRATION 1995–96

	Gujarat	MP	Rajasthan	Total
Villages surveyed	8	13	21	42
Households surveyed	784	688	1,116	2,588
Adults surveyed	2,558	2,448	3,622	8,628
Households migrating (no.)	496	448	745	1,689
Number of migrants	1,366	1,214	1,590	4,170
Households migrating (%)	63	65	67	65
Percentage of population migrating	53	50	44	48
Female migrants (as % of total)	45	43	39	42
Average migration months per family	15.9	16.4	9.4	13.2
Average migrants/household	2.8	2.7	2.1	2.5
Average migration months per person	5.8	6.1	4.4	5.3

1995–96) varied from one to two months to over 60 months (Figure 1).
Overall, there is a striking bimodal pattern with peaks at three to four and
11–15 months. This seems to correspond to the two most common patterns
of migration: namely, the migration of young adult males and the migration
of whole families. As explained below, this in effect reflects the strategies
of differently placed households.

Another characteristic of Bhil migration is the comparatively high level
of female migration. Forty-two per cent of seasonal migrants in this survey
were female, and this varied little between districts. The high proportion of
females (women and girls) relates to the migration of family groups which
itself arises from the need for poor families to maximise the productivity of
their labour power [*Breman, 1996: 45, 86*]. For many families, only the old
and those who are less employable because of injury or illness remain at
home to look after land, cattle and other assets.

Turning briefly to the question of the type and place of work involved,
migrants are engaged in a wide range of occupations including agricultural
labour, construction site work, railway and road work, brick-making and
quarry work, stone-breaking, casual work in factories, paper-picking,
operating hand carts, working as watchmen and many others. The pattern of
work is complicated by the fact that many migrants shift from one job to
another in the course of a season. Employment in agriculture plays a

FIGURE 1

DISTRIBUTION OF MIGRATION MONTHS PER HOUSEHOLD (HH) IN 1995–96

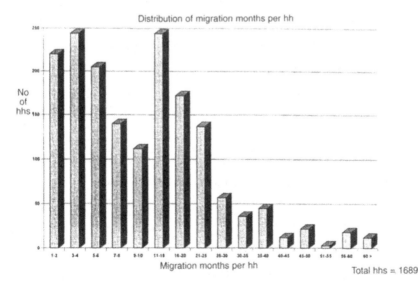

Distribution of migration months per hh

No of hhs

Migration months per hh

Total hhs = 1689

relatively minor part (accounting for only 11 per cent of migration in 1995–96). Most work is provided by the building industry in its widest sense – including ground preparation, earthwork for pipelines, electricity and telephone cables, quarrying and brick-work – and focuses on the major regional cities of Baroda, Surat and Ahmedabad. Over 65 per cent of all migrants from these Bhil villages were involved in urban construction labour[6] (Figure 2). Disguised in this broad picture are more location-specific patterns in which particular clusters of villages link to particular work-sites – brick kilns, quarries or agricultural areas.

Labour is not only mostly urban and building-related, but overwhelmingly casual, unskilled and low paid. Less than three to five per cent of Bhil migrants in our survey obtained skilled work as masons, plasterers or labour contractors, and – for reasons discussed shortly – even after migrating for over 20 years Bhil labourers are unable to achieve upward mobility to skilled labour. Tribal migrants are virtually absent from the formal sector employment. In industry, tribal migrants form a large ancillary body of unskilled labour not engaged directly in the production process but hired through contractors and involved in construction, maintenance, loading/unloading and similar tasks.

FIGURE 2

STATEWISE DISTRIBUTION OF TYPE OF WORK
(STUDY SAMPLE)

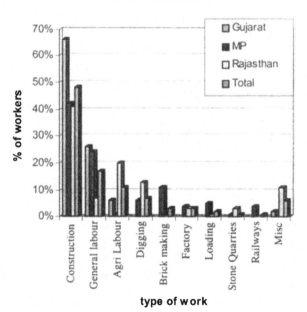

Migration is also unambiguously seasonal, linked to the monsoon cycle which shapes both farming and (to a degree) urban construction work. Hardly any migrating families put down roots in the work area, settle or obtain permanent jobs.

Migration tends to focus on a few urban centres (Table 2). Seventy-four per cent of migrants from villages in Limkheda Taluk (E.Gujarat) travelled to Baroda, while Kota and Surat are preferred destinations for migrants from Thandla Taluk (MP) and Kushalgarh Taluk (Rajasthan); although migrants from these latter Rajasthan villages are dispersed to a larger number of smaller locations (that is, the 745 migrants from Kushalgarh surveyed travel to 63 different locations).

The point to emphasise is that the pattern of migration is not explicable in terms of labour markets organised on the basis of *local* demand and supply. Migrants do not find work in local towns. Indeed, local labour is often at a disadvantage in relation to the cheaper labour of distant migrants [*Breman, 1996*]. From the employer–builder–contractor's point of view, migrant labour has the advantage of low cost (migrant wage rates undercut local wages). But more than this, the system of advances and the insecurity involved in long-distance migration creates an amenable dependency among tribal migrants.

When interviewed, contractors and builders referred to the hard and trouble-free work of Bhil migrants. Indeed, employers routinely opt for longer-distance migrants over local labour. 'TG', for example, who owns a stone processing plant in Kota explains how he sends his *munshi* (accountant/ manager) to Meghnagar (in Jhabua district) to secure labour for the whole season, in bulk and at lower wages than would be possible though the town's labour markets (*naka*s) (he can pay village-recruited migrants Rs

TABLE 2

DESTINATION OF MIGRANT HOUSEHOLDS (HH)

Place	Gujarat	MP	Rajasthan	Total
Baroda	74	3	6	25
Surat	4	27	32	22
Kota		38	1	11
Ahmedabad	12	4	5	7
Ratlam		1	7	3
Neemach			6	3
Mandsor			5	2
Kheda	4	1	1	2
Other smaller destinations	6	24	37	24
Total (%)	100	100	100	100
Total no. of destinations	17	33	63	96

40–45 per day as against the daily wage labour rate of Rs 60). Needing to maximise earnings, tribal migrants are also prepared to work longer hours and take fewer holidays.

Bhil labour migration follows well-defined routes. Each village tends to have only two or three main destinations. In 1995–96, for example, 36 out of 46 migrants from the village of Kakadia (Madhya Pradesh), travelled to specific construction sites in Kota. Individual Bhil villages (or localities) are linked to work sites through specific sets of intermediaries and personalised networks of recruitment. The migrants from Bahadurpada village, for instance, recently shifted from the city of Surat to Rajkot when their contractor moved his business there. We will return to the question of labour recruitment in a moment, but want first to look at the demand for labour and urban casual labour markets.

The expansion of urban labour migration in western India is closely linked to the post-1970 expansion of an urban-industrial corridor extending from Ahmedabad to Bombay [cf. *Breman, 1996*]. Here, tribal migrants form a sizeable portion of 'informal sector' urban labour. In Surat, for example, Breman estimates that some 20–25 per cent of the one million working population are engaged in casual labour, street work, or domestic service [*1996: 54–6*].

This labour is organised through multi-tier systems of contracting, subcontracting and piece rate, which involve a hierarchy of labour brokers and 'jobbing recruiter-supervisors', labour gang leaders, and piece-rate workers [*ibid.: 157–61*]. Thereby the owners of capital are able to gain profit while being freed from the problems of the management of production and the obligations of employer in relation to a workforce [*ibid.*]. The corollary is the reduced bargaining power of labour. Such a structural view of the determinants of migration is valuable; but it should not divert attention away from the strategic importance for migrant actors of the social relations in their areas of origin. This will be the focus of discussion below.

The urban informal labour markets are themselves highly differentiated and segmented along 'ethnic' lines. Bhil migrants occupy a distinct niche of low paid unskilled labour. In Surat, for example, they are excluded from the comparatively secure work in the principal informal industries: diamond cutting and textile weaving (diamond cutters are mostly Kanbi Patels from Saurashtra, while a majority of powerloom operators are long-term migrants of particular castes from Orissa or Andhra Pradesh [*ibid.*]). Bhil migrants make a significant contribution to the socially invisible and politically silent floating population of tens of thousands of men and increasingly women and children who congregate daily at casual labour markets or *naka*s dotted around the cities and on their outskirts. From here they are hired, individually or in groups by employers, contractors or their agents looking for unskilled labour [cf. *Breman, 1996: 46*]. The present study identified 15 such labour markets (*naka*s) in Kota and 10 in Baroda. In these labour markets, low paid Bhil migrants compete successfully against local labour.

However, most Bhil migrants are unwilling or unable to risk competing for work in daily labour markets and are instead recruited directly in their villages. Indeed it is the network of neighbourhood and kin links involved in recruitment (discussed below) that produces the highly structured casual labour market, reduces competition between employers, keeps wages low, removes the opportunity for mobility, and ensures a carefully selected, accountable and amenably dependent tribal workforce. In this way, the consistently high demand for urban casual labour does not translate into stronger bargaining power for Bhil migrants.

IV. THE MIGRATION EXPERIENCE

In the present section we shift from the broad regional perspective to that of individual villages, and look in more detail at who migrates, why and in what manner.

Despite individual and idiosyncratic modes of migration, two contrasting patterns stand out. First, there are families having a slightly better food security situation in which migration is mostly by young male workers; it is short-term, short-distance and combined flexibly with agricultural work. Indeed, household members may take it in turn to migrate and manage the family farm. By contrast, a second pattern involves entire households (mostly poorer) undertaking longer-term, long-distance migration. For this reason, it is mostly *poorer women* who migrate as members of such family groups.

These contrasting patterns of migration are generated by different patterns of borrowing, and distinct strategies for managing debt (and of course the nature of indebtedness itself reflects differences among households in terms of land holding, domestic cycle shifts and social position within the community). Crudely put, poorer households are forced to migrate immediately after the harvest in order to service high interest loans taken during the monsoon season to meet subsistence food needs and (often medical) emergencies. The borrowing of poorer tribal households can be shown to peak in the monsoon season (July–September). Such families lack a credible credit standing or collateral in the form of jewellery. In consequence they pay higher interest (12.5 per cent per month), access loans only through the services of intermediaries (for example, better-off relatives) willing to negotiate the loans or lend them silver, and often have to sell marketable crops to the same lenders at low prices.

The uncertainty of borrowing among the poor means that loans are not taken for cultivation (seeds or fertiliser) where timeliness is critical. Access to credit is a huge problem for the poorest, and it is for this reason that families increasingly meet urgent needs through cash advances on migrant labour.[7] Since, credit payments and emergencies demand the mortgaging of ornaments, bullocks and land (in that order)[8] often to better off members of the same village, earning from migration is necessary not only to service existing debts but also to repossess mortgaged assets. In more extreme circumstances debt demands the advanced sale of labour through one or other form of attached labour or 'bondage', the marriage of daughters (in return for bride price) or the sale of land.

In contrast to the migration strategy of poorer households for whom migration is critical to the management of debt and social dependencies, among households with at least minimum food security, migration provides a means to manage risk, and build assets. Younger (male) members undertake migration flexibly to repay seasonal and longer-term loans taken for agricultural inputs (that is, seeds, fertiliser, implements), the purchase of assets (for example, cattle, well digging, house building or bride-price payments) and to meet social obligations and emergencies. This borrowing peaks in the pre-monsoon period (April–June), is at lower interest against mortgaged silver and does not, generally, take the form of advances on labour. These households are also better placed to participate in indigenous financial institutions (for example, *chandla*) through which large sums are raised for one-off expenditures (typically marriage).[9]

In short, migration is highly differentiated. At the extremes, for poor farmers migration is a defensive coping strategy [cf. *Breman, 1985*], providing the principal means for servicing high interest subsistence-related debts; while for better-off farmers, migration supplements income from agriculture, helps cope with inter-year fluctuations and the management of large expenditures, and contributes to agricultural production or the investment in assets.

Village-level work on livelihood strategies suggests that the balance between these two strategies (which are really extremes of a continuum) varies from village to village. Where, migration is predominantly a defensive coping strategy, overall levels of migration in a village are found to vary with socio-economic position (landholding, etc.). Where, by contrast, migration supplements income, the patterns of migration tend to correlate with household size (that is, available labour). The nature of migration is also strongly influenced by the stage of a household in the domestic cycle. Newly-formed households are smaller, have fewer resources and higher dependency ratios. They are forced into longer-term migration to acquire resources for houses, cattle and implements.

While, therefore, the picture of debt-induced migration holds true for the Bhil area in general, what emerges from our village studies is the need for a more differentiated view of migration experience and outcomes. Poorer families have more members migrating for longer periods (and usually further afield), but the productivity (earning power) of this migrant labour is lower because of systems of advanced payments, the higher costs of migrating as whole families to distant work sites, and because earnings are almost entirely diverted into the servicing of outstanding debt.[10] The poorest are in a trap: they migrate most, work hardest and yet, because of their weaker bargaining power, get paid least and save next to nothing. It is clear that migration is strongly determined by existing social inequalities (within and between villages), and also has the effect of amplifying these. As will become clearer in later sections of this paper, while for a few better-off households migration earnings provide a means, not only to deal with risk and uncertainty, but also to enhance social position, for the poorest, migration serves to perpetuate debt and dependency.

The issue here is not merely the existence of a connection between rural indebtedness and migration, but also the way in which this operates, the mechanisms and the dependency relations involved. It is not just the existence of debt with forces Bhil tribals to migrate, it is equally a matter of to whom and how they are indebted. As David Hardiman's [1987b] work shows, credit relations with trader/moneylenders have long been a feature of tribal social life in western India. What our study suggests (following Breman) is a recent development in this nexus, in that the servicing of debt and the social relations involved are increasingly tied to labour recruitment and urban casual labour markets.

Moneylenders have always been concerned to press their priority claim on migrant earnings, and have often done so by travelling to migration sites to retrieve interest payments. But increasingly moneylenders secure more direct and profitable control over their creditors by linking credit to migrant labour through systems of advance payment and labour contracting (see below).

The advanced sale of labour weakens migrants bargaining power, so it is unsurprising to find that poorer migrants obliged to accept advances and being tied to brokers and contractors end up in the least well paid and harshest working environments (for example, piece rate slab work, quarry work). It is also the very poor who get recruited to labour-intensive agricultural work (for example, soya bean extraction) attracted by cash advances, the existence of food as part of the wages, and low transport costs. We will now turn to the issue of labour recruitment.

V. SYSTEMS OF LABOUR RECRUITMENT

Whether or not it involves advance payments, the recruitment process is complex. Broadly there are three scenarios: first, migrants are recruited as a group through a contractor-'recruiter' (*mukkadam*); second, individuals or families go and secure work on their own using previous contacts or kin-links; and third, migrants travel individually as daily wage earners getting employment through *nakas* (urban casual labour markets). We will comment on each of these in turn.

Mukkadams: Labour recruiters or *mukkadams* are, in most cases, better-off tribal villagers, formerly workers, or supervisors. They have *contacts* through kinship or patronage with urban construction contractors and are involved in site-specific recruitment. The village of Bahadurpada, for example, has three *mukkadams* recruiting labour gangs in three distinct areas: for 'slab-work' in Surat, construction work in Rajkot and agricultural labour in Badnavar.

Becoming a successful *mukkadam,* operating a well-established network requires both capital and charisma. A critical part of the process is the ability to cement hold on migrating groups through advance payments. Using kin networks *mukkadams* make their rounds of Bhil villages to identify workers during the monsoon season. At this time of acute shortage, they make advance payments to labourers or make arrangements with shopkeepers to advance grains. *Mukkadams* return immediately prior to the migration season to ensure availability and exert pressure on reluctant labourers, or make further advances [*Mehta, 1996: 23; Breman, 1996*]. *Mukkadams* are often already moneylenders in their villages, able to extend their operations by entering the labour recruitment business.

Now, while a well-established *mukkadam* may receive advances from the contractor/employers to whom he supplies labour, newly established recruiters have to risk their own capital in making advances. For a *mukkadam,* establishing credibility is crucial: migrants have to believe that their *mukkadam* has the influence necessary to provide a good chance of finding labour. Only a trusted *mukkadam* who is able to make generous advances acquires a reliably dependent labouring group. Equally, contractors will only rely on *mukkadams* and advance them money if they believe that they will come up with reliable, regular, hardworking and compliant labour gangs. As well as clearly successful operators there are numerous failures – men who have lost credibility by failing to secure work or a reliable work gang.

None the less, from the migrants' point of view *mukkadams* provide a crucial means to connect to sources of urban employment. Mukkadams offer the advantage of relatively secure and regular work even if at lower wages.

Independent (kin-) groups: Another section of migrants, notably from the Gujarat villages studied, are not recruited through advance payments by *mukkadams*, but travel in groups with experienced migrants or friends and exploit existing and kin-based contacts with contractors, or find work through urban-based kinsmen.

These groups are often themselves drawn together though kin links. Just as kin ties are an important for Bhil households in carrying out land-based production – especially to meet peak demands for labour, or the urgent need to borrow seed or bullocks [cf. *Sjoblom, 1999*] – so they are also important in accessing distant urban labour markets. Interestingly, in some of the migrant groups studied, patrilineal connections – generally fundamental to the organisation of land and society in Bhil villages and hamlets – seem to be less important than affinalal kin links. Affinal links through a man's mother's or wife's family play a role in bringing together migrants from different villages in a locality. Male migrants in these groups found themselves recruited by their *mama*s (maternal uncles or *behnoi*s (sister's husbands). For example, in the migrant groups in which Jharola villagers were involved, it was rare to find patrilineally linked cousins travelling for work together. Even where, as in Bahadurpada village, groups are not kin-based, migrants tend to avoid village *mukkadams* who are related to them as part of the same patrilineage. Resort to affinal kin networks may have the effect of protecting the socially and culturally primary patrilineage from the acknowledged disruption and dispute associated with migrant labour and earnings (see below).

In general membership of a group is a ticket to access the urban labour market and to finding regular, more secure work under better conditions. However, gaining access to such groups depends upon having a relationship with a *mukkadam* and/or being part of a kin network. And kinship relations themselves have to be maintained through the investment of time and resources – in visiting the sick, reciprocating gifts and loans, exchanging labour and so forth. Certain families having a low credit rating, or being marginal to dominant kinship structures (clans, lineages, etc.) or unable to invest in supporting social networks can find it difficult to gain entry into migration groups.

Individual migrants: Some migrants, who do not depend on cash advances, desire the freedom to choose when and where to migrate themselves. Several have established their own urban contacts for securing employment, others depend upon getting work through the casual labour markets or *nakas*. Despite unpredictability, this has the advantage of flexibility, better wages and immediate payment (and was more commonly found among young male migrants in Panchmahals [Gujarat] villages migrating to close-by Baroda). Other migrants depend upon *nakas* because they have failed to secure membership of more stable groups linked to contractors and work.

Different types of recruitment present different opportunities in the search for work, and involve different types and degrees of obligation (for example, reciprocal relations with kin *versus* dependence on *mukkadams*) which, in turn, effect net earnings. Membership of kin networks and independence from debt and dependence assure more secure work, under better conditions and higher net earnings, than recruitment via advances from *mukkadams*, which tend to be the only options for the economically poor and the socially excluded.

In sum, the organisation of labour recruitment ensures unequal access to earning from migration. Links to recruiters and kin are crucial and certain households who are unable to establish the stable relationships necessary to get regular work find themselves pushed into the more casual, poorly paid work. Equally (as shown below), without social networks, migrants have problems with living/sleeping arrangements, are more vulnerable to intimidation, underpayment and non-payment of wages, not to mention isolation and loneliness – all problems reported in our survey. In other words, access to secure employment and the experience of migration is influenced by the position in the village, and social and kinship ties that households command.

VI. EARNINGS FROM MIGRATION

Household earnings from migration depend upon the period of migration, the regularity of work, number of workers, type of work, advances taken, costs incurred and so forth. Casual labour on construction sites is better paid (Rs 40–60 per day) than agricultural labour (approximately Rs 30 day in 1996); while skilled workers (and supervisors) may earn Rs 90–120 per day. In some places there are differential rates for women (20 per cent lower than men, for example, Rs 10 less) and younger workers. Varying wage rates for different work have to be set against divergent costs of living in the sites of migration. Costs incurred in *rural* migration during the stay away from the village are significantly lower than for urban migration. Wages also vary with location, season and labour demand. At the informal labour markets wages may even vary during the day, falling significantly after 10 a.m. as job opportunities are filled up [*Breman, 1996: 145*].

For many types of work *piece rate* payments (cash or kind) have replaced daily wages, for example in brick-making, well-digging, slab-working and some types of agricultural labour (for example, cutting, threshing, packing or loading). This not only forces workers into a degree of self-exploitation in order to achieve a satisfactory wage, but it also removes from the employer the need to supervise work rates,[11] to cover the cost of stoppages and the obligation to provide meals, tobacco or other support to labourers.

Unless bound to a contractor, migrant workers are not assured work each day, and even for tied workers there is nothing in the nature of a guarantee of continuous employment. Workers often face many unpaid days because of sickness, poor ground conditions, or mechanical failure. Uncertainty in employment is aggravated by the dependence of contractors on builders, builders on suppliers all operating within wider chains of interdependence. Individual migrants, not tied to a particular contractor face even greater fluctuation in the availability of work, or the risk of replacement by other workers willing to work longer hours at lower wages. None the less, in the present study Bhil seasonal workers migrating for five to six months on average obtained work for around 100–120 days [cf. *Breman, 1996: 145*].

Reported annual earnings for a household ranged from Rs 7,900 to 25,200. Net earnings, deducting expenses and travel, are invariably much less. Most migrants take advances, both before migrating and while working to meet urgent needs back home. At the end of the month (or season) advances and any allowances for subsistence are deducted from wages. Aggregate household remittances for the season vary depending upon the duration of migration, number of people migrating, and the type of work, but a family with three migrating members could expect to return to the village with Rs 2,000 to 3,000 after three months' work. Often after the deduction of advances and allowances migrants will return home with far less, and in extreme cases with nothing or even in debt (see note 10; Breman [*1996: 156*]).

Wage payments are routinely delayed, reduced or withheld, particularly by the end of the season when the balance of power has firmly shifted from employee (coaxed with advances) to the employer, especially since migrants are under pressure to return home for the agricultural season. Indeed advances and complex payment arrangements are explicitly used as a mechanism to control a fluid labour force, and debt, as Breman suggests, is an 'instrument of coercion' producing a new form of agrarian labour bondage or 'neo-bondage' differing from agrarian bondage in being less personalised, more contractual and monetised and lacking elements of patronage and protection of earlier forms of clientship [*1996*].

Precisely because of the risk of non-payment and other forms of coercion, and because of the limited powers of redress, migrants place great store on the reputation of contractors and are willing to tie themselves to exploitative conditions, low wages and poor working conditions for the security they appear to offer.

VII. WORK AND LIVING CONDITIONS

In general, working conditions at the sites of migration are indeed harsh and hours long and irregular. Men and women work together, but often have separate tasks (for example, men digging and women carrying in earthwork or on construction sites). Migrants are expected to work hard, and to show flexibility including working unpaid overtime. Supervisors demand near impossible working rates and forbid rest-breaks. One stone quarry visited at Kota presented a dramatic sight – over 400 people (men, women, children) engaged in different tasks: machine cutting the upper layer of stones, chiselling stones and slabs to the right shape and size, loading and transporting, collecting and carrying waste stone and so on. (Very few, if any, of the Bhil migrants were undertaking the skilled work as masons.) Women headloading broken stone were expected to carry 400 head loads of stones in a day. Their work was closely monitored in that women were given a stone 'token' for every headload carried. If the loads carried were fewer than the target, wages were reduced proportionately.

Work-sites (whether quarries, construction sites, factories or mines) are far from safe environments. Employers do not provide protection against risks of injury from the hazardous equipment, chemicals, or poisonous gases with which they are involved [*Mehta, 1996*]. Quite apart from work-related risks, living on insufficient allowances, eating an extremely limited and poor diet, living in the open, exposed to contaminated water and lacking sanitation, it is unsurprising that migrant workers suffer ill-heath for which they have to cover the high cost. Employers rarely contribute to medical expenses, and have offered very limited compensation in the case of severe injury or death (merely Rs 10,000 in one case).

While the conditions of migrant labour are universally poor, the extent of deprivation is strongly shaped by existing social position and the means of access to urban employment which this allows. For example, an organised migrant group from a nearby Panchmahals village, being well-connected to contractors through kin links, manage to secure shelter in an unfinished shopping-office complex or residential building in Baroda with access to clean water supply and fuelwood from ongoing construction. By contrast, families from a Madhya Pradesh village working in Surat live in the open away from work sites along with hundreds of others. They bivouack under plastic sheets. Migrants involved in digging works invariably camp temporarily beside the work site, along roadsides or in nearby open spaces. In most of these sites water is an acute problem, firewood is expensive, and there is no security for their limited possessions (a plastic sheet, blankets, food grains, utensils). The story of one family who returned from work to find their shack burned and most of their belongings removed does not stand alone. Migrants working on well-digging stay at the site and often find themselves having to do petty chores for landowner-employers. Long-distance migrants without connections to *mukkadams* or contractors and dependent upon daily visits to the *nakas* (labour markets) face the most precarious situation of all. They stay with acquaintances, take temporary shelter in railway stations or live on the roadsides.

Mukkadams or supervisor/caretakers might get better conditions; others may have to pay a rent for staying at a site provided by the contractor. Where good relations prevail, a contractor may allow migrants to stay on at a site where they previously worked and travel for new work. If they have a secure place to stay, migrants are often willing to walk two hours or more for work. Daily-wage workers have to set up temporary shelters (for example, under plastic sheeting) wherever they can. They often have to move from site to site.

Migrants bring what they can in terms of food grains. This is easier for Panchmahals migrants working near Baroda, who can have grain sent from home. The migrants working far from home depend upon cash advances or subsistence payments from *mukkadams* or contractors to purchase more expensive local grain. Migrants also buy tobacco and other items from local shops on credit.

Equally difficult as the physical hardships faced by migrants is the social isolation, lack of respect and humiliation received from outsiders. Tribal migrants are generally regarded as ignorant, uncivilised and ill-washed. However, migration is sometimes viewed as having emancipatory potential, providing a means to challenge agrarian hierarchies, alter traditional structures of oppression or engender social mobility or culture critique [*Gidwani and Sivaramakrishnan, n.d.*]. With Bhil migrants this is less clearly the case. Indeed through migration these workers move into a world in which hierarchical distinctions (Bhil/non-Bhil; tribal/non-tribal) are more keenly felt, generalised and amplified; a world in which the culture of poverty is newly experienced as *jati* (caste/'ethnic') discrimination.

If there is a desire for emancipation and cultural critique, it is manifest not in protest/resistance against the hierarchical order within hinterland villages (or the traditional oppressions of moneylender, forester or police), but as instances of a longer tradition dating back to colonial times in which Bhils – responding to external characterisation of Bhil identity and cultual practices as backward – have sought distance from the stigma through affirming Rajput connections, religious conversion, or participation in religious movements. From the mid-nineteenth century these have focused on a reform of stigmatised Bhil practices such as the consumption of meat and alcohol, personal hygiene, 'traditional' dress, and the worship through sacrifice of village *bhuts* (ghosts and demons) and deities [*Hardiman, 1987a*].

Several of these movements focused on new manifestations of the goddess (Salabai), most notably the Devi movement of 1922 analysed by David Hardiman [*1987a*], but also briefer or more localised cults which occurred as recently as 1992–93 in the KRIBP project area. Through her possessed devotees the goddess makes demands for reforms. These movements suggest [*Skaria, 1999: 256*] simultaneously a distancing of Bhils from a 'tribal' wildness now associated with marginality, and a hostility to upper castes in relation to whom Bhils suffered new forms of subordination.

Migration does little to emancipate Bhil women. Irrespective of the forms of recruitment, gender structures tend to remain intact during migration, meaning that women have to continue to fulfil reproductive and domestic roles alongside waged labour. Women from the poorer households migrating as a family face additional stress and work in continuing to meet domestic responsibilities in a difficult environment (for example, problems in securing water, fuelwood, the absence of shelter, managing personal hygiene, child care and exposure to harassment from contractors and male migrants). Women face many migration-induced health problems.[12] Reproductive tract infections, miscarriages and pregnancy complications are some of the problems women discussed during fieldwork. They also have less access to treatment or the cash to pay for it. Moreover, women are at a disadvantage in relation to the work environment. They face segregation, lower wages, and fewer work opportunities. While excluded from the 'public' spaces in which labour negotiations that affect them take place, they are also vulnerable to abuse and sexual exploitation, especially by employers.

Equally, child care is always a problem for poor migrant families. Occasionally a migrant group brings an 'older' child (eight to ten years) to take care of younger children and infants in return for Rs 100–150 per month, but usually children accompany adults to the work-site. Children spend an increasing amount of their childhood in the unfamiliar and insecure migrant work-sites. From seven years or younger they begin to work on construction or brick work-sites, and are deprived of play, leisure and schooling.

Seasonal migrants are separated from the legal protection offered to employees in the formal sector. They can expect little support from government labour officers who, as mentioned, know little about the plight of informal labour, and often ally with employers rather than workers. The Registers of labourers are rarely complete, which serves to limit the responsibility of the employer. The chances of the government Labour Inspector visiting are in any case very limited indeed. Given the general absence of proper records, workers have no proof of employment, and are not in a position to take legal action even if they could afford to do so.

VIII. THE WIDER IMPACT OF MIGRATION

It would be surprising indeed if the massive seasonal exodus of people from villages and the social disruption this involves did not have profound effects on Bhil society. This is properly the subject of a separate empirical study. None the less the direction of such a study can be outlined on the basis of the present work The most important thing to highlight is the highly contrasted social outcomes of long-term migration.

The economic productivity of migrant labour and the net economic gains from long-term migration vary. Migrants working the same amount of time end up with very different amounts of money depending upon the nature of recruitment, advances and pre-existing debts. For most, many years of migration have not led to any long-term increase in assets or any reduction in poverty. Indeed, an important aspect of the system is that poor migrants are not able to work themselves out of debt, even though migration offers a short-term means to service debt and avoid the more extreme forms of dependency and bondage.

However, for a number of farming families with more livelihood security, labour migration strengthens their position, especially where labourers can become (through kin networks) gang leaders and 'recruiters'. For these families, migration significantly increases the household's earning capacity, its creditworthiness and its ability to manage crises. Migration earning compensates for irregular agricultural production on smallholdings, allows small farmers to retain assets and, perhaps, arrests economic differentiation.[13]

In a few cases migration allows new investments in wells, diesel pumps, land (through mortgage tenure), silver or good marriages, as well as investment in social networks (for example, *chandla*) to consolidate prestige and social position. For a few with luck, talent, tenacity and the right contacts, migration provides the means for upward mobility through roles of group leader, supervisor, middleman and *mukkadam*, and the rewards of participating in the lucrative business of labour contracting and local moneylending. (Although the most successful operators have tended to be those few who have cut themselves free from village residence and obligations, moving to the towns and cities.) Such successful migrant families are invariably those from relatively privileged households having more land, surplus adult labour, assets and social links with contractors in the cities.

On the other hand, poorer households face insuperable obstacles to mobility through migration. Migration – through long absence and dependence on distant patrons – entails the loss of reputation, status and social position. The failure to participate or invest in institutions of labour exchange (*halmo*) or *chandla*, or festivals which define in some general sense membership of the community, means increasing marginality from the networks through which credit, or for that matter good marriages, are obtained. All but the very poorest return to villages to celebrate the festivals of *holi* (March), *navaratra* and *diwali* (November). As a Bhil man from a village in neighbouring Dungarpur district told Disa Sjoblom,

> if you neglect coming to the village for important events in the village or [in] other households people will speak badly of you. If you do not show your presence [to] *mataji* [the goddess] during Navaratra people will think you are not interested in village life ... [and] life here is such that you cannot manage on your own [*Sjoblom, 1999: 178*].

In a society where people identify themselves as cultivators, and where an interest in land and involvement in agriculture is necessary to retain social position, or in Bourdieu's terms, to ensure the 'defence of symbolic capital' [*ibid.: 197*], to lose this through migration is to lose respect, status and risk social exclusion.[14]

From this perspective migration is viewed as potentially disruptive of co-operative agricultural life. For example, people point to a weakening of local systems of labour exchange and the greater need for cash to employ labour (that is, the growth of an off-season labour market); to a decline in joint cultivation or jointly-dug and co-operatively-managed wells [cf. *Sjoblom, 1999: 170*]; or to the strain placed on land sharing arrangements and disputes over inheritance [cf. *Dandekar, 1986*]. Undoubtedly migration has some impact on the social organisation of agriculture and the kin and property relations on which this is based (although arguably such changes most affect male patrilineages and leave female support networks more in tact). It would be hard, however, to judge the extent to which migration *actually* diverts interest away from agriculture or reduces the intensity of kinship co-operation rather than underlying a *perception* of the risk of these culturally negative changes. Talk of 'depeasantisation' and the erosion of agricultural livelihoods in upland Bhil areas are clearly unfounded. Wherever they can, Bhil households are found to intensify cultivation and use migration earnings to invest in land and in the social relationships which make it productive.

Up to this point, the evidence clearly reminds us that migration is not an external factor impinging upon or undermining agrarian society. It is profoundly shaped by existing social relations and inequalities which define differential opportunity, contrasting experience and social outcomes. Moreover, migration contributes to the continuation and intensification of agriculture and the social networks on which it depends. So much for inter-household relations; what of relations within the household?

IX. INTRA-HOUSEHOLD RELATIONS

At the outset, it should be said that our understanding of intra-household relations whether concerned with gender or age, in Bhil migration, has benefited enormously from Mona Mehta's work among tribal migrants in south Gujarat. Here there is only space to highlight some of the key issues.

First, village case studies give strong testimony to the observation that in migrating households where women do not migrate, their share of the domestic and agricultural work load increases. This is exaggerated by the sense that men involved in long term migration sometimes have, that the village is a place of leisure and relaxation.

Indeed Agarwal [1994] suggests that migration may contribute to a longer-term re-definition of women and men's roles in agriculture, and a sharpening of an existing gender-linked division between paid and unpaid work (that is, men engage in productive work; women in low-status, mundane tasks). Increased dependence on migrant earnings may be seen as enhancing male authority in the household, and rendering women more dependent on men for cash, for heath care, etc. (especially as alternative sources of local cash income, such as from the sale of forest produce, are cut off). Women's bargaining power declines just as responsibilities increase. Cash earning becomes the measure of entitlement to household resources. In other words, by virtue of their limited participation in labour migration, women and older people can find entitlement to household resources reduced. Under certain conditions, such weakened entitlements can produce a serious threat to well-being, nutrition or health. Older people therefore find themselves looking for alternative, independent means to earn cash for themselves (for example, participating in project soil and water conservation work, collecting and selling fruit, or migration; but where physical strength counts for much and experience little they are at a disadvantage).

But if migration amplifies gender inequalities it may also *reverse* gender and age hierarchies of status and authority. Young male migrants or *mukkadams,* for example, gain status *vis-à-vis* household heads of an older generation by virtue of their ability to secure resources and to finance major family investments (for example, housing or bride-price). These capabilities of younger migrant men may also enhance the position/independence of their wives *vis-à-vis* their mothers-in-law (unless – which is rare – a man uses new income to pay bride-price and gets another wife). Case histories suggest that the inevitable inter-generational tensions tend to accelerate the division of households into nuclear units. Indeed, it is precisely because migration is perceived as so disruptive of core kin relations (for example, the aggravation of disputes over land between brothers, unequal investment in bride-price or housing) that affinal rather than patrilineal kin seem to play such a prominent role in some Bhil villages..

At the same time, whether or not women accompany men, migration itself creates a strain on the marriage relationship. Overburdened, women at home have left for their natal homes, new liaisons are formed in the context of migration, and insecurity and suspicion generates domestic violence and abandonment.

At the root of many of these effects, perhaps, is the fact that migration involves a type of income accrual which (unlike agriculture) is both highly *unequal* and *individualised* within the family, and yet which has to contribute to a livelihood strategy which demands pooling and joint control. It follows that the potential for conflict is greatest where household members have very different levels of involvement (for example, when only men migrate), and is least where all family members migrate equally. In the former instance, young men (and even women) are able to make effective claims on their own earnings at the expense of the group. Indeed in the villages studied this was sometimes a strong motivation for migrating, although the degree of control exerted depends upon the composition of the migration group. A women travelling with cousins will have more control than if travelling with her father (or with her natal rather than her marital kin).

There is little doubt that the majority of villagers interviewed concur with the present description of migration as harsh and risky. Only a few younger men (and women) perceive migration more favourably as an opportunity to experience city life. Several years of experience of hard conditions, high cost, and lack of mobility usually challenge such youthful enthusiasm. Most would not actively choose migration over cultivation and, when given the opportunity to increase agricultural earning, are keen to substitute work on the land or local wages for wages from migration. Moreover, as I have argued, the conditions for successful migration lie in *village*-based social networks. Despite social tensions, therefore, there is no sign of migration engendering alternative non-agrarian identities.

However, as the following section shows, this perspective rarely implies withdrawal from labour migration as a livelihood strategy. Although the patterns may change, involvement in migration continues and in some respects increases even while other economic opportunities develop locally.

X. PROJECT IMPACT ON MIGRATION

As explained at the outset, the particular context of the present study is a development project oriented towards the improvement of the livelihood of rural Bhil farmers. This raises some rather specific questions to which we turn now. First, what impact has the KRIBP project had on the extent and pattern of seasonal labour migration. Second, if it is accepted that seasonal labour migration is integral to rural livelihoods, what implications are there for the design of rural development interventions, and for KRIBP in particular.

As already mentioned, during its first phase the KRIBP project largely viewed seasonal migration as an unfortunate consequence of the decline of natural resources based livelihoods, the reduction of which would be a sure measure of success of its strategies of agricultural and watershed development. How successful has the project been in its own terms? What evidence is there of sustainable impact of project interventions on patterns of migration?

It is rather difficult to answer this question (a) because this project only began in 1993, and (b) there is anyway much inter-year variation in the degree of migration. None the less it was a question addressed in a series of detailed village-level project impact assessment case studies undertaken in 1996. Let us highlight some key points.

In two case-study villages in Madhya Pradesh there was an *overall* decrease in the amount of migration between 1992 and 1996 in terms of the number of migrants and especially the *duration* of migration (for example, a decline in the average duration from 6.5 to four months per year in Naganwat Chhoti village), which reversed a previous upwards trend. However, in both villages the decline in male migration was greater than in female migration. Indeed in one of the villages there was a slight increase in the number and duration of women migrating. The decline in migration has also, as one might expect, been more among better-off landed households. In one village, however, the reverse was true. Migration among the poor decreased and among the better-off increased. This was a better-off village where minor irrigation allowed winter (*rabi*) cropping, and where migration mostly offered positive opportunities to enhance income rather than secure subsistence. In these circumstances (as already mentioned) the extent of migration varied with the availability of surplus labour, varying both with household size and 'age' (in relation to domestic cycles) rather than 'wealth'.

The reasons for these apparent changes are complex, but in the perception of the people questioned, the factors that figure prominently in explaining localised decline in migration are: the availability of local wage labour on soil and water conservation and forestry works, increased effort in agriculture arising from the availability of credit from new farmer self-help groups, and irrigation for *rabi* cropping. All of these benefits are skewed towards land and labour-rich households. While many of these impacts are short term, one programme – lift irrigation with its demand for labour for a second (winter) crop, and income increases seriously able to offset migrant earnings – is likely to compete directly with (and so reduce) migration in the long term.

But overall it tends to be better-off men who have reduced migration to participate in project activities, who have reduced the discomfort and expenditure of migration in order to spend more time on their farms; those whose need to migrate was anyway less. However, the slight reduction in the migration of males (notably higher-status, articulate males) contributes to a local (recorded) *perception* that migration has reduced far more as a result of the project than it actually has.

In a Panchmahals (Gujarat) case-study village, a quite different picture emerges. Over the last four years there has been an increase in the number of migrants, but most of this increase (87 per cent) derives from additional *women* migrating. Despite this, for the reason mentioned above, in group interviews people expressed the contrary view that labour migration from the village had *fallen*. From one perspective, this could be viewed as a failure of participatory research methods in that the view of household heads (who have been substituted in migration by women or other socially less visible individuals) dominate. But from another perspective, changes in the *number* of migrants is, in any case, a good measure of change. Although more people are migrating, they are migrating for shorter periods, more flexibly and retaining more of the income earned. This is a more important positive change than a reduction in absolute levels of migration would be.

XI. WHAT TO DO?

Our research has demonstrated that seasonal labour migration is irreversibly a critical aspect of rural livelihood strategies among Bhil farming families of the inter-state border districts of Madhya Pradesh, Rajasthan and Gujarat. It is unlikely that any rural development initiative will emerge as a complete economic alternative to labour migration, or even that a combination of income- enhancing measures (improved crops, agro-forestry, livestock, etc.) that will have a long-term impact on a phenomenon as complex and socially embedded as Bhil seasonal migration. Rather, such measures are shown to result in some adjustments to the organisation of migration: who travels, where, and for how long, and who remains in the village taking care of new assets and so on.

But our research has also shown that, because of its tie to long-term debt, migrant labour is often extremely unproductive and unprofitable for those involved. The experience and outcome of migration varies widely depending upon the resources a household can command, both the economic (for example, productive land) and social resources. The social resources include membership of groups of kin, good credit status, links to contractors or brokers, access to information, or patronage through which secure waged work in distant centres is obtained. In short, the security and remuneration of migrant labour depends upon bargaining power determined by social position (and social capital – in Bourdieu's rather than Putnam's sense) in the home villages.

Our study and project experience suggests that the critical rural development issue is not how to *reduce* migration, but how to reduce its costs (social and economic) and increase its returns especially for the poorest. This is not the place to develop these thoughts, but we will close by referring to a pilot strategy for support to migrant labour currently (in 1998) under negotiation for a second phase of the KRIBP project. In the broadest terms this has four aims. First, to increase the productivity of migrant labour (that is, raise net earning) for the poorest by gradually de-linking it from debt, the advanced sale of labour and high interest repayments. The principal approach here is likely to involve building upon a programme of micro-finance focused on hamlet 'self-help' groups linked to low cost institutional credit through banks [cf. *Mosse, 1996b*].

The second aim is to improve the bargaining power of migrants in relation to *mukkadams* and increase direct access to employers through shared information, collective negotiation and co-ordinated group responses (for example, group child care, fuel and water provision at work-sites). Rather more work with Bhil farmer groups (men's and women's) is needed to appraise risks and establish appropriate action for this.

Third, the aim is to increase legal awareness of labour legislation and rights, through training programmes, links to government labour offices and contact with NGOs working in urban sites and supportive of construction workers' interests. A critical (although risky) step would be to ensure that workers are registered and work recorded (women separately). Again, participatory planning work is needed both with migrants as well as contractors and employers to pave the way for positive-sum gains from a better informed and skilled labour force.

The final aim is to improve conditions of employment through on- and off-site arrangements for child care, health and hygiene, education and skill training. It is not expected that these initiatives will be easy, or their effects dramatic in the short term. Any venture into the complex networks of migrant labour have to be tentative and sensitive. At the same time, however, it is no longer possible for a rural development project to dismiss seasonal labour migration as a marginal side-effect of environmental decline.

NOTES

1. Various aspects of the Western India Kribhco Rainfed Farming Project (KRIBP) have been described elsewhere: Jones *et al.* [*1994*]; Mosse [*1994, 1996*] Joshi and Witcombe [*1996*].
2. Village studies carried out in the tribal areas of the KRIBP project in the 1980s indicated that only 12–20 per cent of village households were able to depend upon cultivation alone for their livelihoods; between 40 and 80 per cent had to supplement agriculture with the sale of labour, and as many as 40 per cent were almost entirely dependent upon the of their labour [*Lal, n.d.*]. These findings are strongly born out by the experience of the project itself.
3. Above 14 years.
4. This assumes an average wage of Rs 45 per day and expenses of Rs15/day for 24 days a month. As we will indicate below, this is not an indication of household *income* from migration.
5. A study of a Panchmahals village in 1993–94 recorded 76 per cent of households and 44.1 per cent of the labour force engaged in migration. These figures are well within the range found in the current study [*Shylendra and Thomas, 1996: 87*].
6. This figure includes both the work categories 'construction' and 'general labour', the latter mostly comprising construction site work.
7. It has to be said that default on loans is extremely rare, although loans are often renegotiated at higher interest rates (for example, 25 per cent per month). Since they borrow from one source to repay another (or to keep up interest payments) poor Bhil households find themselves tied into an expanding network of credit dependency.
8. Villagers describe a hierarchy of options for the raising money to repay loans. First is the selling of agricultural surpluses or cash crops. For the majority who have no such surpluses, the principle option is migration (of a few members). Increasingly desperate strategies to raise money involve a downward spiral of mortgaging or selling silver, selling livestock (chickens then goats), mortgaging or selling bullocks, migration of the whole family, entering into bonded labour, mortgaging and eventually selling land ('Project Impact on Farming Systems and Livelihoods'. Report to Kribhco Indo-British Rained Farming Project: Jharola case study, Dahod, Jan. 1997, p.25).
9. Poorer households tend to have lower stakes in the indigenous financial systems such as *chandla* which demand reciprocating borrowed money at high (150 per cent) interest. Such households are correspondingly limited in the claims that they can make on these credit systems.
10. With sizeable loans (up to Rs 20,000) taken to meet emergencies, bride-price or food subsistence at up to 150 per cent interest per annum, poor families rapidly face debts on which the interest due is barely covered from their entire season's earnings. For example, after three months 'slab work' in Surat a young couple from a Madhya Pradesh village were able to contribute only Rs 4,000 towards the Rs 7,500 interest due on a Rs 15,000 family loan taken to cover marriage expenses. In the meantime fresh debts are routinely incurred to meet subsistence needs, crop failure or illness.
11. This is passed on to the *mukkadam* who has to ensure that each worker in the group contributes equally to the task, and distributes the earnings to group members.
12. Several studies found women workers, for example, in rice cultivation, were more susceptible to gynaecological infections, intestinal and parasitic infections, arthritis, rheumatic joints, and leech bites (Mencher and Savadamons [*1982*]; UNDP cited in Agarwal [*1994*]).

13. In a recent survey of land sales in Bhil villages in Jhabua, Jhalod and Banswara it was found that 80 per cent resulted from outstanding debt [*Doshi, 1990: 185*].
14. Moreover, long absence from the village makes the poor marginal to local 'poverty reduction' development initiatives such as the KRIBP project. Indeed in the project's own participatory 'wealth ranking' exercises migration was universally used as a negative indicator of status.

REFERENCES

Agarwal, B., 1994, *A Field of One's Own: Gender and Land Rights in South Asia*, Cambridge: Cambridge University Press.

Bhamania, 1976, A Study of Migrating Rural Adivasi Bhil labourers of Dohad Taluka', unpublished MSW thesis, Gujarat Vidyapith, Ahmedabad.

Breman, J., 1985, *Of Peasants, Migrants and Paupers: Rural Labour Circulation and Capitalist Production in West India*, Delhi: Oxford University Press.

Breman, J., 1996, *Footloose Labour*, Cambridge: Cambridge University Press.

Bureau of Economics and Statistics, 1974, 'Final Report of the Survey of Seasonal Migration of Labour in Panchmahals district 1971–72', *Quarterly Bulletin of Economics and Statistics*, Vol.14, pp.1–25.

Dandekar, H., 1986, *Men to Bombay Women at Home: Urban Influence on Sugao village, Deccan Maharashtra, India 1942–82*, Ann Arbor, MI: University of Michigan Press.

de Haan, Arjan, 1999, 'Livelihoods and Poverty: The Role of Migration – A Critical Review of the Migration Literature', *The Journal of Development Studies*, Vol.36, No.2, pp.1–47.

Doshi, S.L., 1990, *Tribal Ethnicity, Class and Integration*, Jaipur: Rawat.

Gadgil, M. and R.Guha,1995, *Ecology and Equity: The Use and Abuse of Nature in Contemporary India*, London and New York: Routledge.

Gidwani, V.K. and K. Sivaramakrishnan, n.d., 'Body Politics: Circular Migration and Subaltern Identities in India', unpublished manuscript.

Hardiman, D., 1987a, *The Coming of Devi*, New Delhi: Oxford University Press.

Hardiman, D., 1987b, 'The Bhils and Sahukars of Eastern Gujarat', in Ranajit Guha (ed.), *Subaltern Studies V: Writings on South Asian History and Society*, New Delhi: Oxford University Press.

Jones, S., Khare, J.N., Mosse, D., Smith, P., Sodhi, P.S. and J. Witcombe, 1994, 'The Kribhco Indo-British Rainfed Farming Project: Issues in the Planning and Implementation of Participatory Natural Resource Development', *KRIBP Working Paper No.1*, Centre for Development Studies, University of Wales Swansea.

Joshi, Arun and J.R. Witcombe, 1995, 'Farmer Participatory Research for the Selection of Rainfed Cultivars', paper presented at the International Rice Conference, International Rice Research Institute (IRRI), Philippines, Feb. 1995.

Lal, R.B., n.d., 'Role of Minor Forest Produce in Tribal Life and Culture', mimeo, Tribal Research and Training Institute, Ahmedabad.

Mehta, D., 1982, *Seasonal Migration of Labour: A Case of Dangs District (a Summary Report)*, Ahmedabad: School of Planning, Centre for Planning and Technology.

Mehta, M., 1996, 'Seasonal Labour Migration and Gender Relations in Dahanu Taluka', unpublished paper.

Mosse, D., 1994, 'Authority, Gender and Knowledge: Theoretical Reflections on the Practice of Participatory Rural Appraisal', *Development and Change*, Vol.25, No.3, July, pp.497–525.

Mosse, D., 1996a, 'The Social Construction of "People's Knowledge" in Participatory Rural Development', S. Bastian and N. Bastian (eds.), *Assessing Participation: A Debate from South Asia*, New Delhi: Konark Publishers.

Mosse, D., 1996b, 'Local Institutions and Farming Systems Development: Thoughts from a Project in Tribal Western India', *ODI Agren Network Paper No. 64*.

Mosse, D., Gupta, S., Mehta, M., Shah, V. and J. Rees, 1997, 'Seasonal Labour Migration in Tribal (Bhil) Western India', KRIBP Working Paper, Centre for Development Studies, University of Wales, Swansea (Report to DFID–India, New Delhi).

Naik, T.B., 1956, *The Bhils: A Study*, Delhi: Bharatiya Adijati Seva Sang.

Patel, B.B., 1987, 'Seasonal Rural Migration Pattern and Some Alternatives for Effective Protection of Legal Rights of Migrant Labour', in V. Joshi (ed.), *Migrant Labour and Related Issues*, New Delhi: Oxford and IBH Publishing Co.

Roe, E., 1991, 'Development Narratives: Or, Making the Best Out of Blue Print Development', *World Development*, Vol.19, No.4.

Shylendra, H.S. and P. Thomas, 1996, 'Livelihood in Transition: A Study of Occupational Diversification in Mahudi', *Rural Livelihood Systems and Sustainable Natural Resource Management in Semi-Arid Areas in India*, Anand: Institute of Rural Management Anand, pp.78–114.

Sjoblom, D.K., 1999, 'Land Matters: Social Relations and Livelihoods in a Bhil Community in Rajasthan, India', Ph.D. thesis, School of Development Studies, University of East Anglia.

Skaria, Ajay, 1999, *Hybrid Histories: Forests, Frontiers and Wildness in Western India*, New Delhi: Oxford University Press.

Seasonal Migration and Welfare/Illfare in Eastern India: A Social Analysis

BEN ROGALY, DANIEL COPPARD, ABDUR RAFIQUE, KUMAR RANA, AMRITA SENGUPTA and JHUMA BISWAS

I. INTRODUCTION

This study draws on long-term in-depth research with seasonally migrant manual wage workers in eastern India to examine the welfare/illfare[1] outcomes of that migration. We examine various aspects of illfare/welfare and we do so not only from the viewpoint of migrant workers, but also from that of their employers. Welfare is broadly defined here to include the subjective experience of migration, in particular for migrant workers. We explore the degree to which migrants' sense of themselves as a social group, their collective identity, is enhanced by migration.[2] At the same time, we illustrate ways in which such identities are deployed instrumentally to make the experience of migration, and its accompanying meaning to the migrant, less degrading.

The study attempts a social analysis of the market for migrant workers, and examines how this and other institutions – importantly household and state – mediate welfare/illfare outcomes for migrant workers. The next section provides the context, describing the role of seasonal migration in the

Ben Rogaly and Daniel Coppard are at the School of Development Studies, University of East Anglia, Norwich, UK; Abdur Rafique, Kumar Rana and Amrita Sengupta are with the Pratichi Trust, Deer Park, Santiniketan, West Bengal, India; and Jhuma Biswas is at the Social Work Department, Visva-Bharati, Sriniketan, West Bengal, India. Corresponding address: b.rogaly@uea.ac.uk.

The authors thank Somnath Chattopaddhyay and Sujata Das Chowdhury for logistical support and research assistance and Ranjit Bhattacharya, Samantak Das, Arjan de Haan, Kirat Randhawa, Nitya Rao, Sunil Sengupta, Dikshit Sinha, Glyn Williams and an anonymous referee for comments on an earlier draft, which was presented at the Global Social Policy Regional Workshop on 'Social Policy in Developing Contexts – South Asia Region', Koitta, Bangladesh in March 2000. Discussions with workshop participants were also extremely helpful and are gratefully acknowledged. During the research, Rogaly was affiliated to the Centre for Studies in Social Sciences, Calcutta (CSSSC), for which he is grateful to the Director, Partha Chatterjee. Thanks go in particular to Samantak Das, who greatly improved our translations from Bengali to English, and to Philip Judge for the map. The research was funded by the Department for International Development (DFID), UK. The authors alone are responsible for the views expressed here and for remaining errors.

economic livelihoods of both wage workers and their employers in rural West Bengal. In the third section we contrast the characteristics of four different streams of migrants. Sections IV, V and VI take the institutions of the market, household and state in turn and illustrate how each of these contributes to the welfare/illfare outcomes of people involved in seasonal migration or in employing migrants. We pay particular attention to income flows, health, and personal security. The role of seasonal migration in forging, reproducing and contesting social identities is analysed in section VII.

In conclusion we argue that while seasonal migrants in eastern India are usually compelled to be involved in arduous manual work away from home by the lack of other options, they are not powerless. They make some choices in the market for labour and may be able to use their remittances to reduce inequality in their own home areas. Nevertheless, they are socially excluded in relation to state policies. Genuine policy responses to counter this exclusion should take care not to compound experiences of second-class citizenship through heavy-handed regulation. Local government policies and practices also have important implications for migrant workers. West Bengal's local government institutions, largely dominated by the elected representatives of the ruling party in the state, have developed a reputation among migrant wage workers for ensuring that wage rates agreed are paid and paid on time.

II. SEASONAL MIGRATION AND INCOME FLOWS IN WEST BENGAL

Seasonal migration for employment in rural manual work is one way in which poor individuals and households in eastern India seek out income and, through income, welfare. People who migrate in this way are not 'just' migrants. For example, they may also be own-account farmers, petty traders and processors, school students, gatherers or priests. Seasonal migration can be once in a lifetime, very regular or somewhere in between.

Partly because of this flux, numbers are hard to come by. There is no official source. The extent of seasonal migration is not counted in the Census nor in the National Sample Survey. Nor do district level officials or the elected chairpersons of panchayats have access to such information. Yet our observations during fieldwork carried out between March 1999 and July 2000 in five districts suggest that seasonal migration continues to increase and currently involves over 500,000 people in one of the four main migration seasons in West Bengal's rice bowl.[3]

Over seventy per cent of West Bengal's population of approximately 80 million[4] are resident in rural areas, most of them involved with agriculture as one among many forms of livelihood. There has been relatively little industrial development of district towns, and the old industries based around Calcutta have long been in decline.[5] Rice is by far the most important crop in terms of area sown, volume of output and value. Wet rice production in West Bengal is dependent on manual labour, particularly in the seasonal tasks of uprooting seedlings from nurseries and transplanting them, cutting the rice at harvest, binding it, threshing it and storing it away. In the 1980s West Bengal agriculture experienced a revolution through widespread investment in groundwater irrigation which led to further adoption of high-yielding technologies for the main monsoonal rice crop and a vast expansion in the production of irrigated summer rice [*Rogaly, Harriss-White and Bose, 1999*].

South-central West Bengal, in particular Barddhaman district, where canal irrigation was already widespread before the groundwater expansion, has led the way in terms of increasing the volume of rice produced. More rice has meant more work for migrants and an exacerbated seasonal labour shortage for employers.

Accumulation and Changing Class Relations

Seasonal migration for rice work across Bengal has a long history. However, like Bengal's rivers, the streams of migrants shift. Among the streams included in our study (see detailed description below), the one involving Muslim migrants from Murshidabad district is relatively new. The stream from Purbi Singhbhum and western Medinipur appears to be in decline, while the others are all growing. The pattern of seasonal migration thus varies across the streams, shaped by the contrasting agro-ecologies and social and economic structures of the source areas. Indeed, as is the case in other places [*Massey, Arango, Hugo, Kouaouci, Pellegrino and Taylor, 1998*], these structures are themselves influenced by migration.

As in several other parts of India, the last 50 years have seen a reduction in the average size of agricultural holdings and an upward shift in the economic and political power of cultivators and their tenants as the area of land owned by large-scale landlords has drastically declined [*Rogaly, 1998*]. Since the abolition of zamindari in the 1950s, the land-grabbing movements of the late 1960s and the subsequent state-administered redistribution of ceiling-surplus land, a smallholding peasantry controls most of the cultivated land. In Barddhaman District a landowning household is likely to be considered well-off with anything up-wards of seven acres of land if they have assured access to irrigation water. Many employers operate much smaller land areas. Although even these employers are dominant in relationships with their workforce, they are still the underdogs in relations with large-scale rice traders, mill-owners and

financiers [*Harriss-White, 1999*]. Other, larger-scale, employers have
earned very high margins from agriculture, perhaps combining farming
with service income and/or political position.[6] This is evidenced by
investments in better housing, telephones, other consumer durables and
non-agricultural enterprises. How different classes of employers ensure
their own welfare is important to our understanding of how those they
employ struggle to secure theirs.

Wage Differences Between Source and Destination Areas

Agricultural wages in Barddhaman District are high in relation to wages
for the same tasks in source areas. There are different arrangements
available to seasonal migrant workers but the minimum they can expect is
the rate set down by the ruling party and its mass organisation, the Krishak
Sabha (peasants' union). The rate is intended to apply to the whole
district. Although there are variations across the district, and minor
seasonal fluctuations, this set wage rate is an important reference point.
There is no similar process of effective minimum wage setting in the
migrants' source areas. During 1999–2000, the rate in Barddhaman
District was Rs 27 and 2 kg of rice which comes to around Rs 50 in all
(US$1.15).[7] In migrants' home areas there may be some employment
available depending on the season but the wage, paid in cash or in kind, is
likely to be around Rs 20 per day (US$ 0.45). This varies seasonally, for
different tasks, according to which particular source area, and between
men and women. In as much as women hire out labour, they often receive
a lower rate.

In contrast, cultivators in Barddhaman now pay men and women the
same daily rate. Moreover, in the tasks associated with transplanting (except
ploughing) and with the harvest, there is a less marked gender division of
work among hired labourers in Barddhaman than in most of the source
areas. Taking wages and days of consecutive employment together, there is
a significant difference in the amount migrants can earn at home and at the
destination, which is manifest in the capacity of those who migrate to
muster relatively large lump sums simply not accessible to most of those
who stick to livelihoods based in source areas.

III. FOUR STREAMS OF SEASONAL MIGRANTS

In the present study we have focused on four streams of seasonal migrants
for rice work into Barddhaman District and surrounding areas (see Map
and Table 1).[8] The first, emerging from Murshidabad's Bagri region on the
east bank of the Bhagirathi river, is referred to locally as *rarhe jawa*
(journey to rarh – the land to the west of the Bhagirathi). The

overwhelming majority of migrant workers in this stream are Muslim men. Employment is sought in groups, usually through bargaining at a labour market-place, such as Katwa railway station in the north-east of Barddhaman District. The Bagri region is highly fertile and intensively

MAP OF THE STUDY REGION

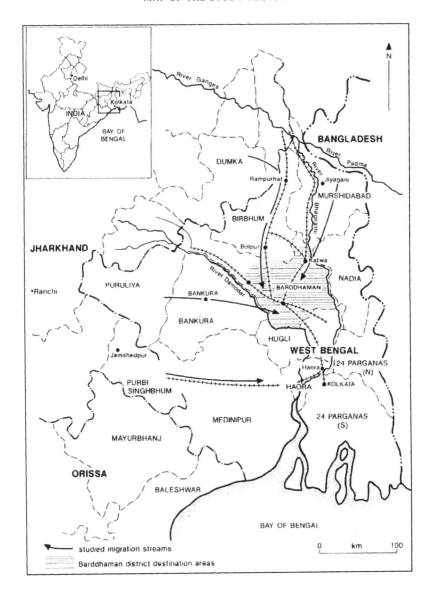

TABLE 1
SOME CHARACTERISTICS OF THE FOUR MIGRATION STREAMS

Stream	Source area pop density per km2 (2001)	Main social groups (*jati*)	Age and sex of migrants	Main labour market place
Rarhe jawa (from Bagri in eastern Murshidabad District)	1101	Muslim	Men	Katwa rail station
Bangla calak' (from Dumka District in the former Santal Parganas)	282	Santal	Men, women and children	Various (but contracts often prearranged)
Pube jawa (from eastern Puruliya and western Bankura Districts)	405	Mixed including: Bauris, Mahatos, Bhumij, Santals	Men, women and children	Bankura bus stand (but contracts often prearranged)
Namal jawa (from Purbi Singhbhum and western Medinipur Districts)	226	Mixed including: Santals, Mahatos, Mals and Sabars	Men, women and children	Various (but contracts often prearranged)

Notes: (1) In Barddhaman District (destination area) population density in 2001 was 985/km2.
(2) Population densities refer to specific parts of the concerned source areas (respectively Murshidabad District; Dumka district; Puruliya district; rural areas of Purbi Singhbhum district – this last figure is from the 1991 census).

irrigated. However, holdings are very small. Population density is even higher than the state average.[9] Moreover, the region is prone to flooding and is experiencing rapid ecological change due to the dramatic shifting of the Padma river south-westwards.

The second stream involves migration from the former Santal Parganas district of Bihar,[10] which lies to the north-west of Barddhaman District. Most of the migrants in this stream are Santals, travelling in mixed sex groups with children. There are at least as many women as men in this stream. The Santals of present day Dumka district refer to the migration as *bangla calak'* (journey to Bengal). Migrants pass through Birbhum District on their way to Barddhaman. They often have pre-arranged jobs with employers they have worked for previously and those employers may have travelled to the source area to recruit them. The journey usually begins on foot and then by bus. Some continue to Barddhaman by bus while many others meet the Sahibganj loop line either at Rampurhat, at Bolpur, or at an intervening station. Migrants who do not have employment fixed up at the destination tend to disembark at Guskara, Khana Junction or Barddhaman rail stations and seek work either there or at nearby bus-stands. There is very little work available in Dumka district. Much land is left fallow in the summer season and the production of rice is far lower than that of Barddhaman in the monsoon season. Many of the migrants complete their own monsoonal rice tasks before embarking on seasonal migration.

The third stream of migrants travels east from the eastern side of Puruliya district and the western side of Bankura district. This migration stream, which is referred to as *pube jawa* (going east) involves at least as many women as men, travelling in mixed sex groups, often accompanied by young children. It is not dominated by any particular social group. The stream includes Mahatos, Bauris, Bhumij, Santals and a few Jola Muslims. Most travel in mixed sex groups with children. The journey begins on foot and by bus, often to the bus-stand at Bankura town. There, especially in the harvest seasons, employers gather to negotiate with the leaders (*sardars*) of groups of migrants. Other migrants in this stream head straight to pre-arranged employment. Previous relations with particular employers may have continued for more than a generation, or be as recent as the previous season. The source area for the *pube jawa* stream is particularly drought prone. Even in good times there is little cultivation of summer paddy, due to the lack of irrigation.

Namal jawa (going to the lowlands) is the fourth stream, involving travel from parts of Purbi Singhbhum district in Jharkhand and west Medinipur District in Bengal to east Medinipur[11] and to Barddhaman. Travel to Barddhaman is by rail via Howrah. This stream is distinct because of its decline (at least in the locality we have selected for study). This may be due to the rapid intensification of agriculture in parts of west Medinipur (for example, Gopiballavpur block)[12] and greater employment possibilities there for former migrants from Chakulia, Baharagora and Ghatsila blocks of Purbi Singhbhum District.[13] The decline is especially significant, given the much longer journey involved to Barddhaman district. Many different social groups are involved in *namal jawa*. Many of the people are Santals, who travel in mixed sex groups with children. However, other groups also migrate, including Mahatos, Sabars and Mals. The latter two tend to travel in men only groups. Work is often arranged in advance with an employer who may have had a long relationship with a particular village (or *tola* within it) turning up in person to recruit labourers.

IV. THE WORKINGS OF THE MIGRANT LABOUR MARKET AND
    WELFARE OUTCOMES

Seasonal migration for rice work in West Bengal can be conceived of as a segment of the regional labour market. Both employers and workers try to use the seasonal migrant labour market to ensure their own welfare. As the monsoonal rice harvest time approaches in Barddhaman District, employers start to worry about where they will get the required amount of labourers from. They start to think about whether to write to the group that came last year, to plan a trip to a source area where they have long-standing relations with the workers of a particular village, or to take their chance at one of the many labour market-places. For some it is time to look for a loan to cover the cost of recruitment. For others it is time to confirm pre-arranged contracts (based on debt) with local labourers to put their rivals – other employers – at a disadvantage. Large-scale employers looking for, say, 40 or 50 migrants, are likely to seek two different sources of labour to avoid the possibility of migrant labour unity in the event of a dispute.

Meanwhile in the source areas, early variety rice may already have been harvested. People are discussing whether they will go away for work this year. How good has the harvest been? How many months will it last them? How much is owed to whom? Do they need a lump sum of money to contribute towards the expenses of a recent illness or a marriage ceremony or new clothes for the festival in mid-January? Discussions are held inside families about whether to go, who will go, when they will go and by which route. Worries are shared about the work involved, how those left behind will manage, which duties it means neglecting and by whom.

The nature and intensity of work and migrant workers' living arrangements combine to make seasonal migration unhealthy. In the *bangla calak'* stream in particular we have observed a negative association between migration and health status. In a study locality (150 households) in Dumka district between March and August 1999, we observed seven premature deaths from tuberculosis, hepatitis or gastroenteritis. There were at least ten people suffering from tuberculosis in the locality in 1999–2000 and all of them migrated before getting the disease. In contrast, there are no cases of tuberculosis among those who do not migrate. A young migrant (under 14 years old) continued working after a cold became a mild fever. After returning, this became a serious bronchial ailment. Depending on the season, labourers encounter extreme heat, cold and heavy rain. Transplanting involves bending continuously while standing in water. Threshing creates high levels of dust and is associated with eye injuries. A middle-aged woman, leader of a migrant gang, sustained eye injuries during the threshing of monsoonal paddy in December 1999. These subsequently developed into serious eye sores and reduced vision. Nutrition also suffers among workers who cut their food intake to increase the quantity of rice taken back home.[14]

Higher wages and the promise of continuous employment for around three weeks in each season are one way in which the market provides for the practical needs of labourers [Wood, 1999]. At the same time few of the labourers would choose this form of engagement with the market if they had alternatives at home. For those who go, seasonal migration is usually a necessary complement to their other means of livelihood. Employers, on the other hand, are likely to have a greater degree of choice. Employment of migrants is used as a route to the accumulation of surpluses from agricultural production.

However, even for employers, the market works messily. They may set out on a day-long journey to recruit workers and return without them, having paid a high cost in terms of travel expenses, health and time. Finding labourers and recruiting them at a wage rate not far above the floor rate mediated by the Krishak Sabha relies either on pre-existing arrangements with known groups of labourers or reaching a labour market-place on a day

---

BOX 1: EMPLOYERS' FEARS

Many employers in Barddhaman District expressed their fears about the journey to recruit migrant workers. As one said, *sat-at din ghure-ghure sudhu muri jol kheye munish enechi. oder khub toshamod korte hoy* (I hung around for seven or eight days without having a proper meal – just puffed rice. You have to go out of your way to persuade them to come here.) Another reported that travelling to Puruliya to recruit migrant workers involved risking one's life. It was alleged by one employer from Galsi block that he was severely beaten and robbed by Sabar people in Puruliya District. The mother of another expressed her concern: *'ami sob samay oder beshi sidha dii bhalo byabohar kori, proti bachor amar chhele okhane munish ante jae'* (I always give more *sidha* (rice) and behave well with labourers because my son has to go to their area every year to recruit people.)

An employer from Bhatar block talked about the risks to his health of recruitment *proti bachor munish ante giye jwar niye phiri, khangrakathi hoye asi* (every year I go to recruit migrants, I come back with a fever (illness), and reduced to a skinny stick).

---

and at a time when there is a relatively high ratio of labourers to employers. There is no precise information about when large numbers of labourers are likely to be seeking work. For example, late onset of the monsoon rains in a source area entirely dependent on rainfed agriculture is likely to mean late departure for migrant workers intent on finishing their own planting. Floods in another area may bring large numbers of workers on to the labour market ahead of time.

Some employers combat their lack of information about labourers by cultivating relations with groups of workers from particular places and engaging in forms of reciprocity, including staying in the houses of workers when they travel for recruitment. A number of labourers reported cases of rough treatment by employers they had met at the labour market – long hours, non-payment of wages (though this is now rare) and intolerable living and/or working conditions. So labourers also benefit from knowing that a particular employer is reliable in terms of payment, will provide bearable accommodation, and will help them out in a crisis. However, some labourers have been made wary of developing long term relations with the same employer because they have experienced the use of such relations by employers to keep wages lower than the market rate or to squeeze out extra work.[15]

Overall, the workings of this segment of the labour market are likely to increase inequality as employers' (especially larger-scale ones') surplus-accumulating production is facilitated, while most of the migrant workers are working hard to stay in the same place.[16] The building of two-storey *pakka* houses (*dalan*) observed in the destination area attest to accumulation by many of the larger-scale employers.

However, migrant labourers are not absolutely powerless in the labour market. Migrant workers travel in groups, ranging in size from two to around 60. These groups are made up of people from the same village or neighbouring villages, who know each other and are brought together by a *sardar* (gang leader) from the same or a nearby village. Travelling in a group provides strength in numbers and some personal security on the journey and at labour market-places. Later, we will discuss how it affects bargaining power over job deals. Groups made up mainly of Santal women on the *bangla calak'* stream often include one or two men, partly for reasons of security. This security may include prevention of injury or attack, including sexual harassment, as well as greatly reducing the risk of remittances being stolen on the route back home. Such men also load and unload the heavy belongings of women in the group on and off buses. In return, women migrants give up their share of *handi* (liquor) often provided by employers to Santal migrants on arrival at the destination. Travelling with others also provides some protection against the worst effects of ill-health in an unknown place.

Locality-based networks of migrants and potential migrants spread information about the appearance of employers in the area looking for workers to recruit. Income flows are enhanced by better information on employment possibilities. Loans from relatives or neighbours may reduce the degree of illfare for migrants who become sick.

As a group, labourers exercise more choice when there is a high ratio of employers to labourers at the market-places. Small variations occur in the same labour market, even within a single day. For example, on 18 July 1999

BOX 2: ON LABOURERS EXERTING POWER IN THE MARKET

One group of Muslim labourers at Guskara rail station, a labour market place in Ausgram block of Barddhaman district, refused to work for a Hindu employer, saying *amra jabona, amader gande gande ghure labh nai* (we won't go; don't hang around us). At a village in Bhatar block, also in Barddhaman District, a migrant worker in the monsoonal rice harvest abused his employer: *besi katha baille jale fele dibore bokachoda* (if you talk too much we will throw you into the (pond) water). *ki karbo; kaj nite hale ektu adhtu sunte habe* (What can I do? One has to listen to (tolerate) these things if the job is going to get done) said the employer, clearly embarassed. In at least two other instances during our research migrants in the destination area have reportedly stopped working during a peak activity in protest at not having been paid extra for working overtime. In one destination village in Birbhum district, an employer lamented the disappearance of the workers he had hired after two nights. Apparently they had heard that the wage at the labour market-place at Katwa station had increased substantially.

---

when we were present at Katwa station, labourers finding work in the morning were able to fix higher wages than those present in the afternoon,when the number of labourers had swollen. A similar process was observed across two different days at Bankura bus-stand in the November recruitment of harvest workers.

In tight labour market place situations, labourers can afford more easily to 'choose' their employer, refusing somebody who talked to them in a way they found insulting, or somebody belonging to a group or from an area which they had decided on previous experience they would not like to work with/go to. We have observed labourers abusing an employer or even walking out on the job after just a couple of days' work.

BOX 3: SEASONAL MIGRATION AND REDUCED INEQUALITY IN A SOURCE LOCALITY

The study locality in Puruliya District in the *pube jawa* stream includes a prominent employer class, descendants of the regional kings (*raja*). The *raja* have long been the principle cultivators and employers of the area. Historically they had strong *jajmani* relations with a group of Lohars, resident in the same locality. The Lohars used to be dependent on the *raja* for employment, and received patronage in return.

During the last 20 years there has been a significant shift in these relations. The increased access to seasonal out-migration for agricultural and other manual work has contributed to the diversification of livelihoods by Lohars and a consequent loosening of their obligations to the *raja*. It is clear that one of the impacts of seasonal migration out of the locality has been the *raja*'s experience of labour shortages during peak agricultural seasons. This has led the *raja*, and consequently other employers, to change the terms of land and labour contracts to the advantage of the Lohars and other labourers in the locality.

Migrant workers may also be able to make small strategic gains in relation to employers of labour in the source area, relations with whom are characterised by unequal mutuality. These arrangements influence decisions about whether and when to migrate. There are often good reasons for doing at least some wage work for source area employers. First there may be no choice – it may be part of an inherited obligation or the other side of an unequal bargain involving a seasonal loan at a time of low employment throughout the region. Secondly, it may be a mutual insurance mechanism – 'I guarantee to be available for your harvest; you provide me with loans to get by when there is no work available anywhere'. In the *pube jawa* stream at least, seasonal migration, while produced – in part at least – by inequality, is also a part of a process whereby labourers once beholden to particular local employers can exercise more voice and gain higher wages.

Meanwhile, Barddhaman employers' behaviour in labour market-places is characterised more by competition than collusion.[17] This is consistent with the high degree of class differentiation among employers and their lack of unity along caste, religious and/or party political lines. It contrasts with the labour-hiring process elsewhere in India, for example in Bardoli taluka of south Gujarat, where sugar cultivators, predominantly of a single jati – Patidar – act together through a 'highly organised recruitment process'.[18]

BOX 4: WHO DECIDES WHETHER TO GO?

During the monsoonal rice harvest in 1999, PM, a Santal man resident in Dumka district, wanted his 16-year-old-daughter C to finish the family harvest before migrating. C refused and left for Barddhaman against her father's wishes. She is the only wage earner in the family. PM suffers from tuberculosis and his wife is also in poor health and cares for their younger child. PM expressed his frustration *cet cikaiak'* (what to do?)

LH, also a Santal from Dumka District, has a daughter, B, aged eighteen. Against her parents' wishes, B has a relationship with a married man, who lives in the destination village. As she earns money from her agricultural labour there her parents have to accept the situation. She cannot be thrown out or otherwise punished.

H, a woman migrant worker from Puruliya District migrated for the same monsoonal rice harvest as PM (above) against the wishes of her mother-in-law. H left behind her one-year-old child. This was discussed publicly in H's village. H and her husband were admonished by one older woman neighbour. *Baccha ke ebhabe phele chole gaechhe. Bar o kichu bole na* (She has just left her child like this. Even her husband says nothing).'

V. RELATIONS INSIDE HOUSEHOLDS

One way in which intra-household relations mediate welfare/illfare outcomes for migrant workers is through the distribution of remittances. This varies between and within the streams. For example,in the *rarhe jawa* migration, where most migrants are men, one woman described how whatever cash her husband returned with was deposited with her on return. She then made expenditure decisions.

In other migration streams much of the migration is in family groups, though not necessarily by members of the entire household. Box 4 provides three examples of the different ways in which decisions about who (if anyone) should migrate from a household may involve contestation of age and gender-based hierarchies.

When groups made up of families from Dumka or Puruliya reach their destination they often split up into families again for cooking purposes. This enables families travelling with fewer dependents to save a higher proportion of that part of the wage which is paid in rice. People travelling without children do not have to sacrifice rice savings just because people from other households have brought children with them.

The household is also an important institution in terms of protecting homesteads and other assets at migrants' homes (see also the discussion of the importance of household composition in explaining migration patterns by de Haan *et al.*, this volume). Some of those who do not migrate regularly give the reason that there would be no-one left at home to look after the security of the livestock, or the house. Others do not migrate because of caring responsibilities within the household, for example, the presence of young children or an elderly relative. In such circumstances seasonal migration is seen as disruptive to existing private welfare arrangements.

Family members who have migrated together are likely to be a first port of call for care if one among them becomes sick. Moreover, travelling with adult family members means greater overall household income from the migration for a given number of days away. Male family members provide some security to women against sexual harassment or robbery on the route.

Members of employer households are variously involved in the process of recruiting, accommodating, supervising, making payment, and, in some cases, cooking for migrant workers. Payment for family groups is divided into daily kind payments made either by men or women from employer households and cash payments paid at the end of the season by a man from the employer household. Employment of groups of all-male migrant workers such as in the *rarhe jawa* stream usually depends on a capacity to provide all meals to the migrant workers during their stay. This is often done by wives of male household heads or their daughters-in-law. Younger brothers or sons are regularly involved in recruitment. Recruitment from labour markets is solely a male occupation. The ways in which employers seek to ensure their own welfare through hiring labourers to make profits from rice cultivation thus also rely, to a large degree, on private, intra-household relations.

VI. THE STATE AND ILLFARE/WELFARE OUTCOMES FROM SEASONAL MIGRATION

Income Flows

The state has little direct involvement in regulating the terms and conditions of seasonal migrant work. The Inter-State Migrant Workmen (Regulation of Employment and Conditions of Service) Act (1979) provides legislative protection for migrant workers travelling across state borders. However, for migrants to access their statutory rights under the Act, they have to be registered. We have not heard of any cases of migrants for rice work from Jharkhand to West Bengal being registered in this way. And much of the migration (the *rarhe jawa* and *pube jawa* streams) is in any case within the boundaries of the state of West Bengal. Although there is an official minimum wage for all agricultural workers in the state, this rate is not a reference point for the workers themselves nor their employers. The minimum wage for agricultural workers of Rs 48.64 per day in December 1997[19] is equivalent to the rate regularly received by seasonal migrants in Barddhaman District in the monsoonal rice season of 1999. This suggests that payment is regularly below the minimum wage. However, inspections by the Labour Department's Minimum Wage Inspectors have only lead to small amounts of compensation to agricultural workers.[20]

Income flows have been positively influenced in some cases, however, by the workings of local government institutions. Several labourers have reported cases of non-payment being taken to the local panchayat and being resolved in their favour. Many migrant workers from Jharkhand are aware that the panchayat system is operative in West Bengal, and that they may be able to protect themselves from the worst abuses through recourse to panchayat institutions. At the time of this research, the Left Front Government had been in power in West Bengal for 23 years. The dominant political party, the Communist Party of India (Marxist) (CPI(M)), had become, in places, synonymous with panchayat institutions. Nowhere was this more true than in Barddhaman District.

BOX 5: CONFLICT RESOLUTION BY WEST BENGAL PANCHAYATS AND THE COMMUNIST PARTY OF INDIA (MARXIST)

In the summer rice harvest of 1997, MK, a Muslim seasonal migrant labourer from Murshidabad, reported a positive experience of conflict resolution by the local panchayat in a village in Barddhaman District. His group of twenty-four labourers worked for a Hindu employer for seven days. When they were asked to wait another day for a payment, they requested the employer to find work for them on that day. On being refused, they asked him at least to give them food, but the employer disagreed. They then approached the local Gram Panchayat member, who took them to the CPI(M) party office. Now acting on the directions from the CPI(M) office they claimed the due, but the employer still refused. To settle the dispute, the police came and ordered the labourers to sell the employer's rice to a wholesaler. The labourers were eventually paid for more days than they had worked. Reflecting on the incident MK said *jani je taka mare bideshe* – (I know the employers in *bidesh*[23] cheat on wages). This is why he decided to seek the help of the panchayat.

TN, who migrates to brick kilns as well as agricultural work in the *namal jawa* stream, narrated another example of the role played by political party cadres in ensuring migrant workers were paid. He reported that in the brick kilns workers buy cards at Rs 5 from CPI(M) party office in Medinipur and the party in turn ensures that employers cannot refuse them payment.

The role of the state could not be separated from the role of the Party in understanding how wage disputes between migrants and employers were resolved in the District.

The agricultural union, the Krishak Sabha, is closely allied to the CPI(M). Of the current Barddhaman District population of approximately eight million, 1.7 million people are Krishak Sabha members.[21] A major contribution of the Krishak Sabha has been the implementation of a district-wide wage floor for men and women agricultural workers. This suits local wage workers in the district as their wages are only very rarely undercut by migrants. It is also in the interests of employers as it encourages labourers' compliance.[22] However, the Krishak Sabha is itself a site of struggle between employers and workers, between the agenda of raising wages on the one hand and reducing input costs on the other. The seasonal migrants engaged in Barddhaman District agriculture contribute to the CPI(M) directly, through 'subscriptions' of five rupees per head, collected at least once a year.

Health

Migrant workers who get seriously ill might go to a government hospital or health centre for medical attention. However, for most migrant workers, health care and medicines are accessed through private sector outlets and are usually dependent on loans from employers.

BOX 6: STATE FAILURE IN HEALTH PROVISION FOR MIGRANT
WORKERS

During the monsoonal harvest 1999, SH from the Dumka study locality migrated to
Barddhaman district with his wife, children and old mother. His mother suffered
from severe body ache and fever. While the workers of his group worked for 26
days, SH could only work for 17 days as he had to organise his mother's treatment.
He spent all the cash he earned (Rs 500) on treatment provided by a quack
(unqualified doctor) in the destination locality. SH told us that *aspatalre ran baku
emok'ak'*—Government Hospitals do not provide medicine [free of cost to poor
people].
Another male migrant from the same village in Dumka District had to spend Rs.
4000 on his treatment at the Barddhaman Medical College and Hospital when he
contracted tuberculosis.
A third migrant, L, suffered from malaria during a season of work in Barddhaman
District. He had to take an advance of aproximately Rs 700 from his employer to see
a private *daktor*, and since he could not work that season the debt was carried over
to the next season. Meanwhile L took home no remittances other than rice.

Back in Dumka District health provision is no better, regardless of whether or not
one migrates out of the district for work:
LH was suffering from malaria in January 2000. Having been verbally abused by the
doctor at the district hospital, he was advised to have a diagnostic blood test done
elsewhere (privately) and was prescribed medicine to be purchased from privately
owned shops. LH had to take a loan of Rs 200 for the medicine and has not yet been
able to repay it.
Now LH is suspected to be also suffering from tuberculosis. He went to the district
hospital. He was advised to get an x-ray done from a private clinic and was also
prescribed some medicine (again to be purchased privately). Though there is a
dedicated tuberculosis hospital in the district, admission requires a complicated
registration process which LH feels unable to undergo. Another tuberculosis patient,
who is registered there, has in any case been told to purchase medicine privately as
well. LH has not yet been able to find the money for his x-ray or his treatment.
In the Dumka study locality people have to rely on treatment by quacks, who give
credit.
In November 1999, RR, a woman leader of a migrant workers' gang was charged
Rs 4,500 by a quack for malaria 'treatment'. She is liquidating all the assets she
had accumulated out of wages earned from migration over several years.

Employers too rely on private sector health care. However, they are
better placed to pay the cost of travel to better quality health facilities
further away and to pay higher fees for the best doctors. Employers with
good contacts in one of the committees of the ruling CPI(M) party are likely
to be able to use those contacts to gain admission to publicly provided
health facilities.

The absence of effective regulation regarding terms and conditions of
work is also a cause of illfare through the intensity of work, overexposure

to harsh weather conditions, and unhealthy workplaces (see section IV). There is also no state provision for the primary school-age children who accompany their parents in the *bangla calak'*, *pube jawa* and *namal jawa* streams. Indeed, discussions with the departments of social welfare and women and child development at the district level revealed a high degree of uncertainty regarding who was responsible for the welfare of workers and their families who were temporarily resident. In one destination locality in Barddhaman district, *anganwadi* workers (providers of free nutrition supplements for pre-school children) were adamant that they were not mandated to provide food to temporary residents.

Children of migrants are, however, included in polio immunisation drives, even when resident at the destination. It was reported that immunisation has also been carried out with migrant children on train journeys. Another, more localised, exception to the absence of state provision for seasonal migrants away from home, was reported at Bankura. The state, in the form of the district administration, has taken the lead in providing health camps for returning *pube jawa* migrants arriving at Bankura bus stand at the end of the two harvest seasons. This has been state action in collaboration with the local bus workers' unions and two non-governmental organisations.

Security

The lack of secure labour market places, overcrowding of buses and poor road conditions combine to make the journeys involved in seasonal migration particularly risky to labourers. If migrants are stuck during a journey they often have to stay at a bus stand or railway station. For example, at Dumka bus stand in the *bangla calak'* stream, migrant workers sleep under the open sky without basic sanitation or access to drinking water. On the return journey in particular there is a risk of theft in all the migration streams, as workers are known to carry accumulated earnings. Non-state actors have also intervened to provide security to seasonal migrants. For example, bus owners at Siuri bus stand in Birbhum District claimed to have organised bus stand security for business reasons when night time attacks on migrants led to fewer *bangla calak'* migrants taking that route. Like the involvement of the Bus Workers' Union and an associated NGO in state-led action on migrants' health at Bankura bus stand this is a rare example of civil society action which is likely to improve welfare outcomes for seasonal migrants.

For migrants of the *rarhe jawa* stream, *in*security at the major labour market-place of Katwa railway station has been further enhanced by the state. On several occasions both in the seasons for recruitment of workers for transplanting and harvesting monsoonal rice, we witnessed workers

---

BOX 7:DESH

RH, a 70-year-old man, spent 30 years in Barddhaman District after migrating there for agricultural work at an early age. He earned much higher wages and had more job security than others from his home village in Dumka District. Yet RH preferred not to remain in Barddhaman District and has come back to his home village, saying *tinan din bideshre tahenak'*– how long can I stay outside the motherland. He always mentions *abo disum* – our homeland and ignores his dilapidated house and poor living conditions. *Bidesh do cet ona in' ge barai* – I know well what the country outside the motherland is (as I have seen it).

Like many other Santals of former Santal Pargana, HR's father settled in a Barddhaman village following regular seasonal migration. HR is a wage labourer, but he is proud of being rich through having a village home in Dumka district as well, unlike some well to do Santals of the same Barddhaman village. *Kisan huyu kate hon unku ak' cet hon banu, aleak' do disum re ora menak' ak'* – they are rich, yet they possess nothing, we have our village home. *Disumredo duk re hon suk* – At the homeland living in hardship is also pleasing. HR carries the idea of his home in Dumka as capital.

---

being *lathi*-charged by the railway police. For these, mainly Muslim workers, many of whom are from the border areas, such treatment added to a sense of alienation, a lack of citizenship (see section VII).

VII. MIGRATION AND CHANGING SOCIAL IDENTITIES

The ways in which identities are deployed in the social process of seasonal migration and the way they are changed through this process is also important in understanding welfare outcomes for seasonal migrants. Migrants deploy collective social identities, a sense of who they are and what they are prepared to do for a living, to create boundaries around who they will work for, where and on what terms.[24] Despite great poverty, such boundaries can sustain a sense of self-esteem and self-worth, which mean much in people's own understandings of their welfare. Boundaries are also contested and change in the process of seasonal migration through interactions with others beyond the territorial limits of one's own locality.[25] In this section, we briefly discuss three dimensions of identity: *desh* (territory), *jati* (social rank) and gender.

Seasonal migration in the study region involves moving from the familiar surroundings of one's own *desh* (home place) to the strangeness of *bidesh* (foreign, other place).[26] Labour recruiters also experience a crossing of territorial boundaries. In the process space-based identities are changed. Going to *bidesh* reinforces a sense of belonging to the *desh*. Observed characteristics of *bidesh* enable the construction of ideas about what it means to belong to one's own *desh*, a process of othering. Without seasonal migration, conflicts between social groups and individuals within the *desh* would assume greater prominence. Interacting with *bidesh* gives meaning to *desh*.

Social identities based around *jati* – including caste, religion and ethnicity – are complex in southern West Bengal.[27] There is no straightforward correspondence between jati and class. The proportion of Muslims (both employers and labourers) is relatively high.[28] Six per cent of the population of West Bengal are adivasis (mainly labourers but also self-provisioners). There is no single dominant rural caste among Hindus [*Chatterjee, 1997*] and caste status is therefore malleable [*Basu, 1992*], making competition and conflict over status potentially fruitful and widespread [*Davis, 1983*].

The capacity to employ manual workers *per se* (employment-based class position) and migrants in particular (as they often require large advances for

---

BOX 8:JATI

The majority of labourers in the *rarhe jawa* stream are Muslim and most of them travel via the labour market-place at Katwa railway station. Identity issues emerge from listening to conversations during recruitment: *do taka maine kam hoi se bhalo tobu muslim barite jabo* (it is better to go to a Muslim employer though the wage rate may be two rupees lower). In another case, following the apparent completion of a negotiation, the leader of a group of labourers was heard to ask *apnara ki jat?* (what is your religion?). They refused to work for the employer when they found out he was from a different religion.

The preference of Muslim labourers to work for Muslim employers is attributed to the lack of dignity some have felt when working for Hindus. Hindu employers tend to serve Muslim labourers cooked food in the open courtyard, even in very cold weather or during the rains. They are asked to clean the place where they have taken food with water and cow dung. Hindu employers also treat Muslim labourers as if they were untouchable. One labourer asked of Hindu employers *jat bhaier moto ora hote parbe?* (could they be like our brothers of the same jati (religion)?)

Identities of desh and jati also overlap. One Muslim worker from the Bagri region (east of the Bhagirathi talked disparagingly of employers from *rarh* (to the west) *rarher sange kutum kora aar balite pechhap kora saman* (to develop kinship with *rarh* and to pee on sand are the same).

---

travel, as well as accommodation and the promise of weeks of consecutive days of employment) may be used as a signifier of power and status. Being able to avoid hiring out labour as a migrant is also loaded with meaning for upwardly-aspiring *jati* in source areas. Perhaps more evident is the way in which conversations, consultations, negotiations over migration, the division of social space for eating and sleeping during recruitment, travel and days of employment create and recreate identities based around religion and ethnicity – seasonal migration involving eating and sleeping away from home inevitably arouses sensitivities concerning the content of the diet of particular social groups.

Gender identities and gendered ideologies of work are also variously constructed, reinforced and changed through the process of migration. Women and men migrate but not uniformly across *jati*. For example, there

---

BOX 9: WOMEN AND MEN IN LABOUR MARKET-PLACES

When we started our field work we expected to find that migrant women were sexually harassed both on journeys and in destination areas. We have not so far come across such sexual harassment.

Observations in the monsoonal rice harvest of 1999, when one of us joined an employer from Barddhaman district on a recruitment trip to Puruliya district, suggested a range of meanings of seasonal migration for women.

Women migrant labourers who were waiting at the bus stand at Bankura for the Barddhaman bus were roaming in and out of the bus stand enjoying the temporary 'mela' atmosphere. Small market stalls emerge in the main seasons of migration, responding to demand from migrant labourers. Women coming from the interior villages of Bandwan block were visibly enjoying the consumption of 'chop' and 'muri' (puffed rice), buying trinkets, towels, Boroline (multipurpose face cream) and small mirrors. Such purchases are unlikely to have been possible without seasonal migration.

One group of women wandered around together without a male escort, just visiting different stalls, bargaining for things and checking out what goods were on offer.

The bus conductors and shopkeepers were cracking jokes flirtatiously with the migrant women. Other observers may have termed it sexual harassment, but the reciprocation from the women showed they were enjoying the interaction.

However, by no means all of the women present enjoyed the time spent at the bus-stand in this way. There were many women sitting aimlessly at Bankura bus stand that day with their children, *'madur'* (mat), cooking pot and *'lathi'* (stick), waiting for prospective employers.

---

are at least as many Santal women seasonal migrants as there are men, but very few Muslim women seasonal migrants. Through the process intra-household power relations along lines of gender as well as age are contested. As mentioned in section V, almost all recruiters are men but women are involved in distributing *sidha* (daily kind payments) to migrant workers (*sidha* is specific to migrant groups of particular gender, *jati* and *desh* but not others). Some women in employer households cook food for migrant workers, involving significant labour inputs, which are resisted by women of other households. This then affects the social processes of negotiation at labour market-places.

VIII. CONCLUSION

Using data from fieldwork with seasonal migrant workers and their employers in West Bengal, we have briefly discussed some of the ways in which seasonal migration contributes to particular illfare/welfare outcomes for the two classes. We have also illustrated aspects of the social process of seasonal migration, in particular the ways it is influenced by, and contributes to, changing social identities.

In order to derive practical welfare gains, migrants rely on the support of other household members and of the groups in which they travel and work. Although there is some evidence of strategic gains, and a greater capacity to decide which form of manual work to perform and for whom, selling labour for manual work is something most seasonal migrants would not choose to do if they had a choice. Their involvement in social and economic ties with employers in source areas, and their engagement in the regional labour market serve mainly practical rather than strategic purposes.

Although the description and analysis in this study has made much of the class distinction between 'employer' and 'labourer', we have also noted the range of wealth and market power within each of the two classes. Most employers are weak players in wider markets for inputs, including credit and products. Smaller employers may have to sell paddy at relatively low post-harvest prices in exchange for loans for inputs, including labour. Even relatively large employers do not wield absolute power in the labour market – experiencing fear and the risk of ill-health in the process of recruitment of workers. But for such employers the hiring of seasonally migrant workers has been a key part of the process of accumulation via agricultural profits, that has characterised the West Bengal rice bowl in the last two decades.

Policies designed to provide adequate health care and nutrition, as well as primary education, have excluded seasonal migrants, who take greater health risks than people who stay at home. Seasonal migrants also have less access to government provision of health services when away for work than others in the destination area. Having low incomes, migrants are not well placed to access good quality private sector care. The continuing lack of security of migrants on the road and at bus-stands, and the *lathi* charging of Muslim migrants at Katwa railway station are further evidence of the exclusion of migrants from welfare-oriented concerns of state action.[29]

It has been implied by the direction of government policies in source areas to date, that the root cause of seasonal migration is the exclusion of people in those areas from rural economic development. Indeed, in the long term, policies which help to bring about greater economic dynamism in source areas are likely to be in the interests of those currently involved in seasonal migration. At present, though, seasonal migration is a necessary reality for many hundreds of thousands of people in the region and also a cornerstone of the prosperity of the state of West Bengal.

However, attempts to reverse exclusion should be aware of attempting a form of inclusion that goes against the interests of migrants. For example, regulation of employment terms and conditions may appear attractive because of its potential role in protecting migrant workers. Yet judging by the current pratices (or lack of them) of minimum wage inspections in agriculture and the record of the Inter-State Migrant Workmen (Regulation of Employment and Conditions of Service) Act (1979), crude regulation is likely to be ineffective in eastern India and could make migration more expensive if it involved a requirement for migrants to register. It might ignore migrants' political citizenship – in terms of their capacity to change the rules[30] – removing the small amount of control which migrants have over their exchanges with employers and thus over the meanings of their migration for rural manual employment. Attempts to delineate what is and is not acceptable in terms of migration movements may run roughshod over the emergence of group identities that can be part of the broader welfare outcome.[31]

Yet, it is imperative that a welfare agenda develops which engages with the existing costs and risks faced by seasonal migrant workers.[32] Emerging initiatives such as the provision of health care for returning *pube jawa* migrants at Bankura bus-stand and security at Siuri bus-stand, which have been started by combinations of different civil society actors and the state, should be learned from and built upon. Greater infrastructure for secure overnight journey breaks, purpose-built labour market-places to move the negotiation process away from the railway tracks (and from violence by the police), more and safer bus routes, and health provision for migrant workers in destination areas, as well as access for their children to existing health and education programmes there, are areas of potential policy action which might improve migrants' welfare outcomes in the short term.

It may also be possible to build on the roles of peasant organisations, such as the Krishak Sabha, and the elected panchayats in Barddhaman District. Although representing employers and local rather than migrant labourers, the Barddhaman District Krishak Sabha has shown itself, no doubt in the interests of its members, to have been capable of establishing a wage floor for seasonal migrants. Meanwhile, the reputation of panchayats for settling wage disputes in Barddhaman District, and the panchayats' close relations with the dominant political party in the district, reduce the risks of non-payment as perceived by people in source areas when considering whether to migrate.

NOTES

1. The authors first came across this term in the title of Harriss-White and Subramanian [*1999*]. Welfare will be used as a shorthand for illfare/welfare in what follows.
2. As in Holmes's [*1989*] study of migrant workers in northern Italy. Holmes found the identification of migrant workers with their homeland to have been reaffirmed through migration.
3. Large numbers of people numbering hundreds of thousands also migrate in the other three seasons. The rice bowl referred to here comprises much of Barddhaman and Hugli Districts, as well as adjoining blocks of Birbhum and Bankura. The figures are estimates based on the following sources: observation and discussion with bus owners and bus workers' associations at Bankura bus-stand in November 1999 and January 2000; four visits to Katwa railway station between March and December 1999 and discussion with railway officials there; the demand for agricultural workers in Barddhaman district (based on detailed crop budgets provided by farmers and state government figures for total area of rice sown); census figures for the number of agricultural labourers in Barddhaman District; the population figures for source areas, especially Dumka and Puruliya Districts; the estimate of the Puruliya District Additional District Magistrate; and observation in five villages spread across five of Barddhaman District's main rice-growing blocks (Galsi, Memari, Barddhaman Sadar; Bhatar; Monteswar). For further details of how we reached this estimate, see Rogaly *et al.* [*2001*].
4. The population figure is from Census of India [*2001*]. The percentage of people living in rural areas was 72.52 per cent in 1991. At the time of the final revision of this paper, the 2001 figure was not available.
5. Indeed, a relatively high proportion of people still employed in these industries are not Bengali [*de Haan and Rogaly, 1996*].
6. Regular income from service enables cultivators of rice better to 'play the market' by avoiding post-harvest sales.
7. In 2000 India's Gross National Product was US$450 per capita, which was US$2149 at purchasing power parity. Using this ratio the equivalent amount paid per day at purchasing power parity was equivalent to US$5.50 in the destination area and US$2.15 in the source area. We are grateful to Arjan de Haan for this calculation.
8. There are other streams including from North Bengal (Malda, North and South Dinajpur), North 24 Parganas, and mixed with both of these, Santals and others from Bangladesh. There is other rural manual work available in Barddhaman District and surrounding areas. This includes brick-kiln work, earth-works (for example road building), stone and sand quarrying, and cultivation of other crops – especially potato, production of which is very high in West Bengal. Seasonal migrants come for these as well, but from our observations travelling with migrants, living in villages with them and with their employers, and spending time at labour market-places, the vast majority of seasonal migrants who come into the district work in rice production.
9. West Bengal has the highest population density of all the Indian states – it was 904 per square kilometre in 2001. The population density of Murshidabad-Jiyaganj block in

Murshidabad District was over 1,100 in 1991, when the figure for the district as a whole was 890. The district's population density rose to 1,101 in 2001 but at the time of the final revision of this paper, block-level figures were not available (Census of India).

10. Santal Parganas has now been divided up into five districts (Dumka, Pakur, Deoghar, Godda and Sahibganj). Bihar itself has been bifurcated, with the whole of the former Santal Parganas included in the new Jharkhand state.

11. Often (in the recent past) via a labour market at Balichowk.

12. See K. Rana [2000]; S. Rana [2000].

13. Observations in Binpur block of west Medinipur in March 1999 suggest this agricultural intensification is not uniform. Binpur remains an area of seasonal outmigration.

14. Of course, this last part does not apply to those migrant workers who have cooked meals provided by employers.

15. Migrant labourers usually travel with others from the same village so that involvement in long-term relations was less a matter of individual choice than collectively followed norms. For example, the bagri study locality labourers almost always sought work at the labour market place, whereas Santals in the Dumka study locality travelled out on the basis of pre-arranged employment.

16. This is in spite of the floor wage set for the main destination area district, Barddhaman. Though this paper discusses some of the small choices migrants can make and their power in the labour market negotiations, most migrants are not able to use these to change what is essentially a class position of being compelled to hire out manual labour.

17. Cooperation is also evident, however. One common form is the sharing of information on when there are large numbers of workers in the labour market places. Another is the loaning of workers contracted by a larger-scale employer to a smaller-scale employer at the end of the former's work. There is usually no explicit charge for this apart from the wage originally agreed. The former employer bears the whole recruitment cost.

18. See Ebrahim [2000: 183]; Breman [1978, 1985, 1996] and Teerink [1995], on which Ebrahim draws.

19. Government of West Bengal [1997: 56].

20. Rs 21,983.50 was returned to agricultural workers by employers following the intervention of the Labour Department in 1997 [Government of West Bengal, 1997: 54]. An anonymous reviewer of this study has commented that in their experience Minimum Wage Inspections in West Bengal have tended to focus on non-agricultural sectors.

21. Interview, Amal Haldar, Secretary, Krishak Sabha, Barddhaman District, 27 Feb. 2000.

22. It is thus in the interests of the Krishak Sabha and the CPI(M), for whom a relatively peaceful and prosperous countryside is a crucial ingredient for electoral success [Rogaly, 1998].

23. Here, bidesh refers to the rarh area, in particular Barddhaman District. For its more general meaning, see section VII.

24. 'Ethnicity ... can become a basis for community, for resistance, for the assertion of self-determination by the oppressed and definitions can be transformed in the context of particular struggles' [Benmayor and Skotnes, 1994: 7].

25. See van de Veer [1998: xii].

26. See use of desh-bidesh in Katy Gardner's work on Bangladeshi migration to the UK [Gardner, 1995].

27. We cannot do justice to this complexity, even as it relates to seasonal migration, in the present study.

28. Twenty three per cent of West Bengal's population were Muslim in 1991 as against 12 per cent of the population of India (Census of India).

29. The all-India National Commission of Rural Labour study group on migrant labour concluded that even for inter-state migration, which is covered by the Inter-State Migrant Workers Act, 'accommodation even if provided is sub-human and arrangement for clean drinking water is an exception'. Moreover, 'provision of adequate health and medical

facilities are exception rather than the rule'. [*Government of India, 1991, Vol.1:119*].

30. For a longer discussion of citizenship as the obverse of social exclusion, see Rogaly, Fisher and Mayo [*1999*].

31. See Ranabir Samaddar's argument that attempting to control seasonal employment and other migration across the Bangladesh-West Bengal border was interfering with the ordinary daily livelihoods of large numbers of people, and serving the interests of statecraft in its struggle to make the nation state more significant in people's identities [Samaddar, 1999].

32. The National Commission for Rural Labour recommended this is 1991 through its call for a migration policy 'with primary focus on smooth migration, greater employment, minimising exploitation and hardships of rural migrant labour. In order to achieve these objectives, certain incentives and facilities will have to be made available by the government to migrant labour' [*Government of India, 1991, Vol.1: 264*].

REFERENCES

Basu, A., 1992, *Two Faces of Protest: Contrasting Modes of Women's Activism in India*, Berkeley, CA: University of California Press.

Benmayor, R. and A. Skotnes, 1994, 'Some Reflections on Migration and Identity', in Benmayor and Skotnes (eds) [*1994*].

Benmayor, R. and A. Skotnes (eds.), 1994, *International Yearbook of Oral History and Life Stories: Migration and Identity*, Oxford: Oxford University Press.

Breman, J., 1978, 'Seasonal Migration and Cooperative Capitalism: Crushing of Cane and of Labour by Sugar Factories of Bardoli', *Economic and Political Weekly*, Special Number 13, pp.1317–60.

Breman, J., 1985, *Of Peasants, Migrants and Paupers: Rural Labour Circulation and Capitalist Production in West India*, Delhi: Oxford University Press.

Breman, J., 1996, *Footloose Labour: Working in India's Informal Economy*, Cambridge: Cambridge University Press.

Chatterjee, P., 1997, *The Present History of West Bengal: Essays in Political Criticism*, Delhi: Oxford University Press.

Davis, M., 1983, *Rank and Rivalry: The Politics of Inequality in Rural West Bengal*, Cambridge: Cambridge University Press.

de Haan, A. and B. Rogaly, 1996, 'Eastward Ho! Migration and Leap-frogging in Eastern India', in G. Rodgers, K. Foti and L. Lauridsen (eds.), *An Institutional Approach to Labour and Development*, London: Frank Cass.

Ebrahim, A., 2000, 'Agricultural Cooperatives in Gujarat, India: Agents of Equity or Differentiation', *Development in Practice*, Vol.10, No.2, pp.178–88.

Gardner, K., 1995, *Global Migrants, Local Lives: Travel and Transformation in Rural Bangladesh*, Oxford: Clarendon.

Government of India, 1991, 'Report of the National Commission on Rural Labour', New Delhi: Ministry of Labour (two volumes).

Government of West Bengal, 1997, 'Labour in West Bengal', Calcutta: Department of Labour.

Harriss-White, B., 1999, 'Agricultural Growth and the Structure and Relations of Agricultural Markets in West Bengal', in Rogaly, Harriss-White and Bose [*1999*].

Harriss-White, B. and S. Subramanian (eds.), 1999, *Illfare in India: Essays on India's Social Sector in Honour of S. Guhan*, Delhi: Sage.

Holmes, D., 1989, *Cultural Disenchantments: Worker Peasantries in Northeast Italy*, Princeton: Princeton, NJ University Press.

Massey, D., Arrango, J., Hugo, G., Kouaouci, A., Pellegrino, A. and J.E. Taylor, 1998, *Worlds in Motion: Understanding International Migration at the End of the Millenium*, Oxford: Clarendon Press.

Rana, K., 2000, 'Gopiballavpur – Anya Mukh' (Bangla), mimeo.

Rana, S., 2000, 'Changing Class Relations in Rural West Bengal – Gopiballavpur Experience', translated from Bangla by Kumar Rana, mimeo.

Rogaly, B., 1998, 'Containing Conflict and Reaping Votes: Management of Rural Labour Relations in West Bengal', *Economic and Political Weekly*, Vol.33, Nos.42/43), pp.2729–39.

Rogaly, B., Harriss-White, B. and S. Bose (eds.), 1999, *Sonar Bangla? Agricultural Growth and Agrarian Change in West Bengal and Bangladesh*, Delhi: Sage.

Rogaly, B., Biswas, J., Coppard, D., Rafique, A., Rana, K. and A. Sengupta, 2001, 'Seasonal Migration, Social Change and Migrants' Rights: Lessons from West Bengal', *Economic and Political Weekly*, Vol.36, No.49, pp.4547–59.

Rogaly, B., Fisher, T. and E. Mayo, 1999, *Poverty, Social Exclusion and Microfinance in Britain*, Oxford: Oxfam in association with the New Economics Foundation.

Samaddar, R., 1999, *The Marginal Nation: Transborder Migration from Bangladesh to West Bengal*, Delhi: Sage.

Teerink, R., 1995, 'Migration and its Impact on Khandeshi Women in the Sugar Cane Harvest', in Loes Schenk-Sandbergen (ed.), *Women and Seasonal Labour Migration*, New Delhi/London: Sage.

van der Veer, P., 1998, *Religious Nationalism: Hindus and Muslims in India*, Delhi: Oxford University Press.

Wood, G., 1999, 'Adverse Incorporation: Another Dark Side of Social Capital', mimeo, University of Bath, Department of Economics and International Development.

Migration and Livelihoods in Historical Perspective: A Case Study of Bihar, India

ARJAN DE HAAN

I. INTRODUCTION

One of the conclusions of my research on migration in India, which focused on the labour market in an industrial neighbourhood in Calcutta, was that unskilled labour was not only migratory, but also that the migration has remained circular. Usually, migration is by single men, part of the family stays behind in the area of origin, and the migrants continue to maintain close links with their areas of origin and invest their savings in the village rather than in the town [*de Haan, 1994*]. This is not a unique phenomenon, and common in many parts of India and elsewhere, as the other contributions in this volume show. But surprisingly, this pattern of migration has existed for over 100 years, and it has existed in circumstances where work offered was relatively permanent. Circular migration is not the transitory phenomenon that many, particularly modernisation theories, expect it to be. I concluded that more attention needs to be paid to the effects of this pattern of migration, on both urban and rural areas.

My recent research has focused on one of the main 'catchment' areas for industrial labour in Calcutta, the western part of Bihar, in particular the district Saran (formerly Chapra), part of the Bhojpur area. One of the central lessons of the research in Calcutta was that to understand migration into the city – and patterns of migration – properly, one needs to pay much more attention to the areas of origin. Moreover, my reading of literature on rural

Arjan de Haan is social development adviser for the Department for International Development, based in New Delhi. This contribution is based on research carried out when the author was at Erasmus University Rotterdam, and at the Poverty Research Unit, University of Sussex. The financial support of the Nuffield Foundation is gratefully acknowledged. Research findings were presented at a conference in Patna in December 1997 and at the Sussex workshop. Comments by the conference participants, as well as the detailed suggestions by Michael Lipton, David Mosse, and by an anonymous referee are also gratefully acknowledged.

development gives me the impression that too little attention has been paid to migration: much analysis and policies have a 'sedentary' bias.[1]

The fascinating aspect of this district in Bihar is that it has had a very long history of out-migration, and my recent ongoing work has been a historical study of this, trying to describe the way migration has determined the socio-economic development of this area, and the livelihoods of the people in it. Emphasising this long history of migration may help to take us away from the sedentary bias of development studies, the assumption, for example, that urbanisation means the start of migration, and help understand migration as a central aspect of rural development. This historical approach allows us to see changing migration dynamics, depending on shifting economic, political and legal circumstances.

This study, therefore, is an attempt to understand the complex relationship between migration from this area, and the wider socio-economic developments, over an extended period of time.[2] The focus is on the situation of the poorer sections of the population. However, it is impossible to limit the analysis to them, for various reasons; most importantly, migration is not restricted to the poor, and the poor are also dependent on the wider process of development, including migration by the better-off. Questions that this analysis aims to answer, are: how do migration and poverty relate? Does poverty cause migration, and how? How does migration affect poverty and people's livelihoods? And how have these relationships changed over time?

The rest of this paper has seven sections. First, I will look at some theories that aim to explain the growth-migration relationship. Second, I present some general socio-economic data on Saran and Bihar, in comparison to the all-India level, before discussing in section IV data on migration from Saran and Bihar. The fifth and sixth sections look into the complex relationship between migration on the one hand, and livelihoods including poverty on the other. Migrations and livelihoods are gendered, however, and section VI tries to look inside the household, to consider different trends in male and female migration, and changing gender relations over time. Section VIII concludes.

II. ECONOMIC GROWTH AND MIGRATION

The literature on the relationship between migration and development is inadequate to understand the complexity the introduction has alluded to. Papademetriou and Martin [1991] rightly gave their edited volume on labour migration the title the *Unsettled Relationship*; they conclude from a large number of case studies that there are no general laws in this respect. All too often, migration is seen simply as a consequence of economic development (and interventions), and too little analysis exists of the effects of migration on, particularly, areas of origin.[3] Development strategies often intend to reduce the number of migrants, neglecting the central role migration plays in the livelihoods of people [*McDowell and de Haan, 1997*]. This is not to deny that labour migrants are often poor people – indeed migrants in Calcutta usually said they had migrated because of a lack of land in their home villages – or that migration does not necessarily solve, for example, problems of indebtedness, as the contribution by Mosse *et al.* in this volume shows. Rather, the analysis here emphasises the contribution of migration to livelihoods, which would suggest, *inter alia,* that development strategies should consider building on this rather that trying to stop migration.[4]

Economic theories often see migration as a sign of imbalance, a disequilibrium. Larson and Mundlak [*1997*] expect migration to come to a halt when inter-sectoral income differentials decline to a certain level. Economic theories expect convergence to result from migration: put simply, if there is free labour mobility, people will migrate until the differentials have disappeared. Cashin and Sahay [*1996*] examine the economic growth of 20 Indian states during the period 1961–91. This shows that initially poor states have grown faster than initially rich states – though Bihar is clearly an exception. The second part of their analysis looks at the role of migration in the growth of different states. They first ask the question: do higher income differentials between states lead to more migration? Migration is measured as net-migration, that is, the difference between in- and out-migration from states. They did not find a significant relation – high income differentials did not lead to high migration:

> This *anaemic Indian response* of cross-state migration to income differentials is most likely due to a combination of several barriers to the mobility of labour: strong local workers' unions that act to keep out competing employees; rigidities in nominal wages (Joshi and Little 1994); lack of housing in fast-growing urban areas; and most important, social, cultural, and linguistic barriers to the cross-regional substitutability of labor [*Cashin and Sahay, 1996: 162*, italics added].

Then they ask the reverse question: how does migration affect relative incomes? They conclude that the process of migration has little effect on the convergence of per capita income: high out-migration has not helped poorer states to catch up with richer ones.

This analysis is helpful as a starting point for an examination of migration. I will try to show below that in Bihar migration has been much more important than the authors assume, though perhaps it has not had the expected effect in terms of economic growth. A first point of critique refers to the level of their analysis: states in India are large units and measuring inter-state migration significantly underestimates total migration. Although this does not make the analysis of inter-state convergence invalid, I would not concur with their idea of an 'anaemic' response. Second, as the contribution by Rogaly *et al.* also argues, Census data, which Cashin and Sahay use, may not be a very reliable source, and may also seriously underestimate the number of migrants, particularly those moving for seasonal occupations.[5]

Third, and more important, they use net-migration as the measure of migration, that is, out-migration *minus* in-migration. In this measure, it does not make a difference whether a state has almost no migration, or large equal numbers of out- and in-migrants. The Punjab is a clear example of the last case. At the same time, large numbers of people have moved to other parts of India, most notably Delhi (600,000 in 1971, for example) and abroad, while cheap labour streamed in (372,000) for the agricultural activities in the Green Revolution area. Both migration streams have contributed significantly to Punjab's growth, and these effects are lost in the analysis if net-migration is taken as a measure.

Finally, and partly following from the above, the analysis is a mechanistic one. It does not specify how migration can affect development, income distribution and poverty. These effects will be dealt with in later sections. Section IV will discuss how much migration there has been, criticising Cashin and Sahay's conclusion about the 'anaemic Indian response'. But first I will present some general data about the area.

III. THE CONTEXT: SARAN AND BIHAR

Bihar is generally known as being among India's poorest state, with the highest levels of illiteracy, defunct health care systems, and a corrupt political administration.[6] This needs little elaboration – although recent developments, in for example, agriculture challenge the popular opinion of stagnation – but what seems important is that this has not always been the case. Two centuries ago, economically and culturally the area seems to have been relatively rich.[7] The economy of Bihar underwent a decline in the nineteenth century. Cash crops declined in the late nineteenth and early twentieth centuries. In the early nineteenth century, weaving and cloth manufacturing sustained about 60,000 people,[8] but this declined, and so did Revelganj, Saran's cotton mart. Other industries also declined: opium production around 1920, and indigo production in the beginning of the twentieth century. Sugar production declined after 1850 because of the growth of indigo, but this was reversed in the twentieth century.

Conditions in Bihar were, according to, for example, the Collector of Patna in the 1880s, relatively bad. The wages in the western districts were much lower than in the eastern parts of (the then united) Province of Bengal, and this was usually attributed to a superabundance of labour. This surplus did not exist, for example, in Burdwan, where population pressure was kept down by endemic diseases, and in a district such as Chittagong where reclaimable wasteland was available. Saran was the most densely populated district in the Province of Bengal, after the metropolitan districts of Hooghly and 24-Parganas. Around 1900, it was estimated that of a population of around 2.5 million in Saran, a quarter of a million had little or no land, and another quarter million lived below subsistence level.

However, the evidence is somewhat contradictory. It was noted that the incidence of landlessness appeared to be low. Hunter wrote that '[t]he Collector is not aware of any tendency towards the growth of a distinct labouring class, who neither possess nor rent lands. There is no class resembling the *krishans* [agricultural labourers] of Lower Bengal.'[9] And in Nolan's view:

> If Bihar has suffered more than other parts of Bengal in this respect, it is because its inhabitants are more healthy and its agricultural resources have been developed at an earlier period, so that the population increases without finding an outlet. The soil in these districts is fertile, there is no want of capital for any enterprise of real promise, the people are industrious and frugal; all the conditions of agricultural prosperity exist except the most essential, that is, the maintenance of a due proportion between the population and the natural resources of the country ... [10]

High population density was commonly seen as the reason for out-migration, and indeed colonial officers used the argument to point out the potential for recruiting labour within the indentured system (discussed below). At the same time, an important characteristic of the region, perhaps cause as well as consequence of the migration pattern common in this area, was that it was characterised by smallholder land-owning communities.[11] A proverb in Saran says that there are as many varieties of Rajputs (landlords) as there are varieties of rice.[12] According to Das [*1997*], following Kosambi's analysis of 'feudalism from below', the area has been marked by 'petty feudalism'. With commercialisation in the nineteenth century, the zamindari communities were among the first to feel the effects, their poverty increased, and they had to resort to manual labour. Between 1870 and 1900 nearly all land-owning communities in Azamgarh for example lost land, which made young men from zamindari families – as well as the lower classes – migrate to cities in search of employment.[13] The Village Notes of the Chapra region in the beginning of this century clearly illustrates that upper castes had to resort to occupations other than agriculture.[14] Rajputs were said to go out for 'service', including as peons and durwans in estates of larger zamindars, and other occupations in Bengal. Despite high out-migration, the average size of holdings has continued to decline.[15]

More research is needed to describe the socio-economic history of the region since the end of the last century, but the evidence suggests that conditions remained stagnant for a long time, until the 1970s perhaps. According to the Dufferin report in the 1880s, agricultural labourers in the western districts of Bengal earned 2 seers of clean coarse rice, and in 1901 the wage was around 2 annas a day. The Village Notes of the southern thanas of Saran district confirm that, by 1918, daily wages were around 2 annas a day, or 3 to 4 kachi seers (that is, 1.5 to 2 pucca seers, or approximately 1 kg.) of grains.[16] According to the 1951 Census, the average daily wage of an agricultural labourer in Saran was Rs 2, and the average annual income of a family of agricultural labourers Rs 534, while their estimated expenditure was Rs 574. On a visit to Saran in April 1991, I learnt that a daily labourer could earn 2 kg. of wheat (money value about Rs 8). In 1998, in southern Saran, daily wages – usually paid in cash – were said to be about Rs 30. This suggests – contrary to what I concluded before [de Haan, 1994a] – an improvement since the 1970s.

The abolition of the Zamindari system after Independence has had limited success and little surplus land has been distributed. According to Das [1986], zamindari abolition turned upper sections of the tenantry into exploiters. He indicates that the gap between a few affluent small landholders and the agricultural workers has widened. According to the

TABLE 1

BIHAR AND ALL INDIA COMPARED: SHARE OF AGRICULTURE,
STATE DOMESTIC PRODUCT AND AGRICULTURAL WAGES

	Share of Agriculture		Domestic product/capita			Agricultural wages (nominal)		
	Bihar	All India	Bihar	All India	Bihar as % India	Bihar	All India	Bihar as % India
1991 prices								
1961	53.6	48.6	2,007	2,857	70.2	1.31	1.41	92.9
1991	54.1	41.2	2,655	4,934	53.8	21.39	22.17	96.5

Sources: Production data – Cashin and Sahay [*1996: 132*]. Wage data – from the data set compiled by Oezler *et al.* 1996. The wage figures are calculated averages for 1960–62 and 1990–92.

1951 Census, 90 per cent of Saran's population worked in agriculture, and there were 427,264 landless labourers (of a population of 3,155,144). Forty-two per cent of the families of agricultural labourers were indebted. The average size of holdings was 4.1 acres, while it was 7.5 at an all-India level. A survey held in 1952 showed that 41 per cent of the households owned less than 0.5 acre of land,[17] and a survey in the 1980s showed that 36 per cent of the population was landless, while 40 per cent had less than 2.5 acres [*Oberai et al., 1989: 36*].

Table 1 shows that economic production in Bihar has stagnated relative to India's – though since 1961 Bihar's per capita product did increase by about one-third. While in 1961 Bihar's per capita state domestic product was 70 per cent of all India's, in 1991 it was only slightly more than half of India's average. And while the share of agriculture in India decreased – though slowly – it increased by half a percentage point in Bihar. However, and one could hypothesise here on the effects of out-migration as a balancing mechanisms, agricultural wages did not show such divergence.

TABLE 2
POVERTY IN BIHAR AND INDIA (HEAD COUNT INDEX)

Round	Period	Rural India	Bihar	Urban India	Bihar
13	Sep 57–May 58	55.16	65.36	47.75	60.70
14	Jul 58–Jun 59	53.26	66.22	44.76	58.63
15	Jul 59–Jun 60	50.89	62.19	49.17	61.57
16	Jul 60–Aug 61	45.40	47.34	44.65	48.13
17	Sep 61–Jul 62	47.20	56.86	43.55	46.14
18	Feb 63–Jan 64	48.53	54.96	44.83	52.26
19	Jul 64–Jun 65	53.66	59.79	48.78	55.03
20	Jul 65–Jun 66	57.60	67.51	52.9	62.88
21	Jul 66–Jun 67	64.30	80.31	52.24	67.85
22	Jul 67–Jun 68	63.67	77.08	52.91	62.36
23	Jul 68–Jun 69	59.00	67.53	49.29	53.15
24	Jul 69–Jun 70	57.61	66.02	47.16	53.42
25	Jul 70–Jun 71	54.84	67.29	44.98	52.55
27	Oct 72–Sep 73	55.36	69.19	45.67	52.61
28	Oct 73–Jun 74	55.72	69.54	47.96	57.35
32	Jul 77–Jun 78	50.60	66.21	40.5	51.90
38	Jan 83–Dec 83	45.31	69.94	35.65	50.32
42	Jul 86–Jun 87	38.81	56.45	34.29	42.78
43	Jul 87–Jun 88	39.60	58.57	35.65	52.95
44	Jul 88–Jun 89	39.06		36.6	
45	Jul 89–Jun 90	34.30	58.57	33.4	42.29
46	Jul 90–Jun 91	36.43	58.29	32.76	41.13
47	Jul 91–Dec 91	37.42		33.23	
48	Jan 92–Dec 92	43.47	67.81	33.73	46.32

Source: Data set compiled by Oezler *et al.* [*1996*].

Although wages in Bihar are lower than the all-India average, the difference decreased between 1961 and 1991.[18]

Household consumption and poverty data, presented in Table 2, similarly show Bihar's stagnation, relative to the rest of India [NSS data, cf. *Datt and Ravallion, 1996*]. At an all-India level, the percentage of people below the poverty line declined from around 55 per cent in the early 1960s to 30-35 per cent at the beginning of the 1990s. Bihar clearly lagged behind in this, with a decline of only a few percentage point. While around 1960, in four states (Tamil Nadu, Kerala, Maharshtra, Andhra Pradesh) the poverty incidence was higher, in 1990 Bihar had the highest poverty incidence, close to 60 per cent.[19]

Arvind Das has described the state of Bihar as an 'extreme case of what has happened to a region subjected to societal stagnation, economic exploitation and cultural degeneration under conditions of long and stifling feudalism, external and internal colonialism and the most brutalising experience of late capitalism ...' [*Das 1992: 5*]. The per-capita income in the state is the lowest in India – Rs 456 compared to Rs 600 in West Bengal for example. Although Bihar has developed, with a modern industrial sector (much of it in South Bihar, now Jharkand), and a high ratio of irrigated area and high use of fertilisers, and an increase of state domestic product by over 30 per cent in 30 years, '[t]he overall picture of Bihar remains one of stagnation, decline and even decay' [*ibid.: 20*].

Because of increasing differentiation and depeasantisation, according to Das, more workers have been forced to migrate, which has led to a 'money-order economy'. Remittances provide some security to the dependants of the workers who constitute the poor and landless peasantry. At the social-cultural level, it has led to 'a dislocation of family life ... an influx of arms into the area and a consequent rashness in the saying *Arrah zila ghar ba, kone baat ke dar baa.*'[20]

IV. A LONG TRADITION OF MIGRATION

Thus, although the state has developed, relative to most other parts of India Bihar has stagnated. It seems logical to expect that this has caused the large streams of migration from Bihar. However, this section will show that the reasons for migration are more complex, and that the migration is much older than Bihar's relatively recent 'stagnation'.

The article by Cashin and Sahay quoted in the first section suggested that much less migration had taken place than one would expect. But as I indicated there, they seriously underestimate the amount of migration that has taken place. Without intending to, I suppose, they subscribe to an old colonial notion of the immobile rural population. In India as in other colonial countries, the authorities often argued that the population was immobile, and, especially during the later part of the nineteenth and early part of the twentieth century, they often argued for measures to enhance mobility.[21] But there is much research showing that the Indian rural population was by no means immobile. Historical evidence, for example, by Habib [*1963*] for the Mughal period, seems to point out rather convincingly that most of the South Asian rural population has been highly mobile.[22] Studies on the early colonial period show that large groups of people moved over large distances. In the second half of the nineteenth century large numbers of people moved to work in agricultural activities, and, in fact, de-urbanisation during the early colonial period also indicates that population movement was the rule rather than the exception.[23]

Western Bihar has been one of the areas where this mobility has been very much present and has formed an integral part of the region's society and economy. In 1891, 15 per cent of the inhabitants of Saran lived outside the district in which they were born – suggesting that about one out of two households had remittances from outside. Out-migration from Saran existed, and may have been more important, before the colonial period. Anand Yang suggests that the population became actually more settled during the Raj, 'when control of land became the fundamental source of power, wealth and status, flight became far less promising an alternative to the raiyats',[24] a trend which may have continued after Independence when rayats became landowners. Desertion was common in the late eighteenth and nineteenth centuries, particularly when indigo cultivation was extended. Many 'indigo deserters', small tenure holders, fled because of indebtedness, poverty, inundation and decrees of the indigo planters. As described by

TABLE 3
MALE/FEMALE RATIO: SARAN DISTRICT

Year	m/f
1901	83.4
1911	86.9
1921	93.8
1931	96.3
1941	92.4
1951	90.8
1961	..
1971	95.1
1981	99.4
1991	105.3

Source: Calculated on the basis of Census figures.
The 1971–91 figures are unweighted averages for the districts Chapra, Siwan and Gopalganj.

Yang, in 1879 complete desertion took place from the Hathwa estate. The Collector of Saran in 1856 noted that large numbers of people worked outside the district in service and as soldiers: '[p]revious to the Mutiny, it is said that as many as 10,000 sepoys were natives of this District'.[25] Finally, as described by Servan-Schreiber [*1997*] trade from the area to Nepal and Bengal has been a common phenomenon.

On the basis of demographic data, we are able to form a relatively detailed picture of the extent of migration from Saran. Migration from this district has been predominantly by men – as I shall discuss more extensively below – which is reflected in a low male/female ratio.[26] For Saran district these are presented in Table 3. This shows that at the beginning of this century migration was proportionally a more important phenomenon for the region than at present – something which was also confirmed in some of the interviews carried out in the district. There was a general decline in the proportion of migration between 1901 and 1931, the year of the industrial crisis that affected Calcutta significantly. Migration picked up again after the War, and has shown a downward trend again since 1951. In any case, this suggests that the migration response has been far from 'anaemic'. Moreover, census data indicate that within the district, migration responses were not even. Within Saran, most migrants came from the southern thanas, where population density was higher than elsewhere,[27] and rent demands were higher than in the northern parts. And in 1911, when the overall male–female ratio was 87:100, a number of villages had ratios of less than 70:100. Some of these villages still had high out-migration (as suggested by the male-female ratio) in 1991, but in others out-migration had virtually stopped.

TABLE 4

OUT-MIGRATION FROM SARAN (ENUMERATED IN OTHER DISTRICTS)

	Total population	total	% of popul.	% male	within state	% of popul.	outside state
1881	2,295,207	191,152*	8.3	65			
1891	2,465,007	364,315	14.8	58			
1901	2,409,365	242,488	10.1	72			
1911	2,289,699	283,000	12.4	72			
1921	2,339,953	209,890	9.0	70	45,998	2.0	164,163
1931	2,486,737	47,000	1.9		29,000		
1941	2,860,537	na	na	na	na	na	na
1951	3,155,144	na	na	na	67,226x	2.1x	

Source: Until 1921, Yang [*1989: 192*], Chattopadhyaya [*1987: 254 ff.*]; 1931–51: Roy Chaudhury [*1960*].

* The 1881 figures do not include migrants outside the state (of Bengal).

x For 1951 figures of emigration from individual districts to other states of India not compiled.

Census migration data for Saran during 1881-1951 are reproduced in Table 4. These also show the relative stagnation of migration during the first two decades of this century. The data also show the predominance of male migration, except for the year 1891. Roy Chaudhury's District Gazetteer of Saran [*1960*] noted that between 1891 and 1911 the district's population decreased, partly due to famine and disease, and partly to an increase in emigration. After that the population started to increase, due to good health but also because of the decrease in the number of emigrants. After 1931 migration again increased.

Census data after Independence is difficult to compare with earlier information, but information for Bihar, 1951–81, is reproduced in Tables 5 and 6. In 1951 and 1961 about four per cent of Bihar's population had migrated (defined as born outside the place of enumeration). In 1971 and 1981, less than two per cent of Bihar's population had moved out of the state less than ten years ago, although in 1981 the total number of migrants was more than double that: over 2.5 million [*Sharma, 1997: 86*].

TABLE 5
OUTMIGRATION FROM BIHAR, 1951–81 (000s)

	Bihar	Out-migrants (born outside)		Out-migrants (moved 0-10 yrs ago)	
	Total popul. (000s)	total	% of popul.		% of popul.
1951	38,786	1,573	4.1		
1961	45,456	2,043	4.5		
1971					
1981	69,915	2,537		1,030,990	1.5

Source: Census of India. Definitions: for 1951–61, data from Census 1961 – emigrants from Bihar to other States – living in other place then born; 1971 and 1981 – from Cashin and Sahay (1996) – duration of residence <1, 1–4, 5–9 yrs. 1981 total number of migrants quoted in Sharma 1997: 86.

TABLE 6
COMPOSITION OF MIGRATION FROM BIHAR, 1981 (000s)

	Total		< 1 yr.		1–9 yrs	
	Total	Empl. based	Total	Empl. based	Total	Empl. based
Male total	1348.3	794.0	98.8	63.5	511.2	296.3
Male rural-urban %	50.8	56.0	31.1	29.6	50.2	54.5
Female total	1086	56.9	49.2	12.2	370.8	21.2

Source: Sharma [*1997: 86 ff.*] (Census Table D-2, Migration Tables).

Table 6 shows the composition of out-migration from Bihar. The majority of migrants were men, although more than a million women migrated as well. Recent migrants formed a relatively small proportion of the total migrants: more than half of the male migrants had migrated more than ten years ago. Among male migrants, the majority had migrated to obtain employment, while this was the reason for only a very small proportion of the women. About half of the male migration was from rural to urban areas.

So far, I have used the term migration without much care. Implicit in the above, however, is that most migration refers to labour migration. Given that in this area – in contrast to, for example, southern India – most migration is by single men, the male–female ratio is a reasonably good indicator of (male) labour migration. Table 6 also confirms that female migration – that is indeed substantial – is usually not for employment.

Historical evidence shows that labour migration has been a common phenomenon in this area for centuries. Destination areas have shifted depending of course on 'pull' factors.[28] In the eighteenth and nineteenth centuries, large numbers of workers migrated to eastern Bengal – Rangpur and Mymensing were major areas of attraction according to Census data at the end of the 19th century – and even to Burma, for agricultural and other manual work. A diversity of occupations was characteristic of most of the population in Saran, and the same goes for the jobs they took up outside their area of origin:

> they took up all kinds of field labor, 'digging and cleaning tanks, repairing roads, making railway embankment and harvesting the winter rice crop. When women go they either work with their husbands, or else earn an income by grinding corn for the Banias.' Much of the earthwork of the Assam-Bihar Railway through Purnea and the Northern Bengal Railway in Rangpur, Bogra and Dinajpur was accomplished by migrant labor ... Many migrants also adopted new occupations in a number of ingenious ways ... [*Yang, 1989: 203*; the quote is from the Bourdillon Report].

Migrants from the southern part of Saran also went to the Sunderbans, though they were not allowed to settle.

The labour migrants usually left for a period of four to six months, from November onwards, returning between March and July. Even in the Village Notes of 1918-19, this was noted as the most common pattern of migration, although by then many people also migrated to Calcutta, where employment was much less seasonal. The timing of leave and particularly of return seems to have been unrelated to demand for labour in the home village. According to Foley [*1906*] – who noted that labour was less in supply during July, August and March – Saran's cropping seasons were *bhadai* in August-September, *aghani* sown after the rain, *rabi* ploughing during the early rains, sowing during the heavy rains, and near the cold season.[29]

With the industrial growth in the later half of the nineteenth century, the destination of migrants from this area changed. It is therefore tempting to see the start of the migration to Calcutta, not as the beginning of a rural–urban transition, but as a diversion of the migration stream which used to go beyond Calcutta, further east. Census figures for Saran show that Calcutta and 24-Paraganas (where the industry was located) came to form major areas of destination. Migrants from Saran went to all industries, except coal mining and the tea plantations which tended to attract migrants from other (often tribal) areas of Bihar and Bengal. Labour was also recruited through the 'new system of slavery' [*Tinker, 1974*], the indentured system during the larger part of the nineteenth century – although the areas of recruitment for indentured labour seem to have been slightly different from those for seasonal and industrial labour in Bengal [*de Haan, 1995*].

After the 1920s, demand for unskilled labour in both urban and rural Bengal declined slowly but the effect of this was probably been felt – except for the crisis of 1931 – only since the 1950s. During the 1960s there was an increasing demand for labour in Green Revolution Punjab, also in other urban centres including Delhi, and even in western India. Most recently some people have started to make it to the Gulf as well. Overall, however, it is likely that there were more opportunities, especially for unskilled migrants, at the beginning of this century than after, say, the 1960s.[30]

These migration movements have been determined by wage differentials – even though non-economic forms of coercion have historically played a role in the recruitment of labour [*Das Gupta, 1981*]. For example, at the beginning of this century, an unskilled labourer in the jute mills could earn almost twice the wage he could get in Saran, and even more during the jute harvest in Bengal.[31]

> For Bihar migrants, the attraction to Rangpur district ... during the cultivating and harvesting season was the possibility of earning as much as 10 annas a day in jute harvesting and retting operations. The gains from factory work, for skilled or unskilled labourers, were also much more than could be attained in Bihar. In jute mills, which had large numbers of Saran hands, ordinary unskilled labour by men earned a weekly sum of Rs 2–4 or over 5 annas per day [*Yang, 1989: 197*].

In 1901, the daily wage in Saran was around 2 annas, while in the jute mills a good weaver could earn up to one rupee per day. And in 1903, according to the Imperial Gazetteer of India on Bengal [*1909: 88*] 'wages offered by the mills are nearly double those obtained by unskilled labourers in the tracts whence they chiefly come'. Cost of living was also higher, but not as much; the industry was thought to be a 'great boon' for the migrants.

With the exception of indentured migration overseas, most migration did not involve resettlement. Migrants went for periods up to six months to work in eastern Bengal. The industries in Bengal often offered more permanent employment, but – as described extensively in de Haan [*1994*] – they did not, or only very gradually, sever links with their areas of origin. Many migrants, even of second and third generations, continue to define their village as their home, and see labour in the city as a village-based family strategy, and an aid to agriculture. The following section will pay more attention to the link between migration and landownership.

Thus, people from Saran migrated because of landlessness, low wages and social oppression, and because of the opportunities offered elsewhere. Out-migration is not a new phenomenon – if anything migration may have been more common at the beginning of the twentieth century than at the end. Saran is generally depicted – particularly by studies which focus on areas of destination – as one of the poorest areas, with a high concentration of population. Yet an understanding of the high rates of out-migration should also take into account that the people from Saran were able to take the better opportunities available within the regional context; work in the jute mills, for instance, was not the worst option and they did not, for example, go in large numbers to the coal fields or as indentured labour overseas.

The districts' earlier contacts with migration destinations seem to have provided the channels for migration, and this still influences migration patterns, including those described in the contribution in this volume on West Bengal. It also contributes to stratification within the villages – where the somewhat better-off have access to Calcutta while the poorest may have to migrate for more local jobs. Moreover, population density is an insufficient explanation for migration. In the context of Saran, I would put forward the hypothesis that this population density was possible *also because of* the income from migratory labour.[32] Migration is not only a consequence of socio-economic circumstances, but also structures these in turn.

V. MIGRANTS: ALL SOCIO-ECONOMIC STRATA

Thus far, little has been said about who migrates, and – despite the suggestion above that higher population densities were enabled by income from migratory labour – about the effects of migration. Therefore, this and the following sections ask two basic questions: who migrates, and who profits? In the absence of survey or household data, answers to these questions are derived from a number of different sources, secondary and historical. The main argument of this section is that, in this area in northern India, migratory work should be seen as a central part of the livelihoods of many sections of the population.

Do the poorest migrate? It seems evident that only poverty will force people to migrate, especially if the job prospects are unskilled work in factories or as rickshaw-pullers. Indeed, Oberai *et al.* [*1989*] conclude that the poor have a relatively higher propensity to migrate from rural areas. In Bihar, Kerala and Uttar Pradesh the bottom three deciles accounted for a relatively high percentage among out-migrants. In Bihar, 15 per cent of the out-migrants belonged to the lowest-income group, as against seven per cent of the total sample population.[33] Migration was also a common strategy of the poorer population in villages in Purnia, North-east Bihar, during the last decades [*Rodgers and Rodgers, 2000*].

On other hand, as has been stressed by many researchers, the poorest often cannot afford to migrate. They may lack the necessary material means to invest in leaving [*Connell et al. 1976: 17*]. Data presented in de Haan [*1997*] indicate that migrants in Indian cities are better-off than the city-born population; this suggests (but not more than that) that they were not also the poorest in the rural areas. Apart from capital, social resources are important. Contacts are essential, and family composition in the village of origin is essential to enable leaving.[34]

Colonial reports referring to this area quite convincingly showed that it was not necessarily the poorest districts from which people migrated, and in the case of Bihar (as described above) it may well have been the earlier development of these districts – and not poverty or backwardness – that provided conditions for out-migration. Areas from which Calcutta attracted most of its migrants, were well connected by railways quite early (and by water in earlier periods), and it is not very likely that these were the poorest districts.[35]

The 'segmentation' of migration streams is important for understanding links between poverty and migration. Because of personal contacts that are essential for successful migration, people from specific areas migrate to specific destinations; hence, in one jute mill in Calcutta 40 per cent of the workers came from the district Saran in Bihar and, if anything, this concentration increased during the last century [*de Haan, 1994*]. Wage differentials or poverty cannot explain why people from Saran went to Calcutta, why people from South Bihar to coal mines or tea plantations, and why from some areas few people migrated. As a consequence, and as described also in the studies on West Africa in this volume, successful migration may provide cumulative advantages to certain areas, excluding others.

There is some historical information about the caste-composition of migrant workers from the area. Indentured migrants, according to Tinker [*1974*] formed a middle strata of the rural population, excluding the trading, clerical and priestly castes, and many of the really downtrodden, the sweeper-folk, the lowest of what used to be called untouchables. In the jute mills, a variety of castes was occupied, including Brahmins [*Census of India, 1921*]. The Village Notes from Saran for the beginning of the last century confirm that people from all castes migrated. In the village Mathampura, for example, that had high out-migration it was noted specifically, as for many other villages in the area, that '[p]eople of higher classes do *grihasthi* supplemented by other service elsewhere'. But for many villages, it was noted also that the lower 'classes' (usually referring to castes), went for manual labour elsewhere. In Rampatti, with even higher rates of out-migration, a similar remark was made about the higher classes, but it was added: 'The lower classes mainly live by agricultural labour and also go for menial labour elsewhere. The Mallahs [boatmen] go to Bengal for work.' More recently, Sharma's [*1997: 103*] survey in villages in Siwan also indicates that the caste (and religion) distribution among migrants and non-migrants is similar.

Similarly, information about the landownership of migrants in this area seems to suggest that the amount of land owned is not a determinant of migration. The migrants I interviewed in Calcutta during 1991 did state that they had migrated because of a shortage of land, but many of them did not belong to the poorest section of their village. Migrants in Calcutta are both landowners and people who work on the land, or at least did so before they left. According to a survey carried out in Bihar in the 1980s [*Oberai et al., 1989*], the landless appeared to be *more* prone to migrate, but the differences were small: the migrants on average had only marginally less land than the total sample population.[36] Owners of small plots of land, probably the majority in the western parts of Bihar, work on their own land, combine this with other income sources, and may hire in labour at peak seasons, or rent out land in sharecropping arrangements. As indicated above, the areas with highest rates of out-migration were not necessarily the areas with highest rates of landlessness – my own fieldwork indicates that migration is often a strategy to prevent proletarianisation, rather than a reaction to it.

Thus, as indicated also by Connell *et al.* for Uttar Pradesh [*1976: 19–21*], the landless and the poorest are not the likeliest to migrate; but most of the data show that all strata do migrate. This correlation is context-specific, depending perhaps primarily on the kinds of migratory work available. Oberoi *et al.* [*1989: 34*], for example, show that the migration dynamics differ between states: in Kerala the middle peasantry migrated more, while in Uttar Pradesh all the landed groups except the highest size of cultivators had a relatively high propensity to out-migrate. Data on changes in inequality in Palanpur, western Uttar Pradesh, show that 'some lower castes had seized the opportunities for outside jobs in earlier years, [but] in 1983/84 the higher castes were more prominently represented and the outside jobs became a source of inequality ... ' [*Lanjouw and Stern, 1989: 17*]. A similar change, over a longer time period, may have occurred for migrants from Bihar: in the beginning of this century unskilled labour found more job opportunities than at present.

The emphasis in this section has been on the diversity of migration streams. However, this is not to deny the segmentation, the fact that some groups have access to better opportunities (like the higher castes even at the beginning of the last century), and the poor may not be able to migrate, or only to take up the least rewarding activities. This differentiation, which deserves more detailed research, also leads to different effects of migration, as the following section describes.

VI. EFFECTS OF MIGRATION ON LIVELIHOODS

It has been noted earlier in this paper that migration should not only be seen as a reaction to socio-economic circumstances, but that it is also a strategy, of households, that is, responsible for structuring and reproducing these circumstances. This area in particular is dominated by its long tradition of circular migration, a constant movement of people to and fro, remittances and other forms of interaction between areas of origin and destination. What kinds of impact has this migration had? As indicated earlier, the stagnation of Bihar – both low levels of economic development and slow rates of poverty reduction – seems to have happened at the same time as the out-migration. But are they interrelated?

Negative impacts often quoted in the literature include the loss of labour due to out-migration, but this does not seem a very relevant factor in the case of Bihar given its very high population density. Yet the relative positive development of wages – as compared to the changes in state domestic product – noted in Table 1 might be related to employment opportunities outside the state.[37] In the Village Notes at the beginning of the century we find occasional reference to such an affect. Further, the District Gazetteer published in 1960 [*1960: 104*] noted that because of out-migration more responsibility for agricultural production went to women, although that seemed restricted to women of lower castes: 'During transplantation of crop season their demand is so great that sometimes they earn more wages than the males.'

However, Bose and Ghosh – whose data showed that the incidence of landlessness was relatively low in the areas with high out-migration – concluded that in the early 1960s labour force participation, especially of women was low in densely populated areas including Saran: 'in place of the idle members of the household, a lot of hired workers has to be employed, who find employment for only about 5 months in the year' [*Bose and Ghosh, 1976: 10*]. Thus scarcity of labour did arise from out-migration in some places, and agriculture was affected by out-migration, but this seems to have been solved by either increasing labour force participation within the household, or hiring in labour from elsewhere.

There is little consensus in the literature about the effects of remittances. Of course, the amounts of remittances vary. Urban-rural remittances are estimated to range from 10 to 13 per cent of urban incomes in Africa, and may be of the same order in Asia [*Williamson, 1988: 432*]. Yet Connell *et al.* [*1976*] suggest that in the villages they surveyed the share of income deriving from remittances was very low. I have no systematic data from my own fieldwork, although I have estimated that workers in the industrial areas of Calcutta *could* save about half of their income, which would imply significant contributions to the incomes of their families in the villages. To show that the wages they paid were relatively high, Calcutta's jute mill managers often quoted figures from post offices about the amount of remittances.[38] According to Oberai *et al.* [*1989*], 72 per cent of the Bihari migrants remitted to their family. Average yearly remittances were in the range of Rs 2,200 (for non-cultivating households) to Rs 2,400 (for cultivating households) – compared to Bihar's average per capita income of Rs 1,513 in 1984–85. Within the lower income groups, the percentage of remitters was higher than within the higher income groups, and remittances formed 93 per cent of the income of the Bihari out-migrant households in the lowest income group.[39]

Research elsewhere indicates that remittances can have positive impacts. Adams [*1991*] argues that the migrants' families invest the remittances, for example to increase agricultural productivity, something which casual observations in Bihar confirms. Helweg [*1983*] shows that the way of remittances of migrants from the Punjab changes over time: first they are spent on family maintenance and improving agricultural production, in later stages they are used to increase the status in the village, and even later remittances are also invested to start commercial, non-agricultural activities. Ballard's [*1983*] research on villages in the Indian and Pakistani Punjab indicates how different economic environments in the areas of origin may lead to different outcomes of migration: whereas on the Indian side remittances facilitated regional economic development, a similar flow of remittances precipitated economic decline on the Pakistani side.

Remittances enhance levels of income, but they also tend to increase inequality, especially if migration destinations are hard to reach, and investments needed for migration high [e.g. *Adams, 1989,* for Egypt]. On the other hand, national remittances may decrease inequality, as recent IDS research in Bangladesh suggests [*de Haan et al., 2000*]. Here, as with respect to the questions regarding who migrates, and how migration affects economic development in the area of origin, the answer seems to be that this is context-dependent. The migration–poverty relationship depends on both the kinds of work taken up by the migrants – for example, in some cases new skills may be learnt which can be put to use once the migrant returns – and the channels for remitting income, and opportunities for investing these back home.

A bird's eye-view of Bihar's migration history suggests that – although there is a great deal of stability in migration patterns *once established* – the outcome of such processes are difficult to predict. During the first half of the century, wages in Bengal's industries remained fairly stagnant, but started to rise during the 1960s, while employment opportunities declined. Jobs became a scarce commodity, and fathers would try to pass on their jobs when they retired – a practice that existed earlier in the century but the premium on succeeding increased. The migrants that started in the unsecure jobs in the colonial industries, over time became part of a labour elite – contributing as suggested above to stratification within the villages. At the same time, as my field research indicated, significant diversification of activities by migrants occurred. Many migrants moved back to rural areas, often because of illness, sometimes with savings. But many found their way into the wider urban economy of Calcutta. In most of the migrants' testimonies, the choice between city and village remains one that continues to exist, their identity being neither urban nor rural, but both.

These interactions between the rural and urban economies deserve more research, including local fieldwork. My hypothesis with respect to this part of Bihar is that migration and remittances have contributed significantly to the particular socio-economic structure in this area, with a relatively slow growing but not stagnating economy, with large numbers of small landholdings which are viable, to a large extent, only because of income from other activities and, of course, with a substantial but not exceptionally large proletariat which finds work locally or elsewhere. This structure should not be conceptualised as a transitional one; the interactions between this rural area, and urban and other rural areas, is a constant feature of the economic structure as well as identity of the migrants: for them, migration is a way of maintaining their 'semi-proletarian' livelihoods, and remittances help to 'plough the land'.

VII. GENDERED LIVELIHOODS

So far, migration has been described as a response to socio-economic circumstances, and a household strategy to manage such circumstances. It has also been emphasised that out-migration has been predominantly by men, and I briefly discussed the effects this out-migration could have on women's labour force participation 'at home'. In some cases, women took over an increasing part of the workload, and some households hired in labour. This section looks at these issues in some more detail.

Fieldwork in Calcutta identified strikingly different patterns of migration, and give some idea of how this has evolved over time. The predominant pattern was of single male labour migration, and the industrial area exists to a large extent of men who left the family behind to live together with other men. But patterns differed [*de Haan, 1994b*]. Whereas single male migration was most common among men – both Muslim and Hindu – from North India, family migration was more common among migrants from southern Orissa, Andra Pradesh and Madhya Pradesh. Whereas the contribution by Mosse *et al.* in this collection shows that such differences can be related to economic differences, in this case such an economic explanation seemed not to suffice. Instead, cultural differences, and ideas about the acceptability of women working were more relevant – although there is also historical evidence that showed that the poorest families moved together. Up until today, women working in industries is more acceptable among communities from southern India than among communities from Bihar and Uttar Pradesh (excluding *adivasi* or 'tribal' women) – although interviews suggested that norms about male breadwinners were becoming increasingly common.

The implications of this for gender relations in Saran – where norms about women's migration and labour are as strong as elsewhere in northern India – remains a topic for further anthropological and historical research. However, some general trends can be outlined. First, it needs emphasising that the demand for female labour in the industry changed over time. Since the beginning of the last century employment opportunities for women in urban areas – particularly the colonial industries such as jute – have tended to decrease, due to a number of factors including changing labour legislation, employers' and trade unions' reactions to this, and probably changes in the perceived acceptability of women working outside the household. The labour elite that came into existence increasingly consisted of (adult) men [*de Haan, 1994b*].

Second, the pattern of male migration has shaped household relations. As Sen notes in her historical study of the jute industry, 'men jute workers, factorised wage labourers, lived and worked in the city while the women and children worked in the village in petty commodity production, services or retail; the household was spatially fragmented ... the working-class household and its strategies of survival straddled the village and the city.'[40] There are some indications that women have taken on more responsibilities in the absence of men. But as Sen's analysis of nineteenth and twentieth centuries suggests, while income from land and crafts declined, and traditional occupations (often carried out by women) disappeared, differences between men's and women's earnings increased. Moreover, women's work was increasingly defined as 'domestic' and 'unproductive', and increasingly women's work was associated (in official reports) with poverty. The long-term devaluation of women's work is, according to Sen, reflected in the movement towards a general practice of dowry, away from bride-price that was common among several agricultural castes in the late nineteenth century (and was still existent among the migrants from Andra Pradesh I interviewed).

It is easy to underestimate the extent to which migration has shaped gender relations in this area. It is reflected in cultural expressions in the area, of songs by women that celebrate the potentials of earnings in Calcutta but also lament the concubine relationships their husbands might engage in while being away, and plays like Thakur's about a woman having started a relationship with a man while her husband was away.

At the material level, migration provided men with income and status, which contributed to a long-term trend which is possibly best summarised as the devaluation of women's contributions. Recent data suggest that rural female – visible – labour force participation is low. Also, in this area female–male ratios have been declining rapidly, suggesting widespread abortion and infanticide of girls. Without more research, we cannot draw any conclusions about these trends, and how they are affected by migration. However, our understanding of migration does need to be sensitive to the way they affect household and gender relations.

VIII. CONCLUSION

This study has made a start in understanding migration as a central feature of the socio-economic structure of a particular region, the western part of Bihar in northern India. This has been done from an historical perspective, which – by emphasising the long tradition of out-migration, and stressing that migration there may be less important now than it was a hundred years ago – indicates that migration should not be seen as a transitory phenomenon, but as a central element of this area's history. The study tries to go beyond seeing migration only as a reaction to conditions in the area of origin, and emphasises how migration affects and reinforces these conditions, including the different ways men and women are disposed.

It is tempting to posit a link between the underdevelopment of and poverty in Bihar and its high rates of out-migration. However, the evidence in this study suggests that this relationship is not straightforward. In the first place, the early out-migration was not necessarily the result of underdevelopment – rather, there is historical evidence to suggest that it was its early development which contributed to out-migration. Conversely, the income that was derived from this migratory work helped to maintain a high population density. In this sense, high out-migration and population density reinforced each other.

Many authors have emphasised the distress-nature of migration from this area. In contrast, I would suggest seeing migration as a household strategy that builds on existing migratory links and traditions. In the first place, it should be emphasised that migration, at the beginning of the last century, for example, was a strategy not only of the poorest but also of landowners whose sons looked for 'service' elsewhere. For many of the migrants I interviewed in the urban areas, and those interviewed for colonial reports, migration was a way of maintaining the family back home, and a way of aiding agriculture, of keeping, in other words, a foot in the rural areas. To understand migration, therefore, one needs to see this from the perspective of the rural base, of households employing diverse strategies.

This brings us to the paradoxical situation of a society of small (and declining) landholdings, of households firmly based in their rural origin, but of being simultaneously a very mobile population. I believe that the legal changes around land ownership during this century has enhanced this. With the changes in legislation early in the last century under colonial rule, and with the zamindari abolition after Independence, the 'peasant' has become more firmly rooted in the rural area. However, it is a peasant with – as it used to be in the eighteenth century – diverse livelihoods.

To understand districts such as Saran, much more attention needs to be paid to migration, not only as a consequence of poverty and high population density, but also in the way it defines these areas, in economic, social and cultural terms. More research needs to be done regarding the effects of migration on, first, development and agricultural change. Second, we need to know more about the effects on poverty and inequality, since the evidence – such as the knowledge of diversification and non-farm employment – suggests that some forms of migration lead to rapidly rising inequality. And finally, since migration is a strongly gendered process, we need to know more about the implications of this pattern of migration for the women who usually stay behind. This study has made a start with this analysis, emphasising the dynamic and historically changing interactions between migrations and the migrants' home society.

NOTES

1. This sedentary bias in the development literature is discussed in de Haan [*1999*], and McDowell and de Haan [*1997*]. Among others, Breman [*1990*] has critiqued the 'conventional wisdom' that labour mobility was absent in colonial Asia.
2. This paper draws on both archival and field research carried out with intervals during 1995–97, and on my research in 1991 [*de Haan, 1994a*].
3. De Mas [*1991*] argues that the literature on Moroccan emigrants is characterised by an ethnocentric perspective, which concentrates on the area of destination, and the same appears to be true for the literature on other migration streams.
4. The anonymous referee pointed out that development projects, for example, in Orissa, do not tend to add to skills of migrants from project villages. See also Mosse *et al.* in this volume, and de Haan [*2000*].
5. This has been noted, for example, by Rogaly [*1998*] for Bengal. Moreover, Cashin and Sahay also use vital statistics, for the last year of their analysis.
6. Research was carried out before the bifurcation of the State in to Bihar and Jharkand at the end of 2000. The description concentrates on the north-western part of Bihar, the area known as Bhojpur (a culturally distinct area, which also included the eastern part of Uttar Pradesh).
7. Also, the area is poor despite the abundance of natural resources [*Das, 1997*]. This may be less of a paradox than it seems, since with abundance of natural resources there may be less incentives for policies that promote development. A similar argument may apply for the effects of migration.
8. Collector of Saran, 1856 (quoted in Roy Chaudhury [*1960*]). In Saran, weavers were mainly Muslims. Some were also cultivators, and diversification of activities within households seems to have been common. Grierson mentions that artisans in Gaya derived 44 per cent of their earnings from supplementary activities [*Sen, 1992: 78*]. During the last decades, the decline of household manufacturing seems to have continued (fieldwork notes, March 1998).
9. See Hunter [*1976: 299*]. According to an agro-economic survey during the 1960s in selected villages in eight Bihar districts, the percentage of agricultural labour families in Saran – with the highest rates of out-migration, and densely populated – was lower (69 per 100 cultivating families) than the average (78 per 100) [*Bose and Ghosh, 1976*].
10. See Nolan [*1888*, italics added]. The districts in UP further to the west (except Gorakhpur and Azamgarh) were less able to support the population than the congested districts in Bihar, because there was less land under rice cultivation.
11. See Pandey [*1986: 69*], based on the 1892 Baden-Powell report; also Hagen and Yang [*1976: 77*].
12. *Rajput wo dhan ka oar nahi hai*; Magistrate of Saran to Risley in 1901, Risley Collection, IOL&R MSS EUR E 295/1, pp.630–54.
13. 'This was no longer the migration of villages or communities, 'voting with their feet', and taking up cultivation or other employment in other areas. The migration that now occurred ... was the forced migration of individuals, predominantly single men: in most cases it retained something of a 'temporary' character about it ...' [*Pandey, 1986: 73–4*].
14. The Village Notes, one of the survey and settlement records, are described extensively by Hagen and Yang [*1976*]. I have consulted the Notes in the District Record Room of Chapra, the headquarters of the former district Saran, focusing on the thanas with the highest rates of out-migration.
15. For example, during the first two decades of this century, average size of holdings in Saran declined from 1.8 to 1.4 acres [*Roy Chaudhury, 1960: 141*].
16. Usually, people would be paid about 2 seers of grain and 1 seer of sattoo. Only one of the village notes I consulted suggested that out-migration could lead to an increase in local wages, from 2 to 4 annas daily (Thana Majhi, Village Gora, No.42).
17. 1960 District Gazetteer of Saran [*Roy Chaudhury, 1960*]. In 1930, according to the Gazetteer, an average family of five persons needed 2.5 acres; the average size of land of 'pure cultivators' was 3.8 acres.

18. Rodgers and Rodgers [2000] describe socio-economic changes in North-east Bihar since the early 1970s, based on field research in Purnia. They note a large increase in real wages and rising consumption, and an increase in temporary migration of mainly male agricultural labourers and small landholders.

19. The same publication suggests that the slow decline in poverty was not due to increasing inequality, but to a slow (only slightly above zero) increase in mean consumption. It is also relevant to note that consumption (and not income) is used for the measurement of poverty; this implies that remittances are reflected in the measurement.

20. My home is in Arrah district; what am I afraid of? [Das, 1986: 220]. However, arms have been present in and exported from the Bhojpur area for a long time [Servan-Schreiber, 1997]. The Naxalite Movement seemed to have played much less of a role than in Central Bihar [e.g., Bhatia, 1997].

21. See, for example, Nolan's report of 1888, on 'how to promote' migration from Bengal to Burma.

22. According to Washbrook [1993: 68], interpretations of the history of Indian agrarian social structure have moved from a perspective which saw a static, ageless society of village communities broken up during the nineteenth century towards a view of a highly mobile and economically differentiated society *rendered* stationary during colonialism.

23. A similar point has been made in the historiography of western societies [Lucassen and Lucassen, 1997].

24. See Yang [1989: 182]. His study of Saran is a beautiful analysis of local developments during the Raj, on which I draw extensively. However, in my opinion he pays insufficient attention to the dynamics of migration, and sees it as only resulting from push factors such as famine, oppression, and high population density. In particular, he pays insufficient attention to the fact that migration also was significant among the better-off.

25. According to the Collector [quoted in Hunter [1976: 240] migration explained the fact that the number of females exceeded the males by 3.4 per cent. This excess was the largest in the southern Sadr Sub-division, which was the most densely populated.

26. The figures since approximately 1971 may be a less reliable indicator of migration because of the larger number of surviving boys due to sex-specific abortion and female infanticide. The extent of this needs further investigation. In Manjhi development block (Chapra) in 1991, for which I have detailed Census information, the male-female ratio was 99.0, while the male-female ratio for the 0-6 age group – the best available indicator of demographic balance – was 103.6, suggesting gender discrimination.

27. During 1915-21, in Gopalganj average landholdings were 2.2 acres, whereas they were only 1.4 in Siwan and 1.2 in Chapra Sadar [Roy Chaudhury, 1960: 141]. At the beginning of this century, the Village Notes indicate, there was also migration from North Saran to South Saran, because of plague in the north.

28. However, these pull factors do not explain why this area in Bihar became main areas of migration; as indicated in Section two, it was an area with high population density, but not necessarily the most deprived one.

29. Foley, who was Collector of Saran, noted in 1910 (File No.1-L/2, B-proceedings for September 1910, Nos.42–83, half yearly statements showing the conditions of the local labour market) that it 'is doubtful whether this migration is much affected by the state of the crops in the district, unless these fail to a great extent.'

30. Recently, despite some assertions to the contrary, migration and urbanisation rates have not increased. Kundu [1997] shows for India a slowing down in urban growth during the 1980s, probably as a result of a decline in the rate of employment creation.

31. The average wage in the mills in 1911 came to Rs 13.7 per month [Mukerji, 1960]. Weavers, however, of which Saran provided a large number, earned a lot more than this. In 1918, when the average wage came to Rs 14.8, the lowest wage was Rs 9 and a weaver could earn around Rs 27 [IIC 1916–18: 11].

32. One would not expect a poor district to have a high population density. In the context of Europe's history, Moch [1993] notes that the most intense population increases occurred where rural industry was most dense. Chaudhury [1992] argues that population pressure in UP does not explain the high incidence of migration (eastern UP, like Bihar perhaps, was

one of the most prosperous areas until 1850).

33. However, these data on household income excluded remittances; inclusion may radically change the picture. Of the Bihari migrants, 72 per cent remitted to the family, but within the lower income groups, the percentage of remitters was higher: remittances formed 93 per cent of the income of the Bihari out-migrant households in the lowest income group. Hence, the data are not very convincing, but they do show that the poorer groups migrate as well.

34. This was indicated both by migrants in Calcutta (interviews 1991) and people in Saran (interviews during 1997) who had not migrated. Large families – given a fixed amount of land or other opportunities at home – make migration more necessary, but also enables it.

35. Evidence regarding China's 'floating population' [Mallee, 1995/96] indicates that very poor areas may have lower mobility rates; in China we are able to witness the consequences of the late start of out-migration from these areas. Connell et al. [1976] quote evidence for migration following the nineteenth-century Irish famine: the migrants did not come from the poorest villages in the west.

36. At the end of the 1940s, a survey found that 59 per cent of the jute mill workers were landless, and 21 per cent owned less than two-thirds of an acre [Chattopadhyay, 1952]. According to the last large survey among jute workers in the early 1970s, 42 per cent of the families did not own any land, and 29 per cent owned less than 1 acre [Bhattacharya and Chatterjee, 1972].

37. See Rodgers and Rodgers [2000] for a description of the positive impacts of migration and remittances in North-east Bihar over a number of decades; I thank the referee for pointing this out to me.

38. From the Post Offices serving the Calcutta Jute Mills, the following amounts were sent according to figures reported by the Indian Mills Association: 1921, Rs 1,32,22,237; 1928, Rs 1,73,57,816; 1932 (the year after the great crisis), Rs 1,39,02,627; 1936, 1,55,39,610 (quoted in Benthall Papers, Box XII; and Government of Bengal, Commerce Department, Commerce Branch, April 1930, 3C-1, Progs. A 1–10). The Village Notes from Chapra contain few references to remittances; where they exist, they suggest that the seasonal agricultural labour in Bengal or Assam would help the migrants to maintain their family throughout the year, but save little beyond that.

39. During recent fieldwork in Bihar, I was provided with information about money orders through the post office. During August 1996, almost 46,000 money orders and 37 million Rupees were sent through Siwan district's head post office, an average of about 18 rupees per inhabitant of Siwan. During January 1998, almost 31 million rupees were sent through the Chapra post office, and average of about Rs 12 per inhabitant. This is of course only a part of the total remittances, since many people will carry their money when going back to the village. Bank transfer is another channel of remittances, and more common among better-off migrants.

40. See Sen [1999: 3]. The changing gender labour relations in the industry were not only influenced by employers' strategies, but also elite discourses on femininity and an emerging notion of 'domesticity'.

REFERENCES

Adams, Richard H., 1989, 'Worker Remittances and Inequality in Rural Egypt', Economic Development and Cultural Change, Vol.38, No.1, pp.45–71.

Adams, Richard H., 1991, 'The Economic Uses and Impact of International Remittances in Rural Egypt', Economic Development and Cultural Change, Vol.39, No.4, pp.695–722.

Ballard, R., 1983, 'The Context and Consequences of Migration: Jullundur and Mirpur Compared', New Community, Vol.11, No.1/2, pp.117–36.

Bhatia, B., 1997, 'The Naxalite Movement in Central Bihar: A Note', paper at the conference on 'Bihar in the World and the World in Bihar', Patna, Dec.

Bhattacharya, N. and A.K. Chatterjee, 1972, 'Some Characteristics of Jute Industry Workers in Greater Calcutta', Indian Statistical Institute, Technical Report No.9, Calcutta.

Bose, S.R., and P.P. Ghosh, 1976, *Agro-Economic Survey of Bihar*, Patna: B.K. Enterprise.

Breman, J., 1990, *Labour Migration and Rural Transformation in Colonial Asia*, Comparative Asian Studies 5, Amsterdam: Free University Press.

Breman, J., 1996, *Footloose: Labour. Working in India's Informal Economy*, Cambridge: Cambridge University Press.

Cashin, P. and R. Sahay, 1996, 'Internal Migration, Centre-State Grants, and Economic Growth in the States of India', *IMF Staff Papers*, Vol.43, No.1.

Chakrabarty, D., 1989, *Rethinking Working-Class History. Bengal 1890-1940*, Delhi: Oxford University Press.

Chandavarkar, R., 1994, *The Origins of Industrial Capitalism in India. Business Strategies and the Working Classes in Bombay*, Cambridge: Cambridge University Press.

Chattopadhyay, H., 1987, *Internal Migration in India. A Case Study of Bengal*, Calcutta: K.P. Bagchi.

Chattopadyay, K.P., 1952, *A Socio-Economic Survey of Jute Labour*, Calcutta: Calcutta University.

Chaudhury, P.1992, 'Labour Migration from the United Provinces, 1881-1911', *Studies in History*, Vol.8, No.1, pp.13–41.

Census of India, various years, Delhi.

Connell, J., Dasgupta, B., Laishley, R. and M. Lipton, 1976, *Migration from Rural Areas: The Evidence from Village Studies*, Delhi: Oxford University Press.

Das, Arvind, 1986, *The 'Longue Duree': Continuity and Change in Changel. Historiography of an Indian Village from the 18th towards the 21st Century*, CASP 14, Rotterdam, 1986.

Das, Arvind, 1992, *The State of Bihar. An Economic History without Footnotes*, Amsterdam: CASA.

Das, Arvind, 1997, 'Bihar: A Worm's Eye View', paper for the conference on 'Bihar in the World and the World in Bihar', Patna, Dec.

Das Gupta, R., 1976, Factory Labour in Eastern India: Sources of Supply, 1855–1946: Some Preliminary Findings', *Indian Economic and Social History Review*, Vol.13, No.3.

Das Gupta, R., 1981, 'Structure of the Labour Market in Colonial India', *Economic and Political Weekly*, Nov, 1981, Special Number, pp.1781–1806.

Datt, G. and M. Ravallion, 1996, 'Why Have Some Indian States Done Better Than Others at Reducing Rural Poverty?', Policy Research Working Paper 1594, Washington, DC: World Bank.

de Haan, A., 1993, 'Migrant Labour in Calcutta Jute Mills: Class, instability and control', in Peter Robb (ed.), *Dalit Movements, and the Meanings of Labour in India*, Delhi: Oxford University Press.

de Haan, A., 1994a *Unsettled Settlers. Migrant Workers and Industrial Capitalism in Calcutta*, Hilversum: Verloren (and published by K.P. Bagchi, Calcutta, 1996).

de Haan, A., 1994ab, 'Towards a Single Male Earner: Decline of Child and Female Employment in an Indian Industry', *Economic and Social History in the Netherlands*, Vol.6, pp.145–67.

de Haan, A., 1995, 'Migration in Eastern India: A Segmented Labour Market', *Indian Economic and Social History Review*, Vol.32, No.1.

de Haan, A., 1997, 'Rural–Urban Migration and Poverty. The Case of India', *IDS Bulletin*, Vol.28, No.2.

de Haan, A., 1999, 'Livelihoods and Poverty: The Role of Migration – A Critical Review of the Migration Literature, *The Journal of Development Studies*, Vol.36, No.2, pp.1–47.

de Haan, A., 2000, *Migrants, Livelihoods, and Rights: the Relevance of Migration in Development Policies*, DFID Social Development Department Working Paper, 2000.

de Haan, A., Brock, K., Carswell, G., Coulibaly, N., Seba, H. and K.A. Toufique, 2000, *Migration and Livelihoods: Case Studies in Bangladesh, Ethiopia and Mali*, IDS Research Report 46, Brighton.

de Mas, Paolo, 1991, 'Marokkaanse migratie naar Nederland: perspectief vanuit herkomstgebieden' (Moroccan Migration to the Netherlands: Perspectives from Areas of origin), *International Spectator*, Vol.45, No.3, pp.110–18.

Foley, B., 1906, *Report on Labour in Bengal*, Calcutta: Bengal Secretariat Book Depot.

Gardner, K., 1993, 'Mullahs, Migrants, Miracles: Travel and Transformation in Sylhet',

Contributions to Indian Sociology, Vol.27, No.2.

Glystos, P., 1993, 'Measuring the Income Effects of Migrants Remittances: A Methodological Approach Applied to Greece', *Economic Development and Cultural Change*, Vol.42, No.21.

Government of Bengal, Proceedings, Commerce Department, Commerce Branch and Labour Branch, West Bengal State Archive.

Government of Bengal Unemployment Enquiry Committee, 1925, *Report*, Calcutta: Bengal Secretariat Depot.

Habib, I., 1963, *The Agrarian System of Mughal India*, London: Asia Publishing House.

Hagen, J.R., and A. Yang, 1976, 'Local Sources for the Study of Rural India: The "Village Notes" of Bihar', *Indian Economic and Social History Review*, Vol.13, No.1.

Harris, J. and M.P. Todaro, 1970, 'Migration, Unemployment and Development: A Two Sector Analysis', *American Economic Review*, Vol.60, pp.126–42.

Hatton, T.J. and J.G. Willamson (eds.), 1994, *Migration and the International Labor Market 1850–1939*, London: Routledge.

Helweg, Arthur W., 1983, 'Emigrant Remittances: Their Nature and Impact on a Punjabi Village', *New Community*, Vol.X, No.3, pp.435–43.

Hunter, W.W., 1976, (orig. 1877), *A Statistical Account of Bengal*, Delhi: reprint Concept Publications.

IIC, Indian Industrial Commission 1916–18, 1918, *Report*, Calcutta: Government Printing.

Indian Factory Labour Commission (Morrison Committee), 1908, *Report of the Indian Factory Labour Commission*, Simla: Government Press.

Imperial Gazetteer of India, Bengal, 1909, Oxford.

Kundu, A., 1997, 'Trends and Structure of Employment in the 1990s: Implications for Urban Growth', *Economic and Political Weekly*, Vol.32, No.24, 14 June, pp.1399–1405.

Lanjouw, P. and N. Stern, 1989, 'Agricultural Changes and Inequality in Palanpur 1957–1984', London School of Economics, Development Economics Research Programme, DEP No.24.

Larson, D. and Y. Mundlak, 1997, 'On the Intersectoral Migration of Agricultural Labour', *Economic Development and Cultural Change*, Vol.45, No.2, pp.295–319.

Lipton, M., 1980, 'Migration form Rural Areas of Poor Countries: The Impact on Rural Productivity and Income Distribution', *World Development*, Vol.8, No.1, pp.1–24.

Lucassen, J., and L. Lucassen, (eds.), 1997, *Migration, Migration History, History: Old Paradigms and New Perspectives*, Bern: Peter Lang.

McDowell, C. and A. de Haan, 1997, Migration and Sustainable Livelihoods, A Critical Review of the Literature', *IDS Working Paper*, No.65, Brighton: IDS.

Mallee, H., 1995–96, 'In Defence of Migration: Recent Chinese Studies on Rural Population Mobility', *China Information*, Vol.10, Nos.3–4, pp.108–40.

Moch, L., 1993, 'Migration History Periodisation: Beyond the Industrial Revolution and Toward an Analytical Framework', paper for the conference on Migration and Settlement in Historical Perspective: Old Answers and New Perspectives', Leiden/Amsterdam, Sept. 1993.

Mukerji, K. 'Trends in Real Wages in the Jute Textile Industry from 1900 to 1951', *Artha Vijnana*, Vol.2, No.1.

Nolan, P., 1888, *Report on Emigration from Bengal to Burma and How to Promote it*, Bengal Secretariat Press,.

Oberai, A.S., Prasad, P.H. and M.G. Sardana, 1989, *Determinants and Consequences of Internal Migration in India. Studies in Bihar, Kerala and Uttar Pradesh*, Delhi: Oxford University Press.

Özler, B., G. Datt, and M. Ravallion, 1996, 'A Database on Poverty and Growth in India', Poverty and Human Resources Division, Policy Research Department, Washington, DC: World Bank.

Pandey, G., 1986, 'Rallying Round the Cow: Sectarian Strife in the Bhojpuri Region, c.1888–1917', in R. Guha (ed.), *Subaltern Studies Vol.2*, 1986 (1983), pp.60–129.

Papademetriou, D.G. and P.L. Martin, 1991, *The Unsettled Relationship: Labour Migration and Economic Development*, New York: Greenwood.

Ravallion, M., and G. Datt, 1996, 'How Important to India's Poor Is the Sectoral Composition of Economic Growth?', *The World Bank Economic Review*, Vol.10, No.1, pp.1–25.

Risley Collection, India Office Library and Records, MSS EUR E 295/1 (Magistrate of Saran to
    Risley in 1901, pp.630–54).
Rodgers, G. and J. Rodgers, 2001, 'A Leap Across Time: When Semi-Feudalism Met the Market
    in Rural Purnia', *Economic and Political Weekly*, 2 June.
Rogaly, B., 1998, 'Workers on the Move: Seasonal Migration and Changing Social Relations in
    Rural India', *Gender and Development*, Vol.6, No.1, pp.21–9.
RCLI, Royal Commission on Labour in India, 1931, *Report of the Royal Commission on Labour
    in India*, Calcutta: Government of India Central Publication Branch.
Roy Chaudhury, P.C., 1960, *Bihar District Gazetteers. Saran*, Patna: Secretariat Press..
Sarvekshana, 1992, Vol.XV, No.1, Issue 48, July–Sept. 1991, Vol.XV, No.4, Issue 51, April–June.
Sen, S., 1992, 'Women Workers in the Bengal Jute Industry, 1890–1940: Migration, Motherhood
    and Militancy', Ph.D. thesis, University of Cambridge.
Sen, S., 1999, *Women and Labour in Late Colonial India*, Cambridge: Cambridge University
    Press.
Servan-Schreiber, C., 1997, 'French Studies and Teaching on the Literacy Tradition of Bihar',
    paper at the conference on 'Bihar in the World and the World in Bihar', Patna, Dec.
Sharma, A.N., 1997, *People on the Move: Nature and Implications of Migration in a Backward
    Economy*, New Delhi.
Tinker, H., 1974, *A New System of Slavery: The Export of Indian Labour Overseas, 1830–1920*,
    London: Oxford University Press.
van Schendel, W. and A.H. Faraizi, 1984, *Rural Labourers in Bengal, 1880 to 1980*, CASP 12,
    Rotterdam, 1984.
Village Notes, notes compiled between 1915 and 1921, for Saran District, at the Chapra District
    Record Room (consulted notes from Manjhi, Parsa, Mashrak).
Washbrook, D., 1993, 'Land and Labour in Late Eighteenth-Century South India: The Golden
    Age of the Pariah', in P. Robb, (ed.), *Dalit Movement and the Meanings of Labour in India*,
    Delhi: Oxford University Press, pp.68–86.
Williamson, J.G., 1988, 'Migration and Urbanisation', *Handbook of Development Economics*,
    Vol.1, edited by H. Chenery and T.N. Srinivasan, Amsterdam: North Holland/Elsevier
    Publishers, pp.425–65.
Yang, A., 1989, *The Limited Raj: Agrarian Relations in Colonial India. Saran District
    1793–1920*, Delhi: Oxford University Press.

Daughters and Displacement: Migration Dynamics in an Indonesian Transmigration Area

REBECCA ELMHIRST

INTRODUCTION

Throughout Indonesia, rural livelihoods are characterised by participation in work away from the farm, frequently involving the engagement of farm families in urban labour markets [*Hetler, 1989; Hugo, 1992; Rigg, 1998*]. Evidence suggests that this has long been the case, as historically, rural economies have embraced a diverse array of activities including trade and traditional industries [*White, 1991*]. Yet since the 1980s, the character of the livelihood options available to rural people has shifted as the country has leaned towards export-oriented industrialisation, and following the implementation of a series of structural adjustment packages and reforms that prompted rapid economic development [*Hill, 1994*].

The pace of economic growth following this shift was, until very recently, sufficient for Indonesia to be included in the World Bank's *East Asia Miracle* [*World Bank, 1993*], with gross national product (GNP) growing at an average of 4.2 per cent between 1980 and 1993 [*Rigg, 1997: 6*]. Within this economic context, participation in localised non-farm in rural informal sector activities has been augmented by a rapid growth in the number of nominally rural people employed in large-scale factories in peri-urban industrial zones, and a growth in temporary migration for work reasons [*Manning and Hardjono, 1993; Firman, 1994; Rigg, 1998*].

In 1997 growth was halted as the Asian monetary crisis, coupled with political crisis, slowed down the rate of foreign investment and brought considerable hardship for those who had hitherto been feeling the benefits of growth: those working outside agriculture. Over the course of the late

---

Rebecca Elmhirst, School of the Environment, University of Brighton, UK: e-mail: R.J. Elmhirst@bton.ac.uk. This research was supported by Economic and Social Research Council Award R000222089 (1998 to 1999) and by an ESRC studentship (1994–97). The author is grateful for the support and advice of the Indonesian Institute of Sciences (LIPI), Jakarta and the International Center for Research in Agroforestry (ICRAF) Southeast Asia office, Bogor. Field-work was conducted with the assistance of staff and students from University of Lampung and from University of Indonesia Women's Studies Programme. Thanks to John Connell, Arjan de Haan and Ben Rogaly for comments on an earlier draft. Any remaining errors are the author's.

1990s, urban and industrial regions were characterised by mass worker layoffs, contract-driven 'hiring and firing' by factories, and by labour unrest in response to efforts to curtail worker benefits. At the same time, it has been difficult for people to seek on-farm alternatives, as the agrarian sector itself has been restructured, curtailing agricultural employment opportunities. Yet despite the crisis and its impact on the industrial sector, non-farm income opportunities, including those involving migration, continue to be of central importance for rural livelihoods.

Much of the literature on the contribution of non-farm earnings to rural livelihoods has focused on the situation in Java: an island that is heavily populated, in which the country's main industrial zones are located (Tangerang, Bogor, Bekasi, Bandung and Surabaya), and where large-scale rural industrialisation has become the norm [Wolf, 1992]. Away from Java many rural livelihoods are also characterised by participation in non-farm work, often at a great distance from home [Rodenburg, 1995; Silvey, 2000]. Recent research has shown that this is also the case in transmigration areas, where the economic success of marginal farmers resettled by the Indonesian government is closely linked to their being able to pursue non-farm income generating possibilities [Leinbach and Watkins, 1998].

Transmigration involves the resettlement of land-poor migrants, primarily from Java, into less populated 'outer island' areas, where they endeavour to forge a livelihood (with some state aid) alongside the original inhabitants of receiving areas. Transmigration began in the early 1900s as the Dutch colonial authorities sought to ameliorate poverty and resource conflicts in 'inner Indonesia' and to spur economic development in 'outer island' regions by relocating people, initially at least, from Java to Lampung. The programme was extended by the New Order government from the 1970s onwards, with almost two million people being moved from Java, Bali and Madura to Sumatra, Kalimantan and Irian Jaya (now West Papua) between 1970 and 1990. Accompanying the general transmigration programme has been Local Transmigration (*Translok*), involving the resettlement of people within a particular province, usually for environmental reasons or to make way for an infrastructural project [Pain, 1989].

An underlying thrust of transmigration has been one of land redistribution, enabling those being resettled to become self-supporting, own-account farmers. However, in many transmigration areas, land degradation associated with attempts to establish permanent food crop cultivation on fragile forest soils has made agrarian livelihoods precarious, with many locations blighted by soil fertility decline, pest invasions and crop failure [World Bank, 1988; Sage, 1996]. As Leinbach et al.'s research suggests, it is difficult for many transmigrant households to secure a livelihood without including non-farm work: such work is initially taken up for survival but it is frequently maintained to raise capital, invest in children's education and meet social obligations [*Leinbach et al., 1992*]. While these concerns within the literature on transmigration have focused on the fortunes of transmigrants, there has been little attention given to the livelihoods of the original inhabitants of transmigration areas. Where these have been discussed, it has been largely in relation to shifting resource entitlements and pressures on resource-based livelihoods.[1]

Less has been said about the strategies pursued by these groups to work with or around the constraints and opportunities posed by the arrival of transmigration projects in their midst. This study takes this as a starting point to explore migration dynamics within an 'indigenous' community in an area of Sumatra that has been transformed by the arrival of Javanese transmigrants through local transmigration in Lampung province. Local transmigration in this part of Lampung has involved the resettlement of Javanese farmers who had come to Lampung spontaneously in the 1970s in search of land, and had settled in government forest areas, now designated as protected watersheds. Since the early 1980s, when the programme began, 370,000 people have been moved (approximately 20 per cent of the province's population).[2] Much of the resettlement has been into the relatively isolated north of Lampung where transmigration settlements, accompanied by large-scale plantation development, now dominate the formerly forested landscapes associated with the livelihoods of the original Lampungese inhabitants of this region.

Research conducted in North Lampung in 1994–95, which sought to compare the livelihood responses of indigenous Lampungese and Javanese migrants to the changes associated with transmigration, revealed that a remarkable change was taking place within indigenous Lampungese communities [*Elmhirst, 1997*]. Since the early 1990s, increasing numbers of young, unmarried women had left the village temporarily to take up work in the garment and shoe factories of Tangerang, close to Indonesia's capital Jakarta on the island of Java. While non-farm work and circular migration appeared to be gaining greater importance in the area in general, this particular aspect of female labour migration was all the more notable as it was taking place in a community where it has been customary for unmarried women to be confined to the house, and where there are strict sanctions against their working in the fields. The point is that these young women had only recently become wage earners: at a time when a number of factors have conspired to make generating an income from agriculture particularly difficult. What is driving this change? How are those customs that restrict the activities of young women being renegotiated and reworked? Is daughters' work an indication of a commitment to help their families through difficult times, or a sign of their greater autonomy? What have been the main impacts of their work on land use and livelihoods in the area?

In this study, these questions are explored by drawing on interviews and surveys conducted in the North Lampung village of Tiuh Indah[3] in 1994–95, when the practice of female migration was still relatively uncommon, and comparing these with interviews conducted in 1998, when almost all of the villagee's teenage women were (or had been) working in the Tangerang industrial district in West Java. These time periods are significant, for they allow a comparison between the economic boom of the mid-1990s; when the Indonesian economy was growing very fast and when there was much foreign investment in labour-intensive industry, and the late 1990s when the monetary crisis reversed this growth, bringing with it factory closures and mass unemployment. Figures for early 1998 (coinciding with when this research took place) suggested that of the total eight million unemployed, 5.5 million were 'newly unemployed', and of these, around half were construction workers, with 1.5 million comprising those dismissed from troubled textile and garment factories, mainly in the country's urban and peri-urban industrial zones, such as Jakarta, Bogor, Tangerang and Bekasi [*Ahmed, 1998*].

This broader context has led to daughters' factory work acquiring a new meaning for people in Tiuh Indah, as households faced the critical effects of an exceptionally long dry season in 1997–98, compounded by the monetary crisis and associated price rises for household goods. Emphasis is given to the ways in which an emerging, culturally-conditioned social network linking village and city altered the terms upon which migration decisions and remittance practices were made, and may have cushioned rural and urban people against the worst impacts of the crisis. In doing so, the study uses empirical case-study material that seeks to challenge the assumption that livelihood strategies (including migration) are orchestrated by households operating as a unit, and to invoke the feminist critiques that such assumptions have provoked..

RESEARCH METHODS AND ANALYTICAL CONTEXT

In general terms, the research outlined here considers micro-level labour market interactions between Sumatra and Java, giving particular emphasis to cultural (that is, non-market) considerations which underscore and give meaning to temporary migration and livelihood practices. An analysis of the migration and work practices of unmarried daughters is taken as a 'route in' to consider the economic and cultural dynamics of livelihood and circular migration among Lampungese people in this transmigration area. A central hypothesis at the start of research, based on observations made during field work in 1994, was that daughters' migration and participation in factory work, far from being a mechanism for augmenting overall household livelihood, was leading to their greater economic and spatial autonomy, and loosening the ties that bound them to the household itself.[4] In testing this hypothesis, the research sought to shed light on the complex relationship between three factors: (i) the transformation of social relations in the Lampungese community brought by inward migration of Javanese transmigrants, (ii) daughters' factory work and the income it generates, and (iii) the loosening of constraints on the mobility of daughters away from home and family.

The research draws upon a large literature concerning temporary labour migration as one element within a portfolio of livelihood possibilities [Hugo, 1982; Prothero and Chapman, 1985; Koppel and Hawkins, 1994]. Temporary or circular migration has attracted the attention of researchers in Indonesia for a number of years, where it appears to be increasing in significance as communications improve. As Hugo points out, it is of considerable economic and social importance, both for migrants themselves and for their communities of origin [Hugo, 1992]. In studies of female temporary migration in Indonesia and elsewhere, particular importance has been accorded to the concept of household livelihood strategies [Hetler, 1989; Guest, 1989].

In this approach, strategies are devised around the labour availability of the household, its consumption needs and production possibilities (alternative forms of income) in so far as these are conditioned by wider economic shifts. Migration by particular individuals from the household may be part of a wider strategy, which includes diversification of income sources across activities such as agriculture, petty enterprise and formal employment [Stark, 1991]. Such an approach may well be useful in conceptualising migration and livelihood practices in North Lampung, where new income possibilities emerge as former modes of livelihood become increasingly difficult in the context of the economic changes associated with the Indonesian government's transmigration programme [Elmhirst, 1997]. An important issue here is the relationship between female labour migration in North Lampung and pressures on indigenous rural livelihoods brought about by the Indonesian government's transmigration resettlement programme.

However, while a livelihood strategy approach correctly places migration within the context of household relations and draws attention to population movement as a socially-embedded process [Tacoli, 1995], its emphasis on labour allocation obscures the intra-household negotiations which underlie what appear to be household migration decisions. In particular, it denies women's and young peoples' agency vis-à-vis male and parental control, and masks the intentionality of daughters' migration, which may well have little to do with the household resource system. In this particular research setting, it contributes little towards understanding why it is young women that are migrating and not young men, or how a practice can be accommodated when it appears to be contrary to local cultural practices, and appears (at least, in 1994) to contribute little to the household economy.

A number of feminist studies have pointed to the dangers of assuming that households devise corporate livelihood strategies, and emphasise instead the importance of internal household dynamics and power relations between men and women [*Kandiyoti, 1988; Kabeer, 1991; Wolf, 1992*]. In this type of approach, the household is seen as a locus where uneven power relations between men and women shape the terms of the gender division of labour, of work, resources, responsibilities and rewards. This perspective is complemented by recent work on gender and migration, which argues that gender should be examined 'as a process that is played out through the gendered households, communities, labour markets and projects of neoliberal restructuring through which migrants move' [*Lawson, 2000: 175; Radcliffe, 1991; Ilcan, 1994; Mills, 1997*].

In Indonesia, Hugo has suggested that a number of factors have conspired to increase female migration, including broader structural changes in the economy, coupled with a reshaping of women's roles and statuses linked partly to increased levels of education, but also to shifts in customary law (*adat*) governing female behaviour [*Hugo, 1992*]. Going beyond an emphasis on gendered structures, others have pointed to the importance of gendered subjectivities and the ways in which female migrants are creative subjects, reforging identities and reshaping the structures in which their lives are embedded [*Lawson, 2000; Silvey, 2000*].

This study draws on these insights about intrahousehold relations and gendered subject positions to probe assumptions about migrant remittance pooling between household members, and to question the idea of a single household decision-maker directing the practices of other household members. By considering various axes and affinities in the household, specifically between daughters and their parents, and daughters and siblings, the research adds another dimension to the household picture: that of gendered intergenerational relations. Daughters provide a particularly important focus in the South-east Asian realm, where adolescence is increasingly recognised as a new life-cycle phase, bringing particular types of agency among young women. To consider this aspect of migration, remittance practices between daughters and their families are examined to assess the extent to which migrant earnings are expected to and do provide a key element in the resource system of Tiuh Indah households.

Finally, the research draws on recent approaches to migration which aim to avoid reducing the migration process to the circulation of labour power. A number of writers have looked to migrant networks as a possible middle ground concept, wherein individual decisions are seen as conditioned by structural forces, and where individual migration decisions, as a cumulative force, alter the decision-making context over time. A particularly compelling approach is that adopted by Goss and Lindquist [*1995*] who draw on Giddens' structuration theory to consider the institutional dimensions of migrant networks. They define the migrant institution as 'a complex articulation of individuals, associations and organisations which extends the social action of and interaction between these agents and agencies across time and space' [*Goss and Lindquist, 1995: 319*]. While migrant or social networks might be one part of this, the migrant institution is not reducible to either of these elements.

In adopting various elements of Giddens' structuration theory, emphasis is given to the institutionalisation of migration practices. According to Goss and Lindquist, as individuals regularly invoke rules in everyday social action, social practices are reinforced and sedimented over time into the institutions that constitute the social system. As others emulate migrant experiences, this has the effect of reinforcing the strategies and social relationships on which the migration has been based, such as pre-existing social networks.

This routinisation of the social practices of migration leads to the emergence of recognisable rules and patterns, and over time, informal or formal organisations may attempt to extend control over the process. The cumulative effect of this is the institutionalisation of migration as 'a complex articulation of rules and resources which presents constraints and opportunities to individual action' [*Goss and Lindquist, 1995: 345*]. Although Goss and Lindquist's framework has been devised with reference to Philippine international labour migration, they suggest the concept is applicable wherever spatially extensive relationships link migrants to their home communities.

As this study shows, such spatially extensive relationships between daughters and their rural families are very important, both as a moral and material resource, and as a moral and material constraint. What is apparent in North Lampung is a 'thickening up' of a migrant network comprising knowledge (about particular work opportunities), people and cash flows between Tiuh Indah and the Tangerang industrial zone. In other words, daughters' migration is becoming increasingly institutionalised, and in so doing, is altering the terms of the migrant decision and also remittance practices. Key to this process has been the emergence of a migrant organisation founded to serve the interests of Tiuh Indah villagers now living in Tangerang.

A series of qualitative survey methods applied over nine months in 1994–95, and again over two months in 1998, were used to identify the ways in which daughterss' migration to Tangerang had changed over time, in terms of its representation in the village, and in terms of its material implications. Methods included semi-structured interviews with a sample of 40 households in Tiuh Indah (out of a total population of 250 households) where separate interviews were held with different household members. In addition, peer group discussions involving fathers, mothers, male siblings and women factory workers themselves on the subject of factory work were convened, and individual interviews with young women that were working in Tangerang were conducted.

This latter group was traced using a snowball sampling technique, in which young women introduced researchers to friends also involved in factory work. This revealed the workings of the informal migrant organisation that had been set up in the intervening period between the two field seasons, and which has emerged as an important factor in bringing about changes in migration decision-making and remittance practices in Tiuh Indah. Where possible, the parents and siblings of all young women that had worked or were working in Tangerang were interviewed individually around issues such as the meaning of migration and factory work, and remittance practices.

THE CONTEXT OF FEMALE MIGRATION FROM NORTH LAMPUNG TO TANGERANG

In order to understand female migration between rural North Lampung and the factory zone of Greater Jakarta, and its likely impacts, it is necessary to consider the local political economy of the village area in historical perspective. Until the early 1980s, this part of North Lampung was a sparsely settled area comprising isolated communities of shifting cultivators belonging to the Way Kanan ethnic group, who lived along the banks of the Way Kanan River. Livelihoods were derived from swamp rice cultivation along the fertile flood plains, from fishing and from trade in forest products including timber and rattan from the area's extensive forests.

Overland travel was extremely difficult, and movement in and out of the communities was largely by boat. In the late 1970s, the government earmarked the area for local transmigration: to receive 'forest squatters' from protected forests elsewhere in the province. Over the course of the 1980s, more than 500,000 Javanese migrants were resettled in North Lampung, increasing the region's population sevenfold in the space of just 10 years, transforming agro-ecological landscapes, land tenure structures and livelihood possibilities in the process.[5] While the objectives of local transmigration were ostensibly to remove people from protected forests, the programme was conducted in tandem with a renewed emphasis on large-scale commercial plantation development in Lampung, with migrants identified as a pool of labour for this sector.

The cumulative impact of this transformation on the indigenous Lampungese has been profound. Much of their ancestral lands have been 'sold' for plantation or transmigration settlement development, and any remaining forest has been removed and replaced, either by *Imperata* grasslands (on less infertile land) or by permanent food cropping (cassava, rice and maize) by transmigrants or perennial cultivation by plantation companies (notably sugar cane and oil palm).[6] While transmigration and plantation development have removed certain livelihood options, they have also created others in their wake. Improved overland transport has led to the development of close links with export-oriented industrial areas in West Java, which may be reached in less than 18 hours overland and by ferry. These links mean that people are able to circulate between areas, extending the influence of Indonesia's principal industrial zone into what has hitherto been a remote and inaccessible area.[7]

Interviews with both men and women in Tiuh Indah suggest migration has begun to play a much more important role in rural livelihoods. In the past, migration would involve short-term relocation to other rural areas, perhaps to coffee, clove and pepper plantations in the mountains for the duration of the harvest. Among wealthier Lampungese, migrations associated with education also took place, where sons would travel to the provincial capital to attend high school.

Since the late 1980s, when the full impact of the changes associated with transmigration was felt, outmigration has become increasingly important, with around 21 per cent of total work time spent in non-farm activities requiring temporary migration. In part this is related to a decline in the possibility of deriving an income from agriculture or the forest. Poor people and the landless have been pushed out of agriculture. However, wealthier families have opted out of agriculture, suggesting commitment to land-based livelihoods is being lost [*Koppel and Hawkins, 1994*]. This 'loss of commitment' is in part driven by economic and institutional uncertainty: in contrast to transmigrants, indigenous Lampungese people do not hold official title to their land, and past experience means there is a strong perception that at any time their land might be taken either for transmigration or for plantation development. For these reasons, time and money is invested in activities outside agriculture, particularly in trade, small businesses and non-local factory employment.

More recently, economic and political crisis in Indonesia has transformed both rural and urban livelihoods once again, changing the portfolio of livelihood options, and altering household relations and resource flows in a number of important ways. The fall in the value of the rupiah against the dollar in early 1998 and the impact of measures demanded by the IMF that followed meant prices for most everyday household goods rose dramatically. Yet agricultural incomes did not rise in accordance with this, and as a result, there was a critical cash shortfall in all rural households. Families were no longer able to afford basic necessities such as cooking oil, medicines (including family planning measures) or afford to pay school fees. The need to augment farm incomes thus increased.

At the same time, the economic crisis brought a dramatic decline in urban formal sector employment: as fieldwork began in March 1998, it was estimated that around 250,000 formal sector workers in the Tangerang industrial zone alone were newly unemployed.[8] Although evidence was patchy, interviews in Tangerang among Lampungese migrants suggested that male unemployment was greater than female unemployment as men tended to work in the sectors that were hardest hit, while women working for subcontractors of larger international companies, such as NIKE, had not felt the full impact of unemployment. Rather, employment had become short-term and sporadic.

More specific to rural North Lampung, and compounding the effects of the monetary crisis on prices and employment prospects, was the impact of an exceptionally long dry season in 1997–98. Critically, most households in Tiuh Indah harvested just half of what they could expect in a normal year. Crops were ravaged first by drought, then by flooding, and for the first time in many years, families went hungry. For all but the wealthiest quartile of households, cash earned outside farming assumed a much greater importance, and for this reason, daughterss' migration and engagement in factory work assumed a new importance for rural families. Monetary crisis and the uncertainties brought by a long dry season meant daughters (and their work practices) acquired a new value in Lampung's economy and cultural landscape. The significance of this for the argument being developed in this paper is that it points to the dynamism that underlies the practice of off-farm work and circular migration, not just in terms of who participates and when, but also in terms of shifts in the meaning and value of temporary urban migration, and changes in the kinds of economic and cultural impacts it brings to rural areas over time.

While the wider political economic context was of crucial importance in underpinning daughters' temporary migration, as Hugo's work might have predicted [*Hugo, 1992*], also important were those factors which condition and colour female agency in the community, and the capacity of young women to be architects of their own lives. One way of examining these factors is to consider the cultural and moral prescriptions that define daughters' customary role, and to look at the possibilities for daughters to challenge or comply with these prescriptions. In particular, kinship, and all that it embraces, including gender and generational relations, inheritance and familial obligations, underscores the lives of young women and sets the terms for their work practices [*Wolf, 1992*]. Such a conceptualisation marks a departure from the rather mechanistic depiction of household relations in migration and labour allocation models and seeks to draw together both cultural (kinship) and economic (the household economy) factors together in order to arrive at an explanatory framework that can account for the work practices, including temporary migration, of young women [*Kabeer, 1991*].

Lampungese daughters in Tiuh Indah belong to the Way Kanan group, whose kinship system is patrilineal and genealogy-based, located within a wider *Marga* or clan system to which smaller family groupings defer in many family decisions, particularly those concerning property, inheritance and marriage [*Hilman Hadikusuma, 1989*]. Within this system, property, family status and responsibility all pass down the male line through the eldest son, who is regarded as being responsible for his parents in their old age, although in practice this responsibility inevitably falls upon his wife. Most women co-resided with their husband's parents, relieving the burden of his mother, but taking on much of the domestic work themselves.

In terms of intra-household relations within Lampungese families, lines of authority are both gendered and generational. Mothers may be observed deferring to their sons, and, more frequently, sisters to their brothers. In other words, all female household members are under the guardianship of male household members, whatever their age. As economic units, households are extremely complex, made up of a number of different conjugal units. Within this, the division of labour between men and women is relatively clear-cut. While men and adult women work together in the fields, there are clearly identified male and female tasks, and women are solely responsible for all domestic work including processing the harvest (unless this is done by machine). Although the ideal for women is that they do not engage in agricultural work (they should stay home, keep their skins white and avoid building muscles), in practice this is rarely achieved, particularly among poor people.

Partly, restrictions on women's work practices relate to normative constraints on their mobility. Even married women are not allowed to go out of the village unaccompanied, or go to distant fields on their own. Widows would be seen accompanied by their sons as they made their way to tend their crops. Where these restrictions are particularly strong is in the case of unmarried girls, who, on reaching puberty, are not allowed to go out of the house except with parents or older brothers. Thus, they have no role whatever in the farming system as they are precluded from taking part in any activity that takes them away from the confines of the house until after they have married and borne their husband a child.

Particular considerations appear to be both aesthetic and moral: a protection of young girls' pale skin and delicate constitution and a protection of their honour, as agricultural work is associated with the possibility of being 'bothered' by young men. In this sense, there is little expectation of daughters being able to support themselves economically through their own efforts, were they to remain in the village: in short, they have no *local* economic value. However, the position of daughters is entirely dependent on them making a suitable marriage, as they will have to look to their future husband for their future welfare. In view of this, daughters (and their families) need to negotiate a line of expected behaviours (and aesthetics) which will maintain their respectability and standing in the eyes of others.

In view of the apparent restrictions upon young women, their temporary migration to the factories of Tangerang is notable. The question is, how can it be accommodated within local cultural prescriptions, and why does it not draw the loss of prestige *(gengsi)* that working in the fields (or the plantation) would bring? As the remainder of this paper suggests, what is apparent is that these considerations are shifting: as migration to Tangerang has become increasingly institutionalised, and as political-economic factors have changed, factory work has acquired a new and more acceptable meaning, and daughters have secured a new and more important economic role.

CHANGING DECISION-MAKING PRACTICES: NEGOTIATING MIGRATION AND FACTORY WORK

Factory migration began in the early 1990s when a Way Kanan girl, living in the provincial capital Tanjung Karang, went to work in Tangerang. Effectively, this prompted a steady stream of young women, mostly her relatives and close friends from Tiuh Indah, to follow suit. By 1994 (the first period of fieldwork on which this study is based), around a third of all post-school, pre-marriage girls were going to Tangerang, usually on their own initiative and after pressing their parents into agreeing to let them go. At this point, daughters' decision to migrate was their own: there was no system of labour brokerage being operated by factories or middlemen. Young women moved to Tangerang, stayed in the same hostels as those already working there, and approached the factories themselves, on the advice of friends and peer-group relatives. As other studies have shown [e.g., *Wolf, 1992*], at this point, young women were drawn towards work in the factories for a variety of reasons, few of which were purely economic, and none of which indicated their desire to help their families.

In the early 1990s, when the practice was in its infancy, parents were reluctant to concede to their daughters going. There were fears about daughters' morality being compromised, about parents losing control of their daughters: during fieldwork in 1994, there were many salacious stories circulating about particular young women who had compromised the standing of their families by their behaviour in Tangerang. But the lure of the factories was such that many young women were able to push back at the boundaries imposed by their parents, by selling jewellery to pay for travel and accommodation. Over the course of the 1990s, more and more young women went to work in Tangerang, with interesting consequences for how factory work came to be represented in the village. Effectively, this changed the terms on which daughters and parents were making the migration decision.

From its beginnings as a few 'brave' young women challenging parental authority to go to Tangerang, an informal kinship-peer group network of young women had emerged, setting in motion a migration network which, by April 1998, involved 25 of the 30 young women in the village aged between 15 and 20. Effectively, the social practice of migration was sedimented over time [*Goss and Lindquist, 1995*]. Daughters were able to borrow money from friends already working in Tangerang, enabling them to accompany their friends when they returned to the factory after the Muslim *Lebaran* holiday, and it was certainly the case that parents regarded the main influence on daughters as being their friends.

The very existence of a network, and the fact that it was one based on kinship and common identity (belonging to the same clan) has meant that factory work could now be accommodated within prevailing ideologies concerning young women's work and their obligations towards their natal household. Parents believed their daughters to be 'supervised' by older women for the time that they were at the factory. The leverage used by daughters to persuade their parents to go along with their plans to work in Tangerang was not so much an economic argument, but one which appealed to the parents' duty to appear to be providing well for their daughters, to be 'modern'. By early 1998 it was almost the case that if a girl was not at school, she was working in Tangerang. 'The main thing is the trend in this era, which is for her friends to go there', said one father. 'If you have a feeling like that ... I don't know, they are all talking about it. The main thing is the village fashion.'

A key factor in increasing the flow of young girls to Tangerang appears to have been the setting up of a migrant organisation to look after the affairs of Tiuh Indah migrants in Tangerang. The *Ikatan Keluarga Buay Serunting* (literally, the family ties of Buay Serunting – the ancestral founder of the village centuries ago), was founded in 1996 by a prominent Tiuh Indah man who had left the village in the 1960s to undertake schooling in Jakarta, and who had settled in Tangerang where he worked as a manager in a utility company. It was the intention of Pak Selamat to 'give something back' to his home community, with which he retained strong ties (as a landowner and member of the elite).

The organisation also enabled him to raise his own status within the Tiuh Indah community. The *ikatan* was set up to offer a home from home for young migrants in Tangerang, and, importantly, reassurance to parents that someone was keeping an eye on their daughters while they were in the city. It also acted as an information conduit about possible work. Regular meetings were held at Pak Selamat's home for young migrants, where they had the opportunity to discuss issues associated with life in Tangerang, receive messages from parents, eat traditional Lampungese food and listen to Lampungese folk songs.

A number of features of the *ikatan* indicate the way in which migration to Tangerang has been institutionalised in recent years. First, young women are rigorously 'supervised' by a male authority figure (Pak Selamat) who has taken over the informal supervision offered by friends and other family members, thus securing the trust of even the most concerned parents. Secondly, supervision of young women is highly organised, in ways that mimic government bureaucratic practice. A registration book is kept detailing personal details and employment histories of all members of the *ikatan*. Thirdly, the *ikatan* maintains a presence in Tiuh Indah as all households with children in Tangerang have a large calendar hanging in their homes, displaying the name and address of *Ikatan Keluarga Buay Serunting*. Finally, the *ikatan* has played a key role in the routinisation of remittance practices, establishing 'rules' and conventions for how factory wages are disposed of.

Effectively, the setting up of the *ikatan* has formalised an informal kin-based migration network, and brought it under male parental (patriarchal?) control. The *ikatan* has increased parental trust and smoothed the path of the migration decision-making process between parents and daughters. By drawing on an ancestral name with important connotations for local Lampungese identity and cultural practices, the founding of the *ikatan* has also enabled female factory work to be accommodated within local customary law (*adat*), and lessened some of its negative associations that were apparent in the early 1990s when the practice first began.

The changing attitudes of parents (and the wider community) towards factory work between 1994 and 1998 is striking. What became apparent in interviews conducted in 1998 was how factory work had come to be viewed as an important rite of passage for young women in Tiuh Indah, and as a way of developing a particular kind of Lampungese femininity. In part, this related to prevailing ideas within the village about factory work. It was viewed by parents (and others who had never been to the factories) as clean, light and modern work that required a relatively high level of education (at least high school), and which engaged young women in the manufacture of well-known international branded products, such as NIKE trainers. Tiuh Indah people contrasted this with work in the fields, which was hot, heavy, dirty and hard, taking place under the hot sun, and for which no modern education was required. Working in Tangerang factories was considered important for young women for three related reasons: first, in terms of aesthetics and prevailing ideas about female beauty, secondly, in terms of expanding experience (learning) and developing social skills, and thirdly, in raising the value of daughters on the marriage market.

To elaborate, within local cultural practice, appearance is very important for Lampungese women. For young women in the village, working in factories presented an opportunity for raising their aesthetic value. Contrasts were drawn between the 'rough', dark skins of those people unfortunate enough to have to work as farmers, and the smooth, pale skins of young female factory workers who had no need to work under the hot sun or to carry heavy loads. Moreover, the experience gained from having lived away from the village was highly valued. In part this relates to a Sumatra-wide tradition of *merantau*: migration for employment and education, and a general expansion of horizons. In the past, *merantau* was seen as a rite of passage for young men and was associated with education, but more recently, it has become something that is of value for young women too. Families were proud of the new social skills their factory-employed daughters bring home. 'She's different yes', said one mother. 'She is clever at talking, she knows what to say if we have a visitor. She is more polite, does things more correctly now.'

For these reasons, and in stark contrast to the negative misgivings apparent in Tiuh Indah in 1994, by 1998, ex-Tangerang girls had become valued in the marriage market. In part this related to their aesthetic appeal and their more worldly experience: their brush with modernity. However, it was also linked to more practical and prosaic considerations. At least until the monetary crisis, factory women were able to save money, buying gold (as a future investment) and buying household wares (furniture, bedding and so forth) for when they married and set up home. This made them an attractive prospect for potential marriage partners, and in part dissolved some of the effects of economic stratification on the marriage market in Tiuh Indah. Within Lampungese custom, getting married is an expensive business and both parties welcome whatever contribution a girl can make herself. There have been instances where the daughters' family has been able to ask for a higher bride price because their daughter has worked in Tangerang (in parallel to the higher bride price paid for women with a higher level of education). By 1998, factory work was considered to enhance the social standing of a family in the village, from the perspective of parents, siblings and neighbours: a situation that was very different from that encountered in interviews four years previously.

FACTORY WORK AND THE MIGRANT NETWORK: CHANGES IN REMITTANCE PRACTICES

Interviews conducted among factory women and their families in 1994 when factory work was still relatively unusual suggested that while young women were able to earn a substantial wage in comparative terms, there was little incentive or obligation for them to remit any of this money to their parents. Attitudes towards female factory work centred on its moral implications and there was little acknowledgement among parents that it could yield any sort of material advantage to them. It was rare for parents to make any sort of demand upon the money earned by their daughters from factory work, and this in part related to their having limited expectations about the economic contribution of daughters more generally: as has been pointed out, daughters had little or no role in the farming system. By 1998, the situation was rather different. A pattern of particular 'remittance behaviours' had begun to emerge, in which daughters' direct and indirect economic contribution was increasingly recognised. Furthermore, differences in remittance practices were observable across different socio-economic groups, although any direct link with the farming system (in terms of investment of cash into agriculture) remained tenuous.

While factory earnings compared favourably with what might be earned in off farm work locally, the amount of money that daughters were able to save or send home each month was very small. On average, a six-day working week yielded between Rp 100,000 and Rp 250,000 per month (in April 1998, this amounted to between £10 and £25 per month). Out of this, daughters had to pay for food and accommodation, which totalled around Rp 100,000 per month. Unless these young women were engaged in overtime, they were unable to save any money at all. However, overtime rates meant they could boost their monthly salaries by as much as 100 per cent. This said, on average daughters were able to save about Rp 20,000 (£2) per month for themselves.

The amount of money sent home varied greatly between different young women and different households. Poorer households were able to exert much greater pressure on their daughters to send money home, to the point that some parents visited Tangerang themselves on a regular basis to collect money from their daughters. In one case, the decision to go to Tangerang had been made by the daughters' parents: it had not been on her initiative at all. In this case, the daughter handed over about Rp 30,000 once every two months, some of which was kept for her benefit, but the majority of which was given to her parents. It is notable that there were no instances where this money was invested into the farming system by parents: small sums of cash were used to buy food necessities such as cooking oil and sugar, or to pay for younger children's school uniforms. The likely impact of factory work on land use and farming systems appeared to be limited, and reflected a growing recognition among parents that their children's future would not be land-based.

For the majority of households with daughters working in Tangerang, while similar amounts of money were sent home at similar intervals, this was at the discretion of daughters, who asked that it be spent on particular items: gold jewellery, furniture and cloth items used when setting up home. 'She sends her money to me', said one mother. 'She sends money every few months, with a letter explaining what she wants. She asks for gold, for things for later, for when she gets married. Its her money, and she's thrifty, like most young girls.' Popular purchases were carved wooden wardrobes, in which were stored items such as bedding, plates and so on: the kinds of goods that typically young women bring into their marital home.

Yet young women's wishes were not always obeyed, as mothers were able to exert some sort of control over what happened to the money sent: 'We receive a wage and what is bought is things for us', said one daughter. 'Clothes, soft furnishings, things for us. But often we are angry: how come this wasn't bought? In fact what is bought is things for our younger brothers and sisters like shoes, things for school.' Conflicts between parents and daughters over what the money is spent on were indicative of a growing recognition among parents of the value of daughters' work and how it might help parents make ends meet in the context of pressure on farm livelihoods brought by drought and crop failure. This was being voiced by people weighing up whether to let their daughters undertake factory work: 'I saw people who were already working there [in Tangerang], who had made money', said one father. 'I thought it would lighten the load of her mother, of her father, so I let her go there.' Daughters' access to additional income was translated into a degree of control over what was done with their income, and while management of this income lay in the hands of their mothers, its disposal was at the discretion of daughters (see Pahl [1989] as cited in Kabeer [1997]). At first sight, the principal beneficiaries of factory income were daughters themselves with a smaller proportion of income destined for collective purposes. While this appears to accord with the hypothesis of daughters' greater autonomy, a closer analysis of how remittance practices were becoming increasingly institutionalised calls this interpretation into question.

One of the more striking features of remittance behaviour revealed in interviews and observations made in 1998 was the extent to which a pattern of remittance behaviour was emerging across the community, and across different socio-economic strata. Mention has already been made of the kinds of purchases normally made by daughters with the money they had been able to save. Importantly, it was rare for factory wages to be reinvested into agriculture, and only a small proportion found its way into a collective pot. Instead, major purchases tended to revolve around buying those goods required to set up a new home after marriage: furniture, bedding, kitchen utensils, and in some instances, savings in the form of gold. Comparing this data with that collected in 1994, when purchases from remittances did not follow any clear pattern, suggests that as migration became increasingly commonplace and increasingly institutionalised, particular rules and practices of expenditure began to emerge.

A closer look at the kinds of goods purchased and the meanings ascribed to them suggests the principal beneficiaries of factory wage income were not daughters themselves, but their future households. Daughters explicitly looked towards the future in deciding how to spend their money as they tried to lessen their perceived future burden: 'We don't want to be made "busy" again', said one daughter. Although parents believed 'the advantage is for her', this was only partly so. Daughters did not act selfishly (they sometimes gave money to parents to help out), but neither were their actions wholly selfless. There was a sense of perceived interest in how earnings were spent: purchases were regarded as an investment in the future and the kinds of things that were bought had the effect of raising young women's value in the marriage market.[9] Effectively, the ultimate beneficiaries would be their future husbands, their future husbands' families and indeed, their own families, as less money would have to be raised in order to set up their future home on marriage.

The switch from relatively selfish remittance behaviour (spending money on make-up and clothes) observed in 1994 and relatively selfless behaviour (saving money for a future household) in 1998 parallels the changes noted by Wolf [*1992*] over a similar timescale in her study of rural Javanese factory daughters. Wolf linked this to life-cycle: as factory daughters grew up, their spending patterns tended to change towards being more altruistic. However, in North Lampung, the observations relate to a different cohort of girls to those interviewed in 1994. Life-cycle factors were unlikely to explain changes in remittance practices among very young women. Rather, they were linked to the emergence of a normative framework around factory wages, which related in part to the institutionalisation of factory migration, and in particular, to the founding of the village *ikatan keluarga* (family ties organisation) as outlined earlier. In regular meetings of the *ikatan* daughters were continually reminded of their familial role, their moral obligation towards their parents, and indeed the economic circumstances of the family they had left behind. As the head of the *ikatan*, Pak Selamat, said: 'What we are trying to do with the *ikatan* is to help the village, to help poor people who are still in the village. If these girls can do that, then I am happy.'

One of the ways in which the *ikatan* attempted to secure remittances for parents was through the foundation of a rotating credit savings system (*arisan*). Rather than using a bank account, daughters were encouraged to place a small amount of cash into a common pot, which they would be entitled to 'win' once every few months. This gave daughters the opportunity to have access to a lump sum of money. In meetings, there was much discussion of what was going to be bought, peer group influence was very important, but more crucial was the influence exerted by Pak Selamat himself, in his self-appointed parental role. Also, the *ikatan* provided a conduit for information for parents to hear about the behaviour of daughters and, critically, what their earnings were. This cancelled out any opportunity for daughters to 'underreport' their earnings and thus avoid having to send money home.

Compared with interviews in 1994, four years on, parents were much more astute about factory earnings (including overtime payments). They were increasingly able to exert long-distance power over their daughters through the *ikatan*, truncating any autonomy that factory migration might have implied for daughters four years previously. As such, the *ikatan*, as a new institutional form, represents a similar kind of control over young women from North Lampung as Mather noted for local women employed in Tangerang when recruitment was confined to the villages around the factories [*Mather, 1982*].

As drought and monetary crisis brought considerable pressure to bear on all but the wealthier households in Tiuh Indah, in early 1998 daughters' factory work took on a new significance for almost all families. Most reported agricultural yields of 50 per cent below their normal level, and local off-farm work (that is, logging) had all but ceased, linked in part to the dry season, fire and the destruction of any remaining forest in recent months [*Elmhirst, 1998*]. For the first time, parents began asking for money from their daughters to directly support the household, in particular through the dry season when there was a shortage of food. In about a third of households interviewed, at least over the dry season, cash from daughters' factory work was the only income being received by households.

A growing recognition of the importance of daughters' factory income altered the way factory work and daughters' economic role was represented in Tiuh Indah. Before, daughters' migration was seen as a way of gathering life experience and perhaps saving a little for the future, but it was not part of the household economic equation. Parents' dependence on daughters' factory income over the course of the long dry season in 1998 shifted this representation so that those daughters who remained in the village and did not engage in factory work were the ones that drew comment. 'Here there is no work, in Lampung there's no work for girls, it is very difficult. Better to be there than be here where I am unemployed', said one Tiuh Indah daughter. What is notable from this comment (and many others like it) is how daughters who were once seen as having no economic role (that is, not part of the potential work force) were regarded as 'unemployed' when they were not engaged in factory work. In 1994, the idea that daughters' role in the household should constitute 'unemployment' was unthinkable.

As the dry season came to an end in 1998, household incomes continued to be under pressure but from a different source: one that was equally likely to bring a shift in household relations and remittance flows. By April 1998, monetary crisis was taking its toll on factory employment as factories went bankrupt on a weekly basis and as thousands of workers were made redundant. By the beginning of May 1998, around a third of all of the female members of the migrant organisation had lost their jobs, and nearly all of the young men had already returned to the village. Unemployment, and the prospect of unemployment, was on everyone's minds. The view of the Indonesian government, prior to President Suharto stepping down, was that factory workers could (and should) return to their natal villages, where they would be able to subsist by being absorbed back into a farm household economy. Considerable effort (and government cash) was used in encouraging people to return to their villages. A number of young women from Tiuh Indah followed this path, returning to their parents' homes where once again they had no role in the farming system, and where their parents regarded them as a burden: 'All she does is sleep and eat'. While rural households were able to cope in the short-term, their longer-term prospects, particularly over subsequent dry seasons, when food production ceases, looked very bleak indeed.

As Tiuh Indah women faced unemployment, the role of the migrant organisation (*ikatan*) shifted once more. First, most young women remained in the city, using the *ikatan* as an important information source for tracking down factory jobs, which still existed, but with factories recruiting when orders come in, and laying workers off when there were no orders (that is, rapid hire and fire). While the *ikatan* was unlikely to offer sufficient material assistance for daughters and their families to enable them to overcome the difficulties they faced, it was nevertheless an important source of moral and material support in the face of crisis. Daughters made a trade-off between its rather authoritarian approach towards their behaviour, and the benevolence it could potentially offer in the form of small loans, advice and information: all of which were critically important in the face of political instability and economic uncertainty in Indonesia.

CONCLUSION

At the beginning of this study, a number of questions were posed concerning the temporary migration of young women from North Lampung to work in the factories of Tangerang (Greater Jakarta), West Java. It asked what was driving this pattern in a community where it has been customary for young women to be confined to the house and where strict sanctions prevent them from working in the fields. The answer to this question has changed as migration has become more common place, more institutionalised, and as economic conditions in the village have shifted. In 1994, the initiative for migration was very much that of daughters – young women exerting their agency, with motivations which appeared to be largely self-centred and not altruistic.

By 1998, and particularly as a long dry season and monetary crisis took its toll on rural livelihoods, driving forces had changed. Daughters' factory work has been accommodated within local *adat* (custom) as what began as the actions of a disapproved of minority developed into a practice being followed by the majority of young women in the community. By 1998, the women drawing comment were those who had not gone to work in Tangerang, whilst those that had gone were regarded as worldly (in a positive sense) and modern. Changes in attitudes towards migrants altered the context in which more recent migration decisions were being made, so that young women's agency *vis-à-vis* factory work no longer was confronted by parental resistance: rather, female migration was, by 1998, being actively encouraged.

This shifting moral terrain on which migration decisions were being made was also evoked in the emergence of a set of norms concerning remittance practices: daughters increasingly expected (and were expected) to send money home, which was used to purchase goods that they could take with them when they married and set up their own households. These emerging remittance practices were simultaneously an expression of autonomy from economic dependence on the parental household, but a commitment to help, in the sense that they were relieveing any future burden on their parents to provide the goods required for their daughter to set up home.

Key to these changes appears to be '*institutionalisation*', a thickening-up of contingent social practices, through which parents have been able to reassert parental authority, and wrest control over their daughters' lives and livelihoods once more. As research on migrant networks has indicated, as other emulate migrant practices, this reinforces the strategies and social relationships on which migration is based, leading to recognisable rules and patterns and, over time, the emergence of informal organisations to extend control over the process [*Goss and Lindquist, 1995*]. This has evidently been the case in North Lampung, where the *Ikatan Buay Serunting* (family ties organisation) has attempted to extend village-based parental authority to the city, enabling households to exert a little more control over the activities and remittance practices of young women. This reassertion of control became most notable during the extended drought of 1997–98, when, in the context of crop failure, parents looked to their daughters to remit small amounts of cash to buy food and household necessities. This, coupled with the legitimacy given to young women by the presence of a village network in the city, accounts for the accommodation of female migration within a cultural framework that is generally negative towards female mobility and manual employment.

However, from the point of view of longer-term livelihood sustainability in the village itself, parental control over migrant income is no guarantee of its investment into agriculture, let alone in sustainable farming practices. In a context where complex institutional factors such as land tenure, coupled with environmental degradation, mean indigenous Lampungese agriculture is regarded as inherently uncertain, off-farm work is not seen as a prop to farm incomes. Rather, it is seen as a first step towards uncoupling the link between agricultural success and household well-being, even towards abandoning land-based livelihoods altogether, in the face of a perceived threat from transmigration and plantation development. This challenges any assumptions that the monetary crisis has driven people back to land-based livelihoods in North Lampung, at least. Instead, the broader structural and environmental forces associated with transmigration and commercial agriculture have converged with new patterns of female agency and aspirations in North Lampung, encouraging a shift away from resource-based livelihoods, and a reworking of the material and symbolic make-up of intrahousehold power dynamics.

NOTES

1. See, for example, the collection in *The Ecologist*, Vol.16, Nos.2 and 3 (1986).
2. Figures from *Lampung Dalam Angka 1998* (Lampung in Figures), published by Kantor Wilayah Statistik Lampung (Regional Statistics Office of Lampung), Bandar Lampung, Indonesia.

3. The name of this village and its residents have been changed to protect privacy.
4. These issues are discussed in depth in Elmhirst [*1997, 2000*].
5. For a more detailed discussion of the highly controversial and authoritarian local transmigration programme, see Elmhirst [*1997*].
6. To put this in perspective, between 1986 and 1994, forest cover declined from 70 per cent to 30 per cent, while permanent cultivation increased from 25 per cent to 65 per cent of the land area. Commercial plantations occupy vast areas, between 10,000 and 85,000 hectares, of sugar cane, fast-growing timber, oil palm and rubber. All of these have been developed since the mid-1980s.
7. According to Soegiharto *et al.* [*1997*], who base their analysis on official census data, migrants from Lampung to West Java (where the main industrial zone is located) increased from 15,851 persons in 1980 to 84,290 in 1990.
8. For example, research by *Bakti Pertiwi* and the Jakarta Social Institute. Data reported here are from interviews conducted with staff from these non-government organisations.
9. Thus, they might be said to be striking a patriarchal bargain [*Kandiyoti, 1988*].

REFERENCES

Ahmed, I., 1998, 'The Employment Crisis in Indonesia: Key Issues and Major Challenges', BAPPENAS/ILO seminar on 'Vision of Employment Development in Repelita VII', Jakarta: BAPPENAS, 24 March 1998.
Elmhirst, R., 1997, 'Gender, Environment and Culture: A Political Ecology of Transmigration in Indonesia', unpublished Ph.D., University of London, Wye College.
Elmhirst, R., 1998, '"Krismon" and "Kemarau": A Downward Sustainability Spiral in a North Lampung *Translok* Settlement', paper presented to ICRAF and the 'Alternatives to Slash-and-Burn' research consortium, Bogor, Indonesia, May 1998.
Elmhirst, R., 2000, 'Negotiating Gender, Kinship and Livelihood Practices in an Indonesian transmigration area', in J. Koning, J. Rodenberg and R. Saptari (eds.), *The Household and Beyond: Cultural Notions and Social Practices in the Study of Gender in Indonesia*, London: Curzon Press, pp.208–34.
Firman, T., 1994, 'Labour Allocation, Mobility, and Remittances in Rural Households: A Case from Central Java, Indonesia', *Sojourn*, Vol.9, No.1, pp.81–101.
Goss, J. and B. Lindquist, 1995, 'Conceptualising International Labour Migration: A Structuration Approach', *International Migration Review*, Vol.29, No.2, pp.317–51.
Guest, P., 1989, *Labour Allocation and Rural Development: Migration in Four Javanese Villages*, Boulder, CO: Westview.
Hetler, C., 1989, 'The Impact of Circular Migration on a Village Economy', *Bulletin of Indonesian Economic Studies*, Vol.25, No.1, pp.53–75.
Hill, H., 1994, *Indonesia's New Order: The Dynamics of Socio-Economic Transformation*, St Leonards, NSW: Allen & Unwin.
Hilman Hadikusuma, 1989, *Masyarakat dan Adat-Budaya Lampung*, Bandung, Indonesia: Mandar Maju.
Hugo, G., 1982, 'Circular Migration in Indonesia', *Population and Development Review*, No.8, pp.59–84.
Hugo, G., 1992, 'Women on the Move: Changing Patterns of Population Movement of Women in Indonesia', in S. Chant (ed.), *Gender and Migration in Developing Countries*, London: Belhaven Press, pp.154–73.
Ilcan, S.M., 1994, 'Peasant Struggles and Social Change: Migration, Households and Gender in a Rural Turkish Society', *International Migration Review*, Vol.28, No.3, pp.554–79.
Kabeer, N., 1997, 'Women, Wages and Intra-Household Power Relations in Urban Bangladesh', *Development and Change*, Vol.28, pp.261–302.
Kabeer, N., 1991, *Gender, Production and Well-Being: Rethinking the Household Economy*, IDS Discussion Paper 288, Brighton: Institute of Development Studies.
Kandiyoti, D., 1988, 'Bargaining with Patriarchy', *Gender and Society*, Vol.2, No.3, pp.274–90.
Koppel, B. and J. Hawkins, 1994, 'Rural Transformation and the Future of Work in Rural Asia',

in B. Koppel (ed.), *Development or Deterioration? Work in Rural Asia*, London: Lynne Rienner, pp.1–46.

Lawson, V.A., 2000, 'Arguments within Geographies of Movement: The Theoretical Potential of Migrants' Stories', *Progress in Human Geography*, Vol.24, No.2, pp.173–89.

Leinbach, T. and J. Watkins, 1998, 'Remittances and Circulation Behaviour in the Livelihood Process: Transmigrant Families in South Sumatra, Indonesia', *Economic Geography*, Vol.74, No.1, pp.45–63.

Leinbach, T., J. Watkins and J. Bowen, 1992, 'Employment Behaviour and the Family in Indonesian Transmigration', *Annals of the Association of American Geographers*, Vol.82, No.1, pp.23–47.

Manning, C. and J. Hardjono (eds.), 1993, *Indonesia Assessment 1993 – Labour: Sharing in the Benefits of Growth?*, Political and Social Change Monograph No.20, Research School of Pacific Studies, Canberra: Australian National University.

Mather, C., 1982, 'Industrialisation in the Tangerang Regency of West Java: Women Workers and the Islamic Patriarchy', paper presented to conference on 'Women in the Urban and Industrial Workforce: South and Southeast Asia', University of the Philippines, Manila, 15–19 Nov. 1982.

Mills, M.B., 1997, 'Contesting the Margins of Modernity: Women, Migration and Consumption in Thailand', *American Ethnologist*, Vol.24, No.1, pp.37–61.

Pahl, J., 1989, *Marriage and Money*, London: Macmillan.

Pain, M. (ed.), 1989, *Transmigration and Spontaneous Migration in Indonesia*, Bondy, France: ORSTOM.

Prothero, R. and M. Chapman (eds.), 1985, *Circulation in Third World Countries*, London: Routledge & Kegan Paul.

Radcliffe, S., 1991, 'The Role of Gender in Peasant Migration: Conceptual Issues from the Peruvian Andes', *Review of Radical Political Economy*, Vol.23, No.3/4, pp.148–73.

Rigg, J., 1997, *Southeast Asia: The Human Landscape of Modernisation and Development*, London: Routledge.

Rigg, J., 1998, 'Rural–Urban Interactions, Agriculture and Wealth: A Southeast Asian Perspective', *Progress in Human Geography*, Vol.22, No.4, pp.497–522.

Rodenburg, J., 1995, *In the Shadow of Migration: Rural Women in North Tapanuli, Indonesia*, Leiden: Royal Institute of Linguistics and Anthropology.

Sage, C., 1996, 'The Search for Sustainable Livelihoods in Indonesian Transmigration Settlements', in M. Parnwell and R. Bryant (eds.), *Environmental Change in Southeast Asia: People, Politics and Sustainable Development*, London: Routledge, pp.97–122.

Silvey, R.M., 2000, 'Stigmatised Spaces: Gender and Mobility Under Crisis in South Sulawesi, Indonesia', *Gender, Place and Culture*, Vol.72, No.2, pp.143–61.

Soegiharto, S., Herawati, T. and Wagiran, 1997, *Migration Patterns and Migrant Characteristics in the Province of Lampung (1980 to 1990)*, final report to Centre for Research and Development, Ministry of Transmigration and Forest Squatter Resettlement, Alternatives to Slash-and-Burn (ASB) consortium, and Agency for Agricultural Research and Development, Ministry of Agriculture, Jakarta.

Stark, O., 1991, *The Migration of Labour*, Cambridge, MA: Basil Blackwell.

Tacoli, C., 1995, 'Gender and International Survival Strategies: A Research Agenda with Reference to Filipina Labour Migrants in Italy', *Third World Planning Review*, Vol.17, No.2, pp.199–212.

White, B., 1991, 'Economic Diversification and Agrarian Change in Rural Java, 1900 to 1990', in P. Alexander, P. Boomgaard and B. White (eds.), *In the Shadow of Agriculture: Non-Farm Activities in the Javanese Economy, Past and Present*, Amsterdam: Royal Tropical Institute, pp.44–69.

Wolf, D., 1992, *Factory Daughters: Gender, Household Dynamics, and Rural Industrialisation in Java*, Berkeley, CA: University of California Press.

World Bank, 1988, *Indonesia: The Transmigration Program in Perspective* (A World Bank Country Study), Washington, DC: World Bank.

World Bank, 1993, *The East Asian Miracle: Economic Growth and Public Policy*, Oxford: Oxford University Press.

Gender, Migration and Multiple Livelihoods: Cases from Eastern and Southern Africa

ELIZABETH FRANCIS

I. INTRODUCTION

For the last century, millions of rural households in eastern and southern Africa have depended on labour migration for their livelihoods. In colonial Kenya and Zimbabwe and in South Africa, Africans were pushed into overcrowded reserves. While some households became involved in commodity production, most depended heavily on labour migration to European farms, plantations, and towns and, across much of southern Africa, to the South African mines. Labour migrancy also became common in those countries, like Botswana, Tanzania and Zambia, which did not experience large-scale European settlement. Migrants' wages provided the investment capital for rural commodity production, while the experience of migrancy was a conduit for the flow of new ideas and social practices into rural areas. The literature on agrarian change in Africa has long recognised the importance of labour migration for rural livelihoods and has for an equally long time been concerned to understand its impact on rural life. This was a central issue for anthropological study concerned with social change in colonial Africa [*Eades, 1987; Moore, 1994*].

Steep falls in real wages and job prospects in urban areas since the 1970s have made migrants' remittances an unreliable, and often unsustainable, basis for rural livelihoods. Urban real wages in Tanzania fell by 83 per cent between 1974 and 1988. They continued to fall in the 1990s. Many urban dwellers responded by leaving wage employment for self-employment and urban farming [*Tripp, 1997*]. In Kenya, real wages for workers in public administration fell by almost a quarter between 1976 and 1989, while real wages in manufacturing fell by 42 per cent between the early 1970s and the

Elizabeth Francis, Development Studies Institute, London School of Economics. Her research in Kenya was funded by the Economic and Social Research Council, the Wenner-Gren Foundation, the Royal Anthropological Institute, Somerville College, Oxford and St Anne's College, Oxford. This study draws on material from the author's book, *Making a Living: Changing Livelihoods in Rural Africa* (London and New York: Routledge, 2000).

late 1980s [*Jamal and Weeks, 1993*]. In 1984, it was estimated that two-fifths of urban families in Zambia earned less than they needed to pay for their minimal needs [*Loxley, 1990*].

The downturn in urban economies has led to a slowing of migration from rural to urban areas and to return migrancy. Population growth rates in urban areas have dropped [*Becker et al., 1994; Baker and Pedersen, 1997; Potts, 1995, 1997; Satterthwaite, 1996*]. Changes in the South African mining industry have had repercussions throughout southern Africa. Falling gold prices and the restructuring of the industry have led to large-scale job losses. The yearly average total of miners employed on the South African gold mines fell from 477 397 in 1986 to 324,441 in 1992 [*Crush, 1995: 22*]. By 1999, in the face of a collapsing gold price, this figure may have fallen to around 280,000.[1] From the early 1970s onwards, mine labour employment in Zambia was devastated by the falling copper price [*Ferguson, 1999*].

While labour migrancy remains a critically important strategy, rural dwellers are increasingly diversifying their sources of livelihood [*Reardon, 1997*]. Reardon reviewed 23 case studies distributed over eastern, western and southern Africa and found that the average share of income earned in the non-farm sector was 45 per cent. It varied from 15 per cent to 93 per cent.[2] Diversified livelihoods may involve combining farming with wage labour, trading, selling services and producing commodities for sale. They also involve all the help, transfers, exchanges and information that people get access to through social networks. Most African rural households have long depended on more than one source of livelihood.

In this volume, de Haan, Brock and Coulibaly show how rural households in Mali have for decades combined farming with migrancy, local wage labour and sale of goods and services. Hampshire's research in Northern Burkina Faso reveals extensive, long-term diversification. There is also evidence that livelihoods are becoming increasingly diverse [*Heyer, 1996; Bryceson, 1999; Ellis, 2000; Francis, 2000*]. This study is concerned with the implications of these changes in livelihoods for gender relations and, conversely, the role which gender relations play in making possible, or impeding, people's ability to construct diversified livelihoods.

The emergence of migrant labour economies rested on reorganisations of household divisions of labour [*Murray, 1981; Bozzoli, 1983; Sharp and Spiegel, 1990; Moore and Vaughan, 1994*]. Before large-scale labour migrancy, women in a very large proportion of African societies bore the major responsibility for providing their households with food. Since the large majority of migrants were male, where migrant labour became widespread many women became dependent on men to earn the cash needed for household reproduction. Women, in turn, took on responsibility for holding rural households together in the absence of male relatives.

These changes were negotiated, and contested, in terms of the rights and responsibilities members of a household bore towards one another. They were also bound up with the impact of encounters with mission Christianity, European educational systems and urban life. There are parallels between these long-term changes in women's status and power and the findings of Samita Sen in Bihar, India.[3] Male migrancy in Bihar over the last century appears to have been associated with a long-term decline in women's position. The links between these two processes are not clear, but they are likely to be equally complex and uneven.

When migrancy no longer looks like a safe option, rights, responsibilities and powers must be renegotiated. Changes in the sources of livelihood raise new issues in rural households, and intensify old ones. Deteriorating economic conditions require households to construct livelihoods from many different resources and activities, throwing into question the material basis of household construction and maintenance, and also power relations within households. Changing opportunities for constructing a livelihood may alter the terms on which men and women try to get access to land, labour and money. The focus of domestic conflict lies around questions of who contributes to the household's livelihood and how much. Questions about the authority, rights and responsibilities these contributions confer are contentious. They may also increase pressures for households to fragment, or to reconfigure around relationships other than marriage. In the rest of the study, case studies from migrant labour economies explore the impact of changes in urban labour markets on household relations in rural areas. The case study from Kenya draws on my field research in Kisumu District. Case studies from Lesotho and South Africa draw on secondary literature.

There are some interesting contrasts between this case material and the research findings from West Africa reported by Hampshire and by de Haan, Brock and Coulibaly. Comparing these cases, one can see a spectrum, running from the Burkina Faso case study, through the Malian cases, to the case studies in this analysis, in which migrancy plays an increasingly central role in household reproduction. Hampshire's study of migrancy among the Fulani of Northern Burkina Faso describes a local economy in which migrancy has been significant only since the 1970s and is predominantly seasonal. Seasonal migrancy is, for those households which can spare the labour power, one option among others for improving livelihood security.

In the case material from Mali, de Haan, Brock and Coulibaly found a pattern common elsewhere in West Africa, where migration has been a significant component of household livelihoods for several generations. In one of the villages they studied, migration was predominantly rural-rural, to farms cultivated in other agro-ecological zones. Migrancy appeared to have made a positive contribution to livelihoods, particularly for the better off. In the other village, migration was predominantly seasonal, to rural and urban areas and was most common amongst middle-income households. Poorer households could not spare the labour power and better-off households had other options.

In contrast, in the settler economies of Kenya and Southern Africa, migrancy became a central component in the reproduction of the large majority of rural households from at least the 1930s onwards. Much of this migration was long-term. This kind of migrancy, and the importance of remittances for household reproduction, put pressure on people to renegotiate patterns of living, access to resources and rights and responsibilities. Changes in household reproduction were closely linked to a trend away from large, extended households (as described in the West African material) and towards much smaller domestic units. The authority of elders over younger generations often weakened. Gender relations became the central focus for negotiation. This is also the case for the upheavals and readjustments demanded by the declining availability of urban employment.

II. CASE STUDIES

Gender and Labour Migrancy in Western Kenya

Koguta Sub-Location lies in Kisumu District, in Nyanza Province. Kisumu is one of the home districts of the Luo people. Like many smallholder regions of Kenya, Luoland has been a source area for migrant labour since the early decades of this century. For the first half of the century, the priority of the colonial state in Kenya was to protect European farmers from competition from African producers and secure labour for the European farming sector. Labour supply was stimulated first by force and taxation. From the 1920s onwards, large numbers of men (and some women) began to migrate voluntarily, in search of cash incomes that became increasingly central to household reproduction.

In Luoland, several generations of men have spent the bulk of their working lives outside the district and many women also migrated for employment or to live with their husbands. By the time of my fieldwork in the late 1980s, return migration was an increasingly important trend, however, as it became more difficult to make a living in the towns. The dominance of labour migration in the regional economy undermined agricultural production over the long term. In the inter-war years, some households were quite heavily involved in production for the market, selling and trading maize and livestock. There were still some small-scale commercial farmers, mainly selling vegetables. But farms were small (mean holding size 4.2 acres, median 2.25 acres) and only a few households could provision themselves from farming alone.

Access to off-farm income was crucial for maintaining an adequate livelihood. For many households, this income used to come from remittances for migrants. Men dominated access to this resource. They migrated for work more often than women, while the work they found paid better than the opportunities open to women labour migrants. Few men were willing to allow their wives to undertake independent trading or cash cropping. For these reasons, women's spheres of authority and responsibility in the household had been eroded. When a household's livelihood depended on a man's ability to earn a wage, it tended to become more unified, under his authority. Ideological change both promoted and reflected these changes.

In common with many other migrant labour source areas, rural households in Kisumu had felt the impact of unemployment and falling real wages in the urban economy. Some households, by now a small minority, were able to rely on regular remittances or pensions. In these cases, most of the cash income came from the husband's remittances. Some men had given up trying to find work in the towns and had returned. They did casual work, or grew a few vegetables for sale. Many other households juggled different sources of income – low or intermittent remittances; small-scale trading; basket making; casual farm work; loans and gifts from relatives and friends – none of them very remunerative. In these households, the wife was often responsible for finding cash.

Households differed in the levels of their incomes; in the activities they relied on to build a livelihood; in the responsibilities of husbands and wives; in their power and authority; and in the terms on which they made decisions. To a great extent, these differences could be explained in terms of differences in livelihood. In households where the husband was a migrant and sent regular remittances back to his wife, she tended to be almost entirely financially dependent on him. Remittances usually covered the day-to-day costs of food and other needs, with money specifically allocated by the husband for larger outgoings like school fees.

Changes in Gender Relations

This model of the household as an economic unit, with a male breadwinner and dependent wife, was the one people reached for when asked about domestic divisions of responsibility and power. It seems to be quite different from gender relations in pre-colonial Luoland. Most societies in what later became Kenya were patrilineal and polygynous, with domestic relations resting on a house-property complex, as was a broad band of groups stretching from Sudan to South Africa [*Gluckman, 1950*]. Under a house-property complex, property was divided between the 'houses' formed by a man's wives. Oboler has argued that many ethnographic accounts of house-property complexes in eastern and Southern Africa have overlooked the rights over cattle they gave to women [*Oboler, 1994*].

Similarly, accounts of pre-colonial gender relations which I collected from informants in Koguta suggested that women had considerable authority over the fields allocated to them by their husbands. This was linked to the responsibility each married woman bore for feeding her own house.[4] Women's property rights had been eroded by pressures of demographic change, as land shortage encouraged men to unify their households' fields, usually under their own control.

Changing gender ideologies also undermined women's control over productive resources. The more unified, 'breadwinner model' represents an ideology of gender which has grown in importance in Kenya through a host of influences. Mission Churches promoted a Victorian, patriarchal ideal. Missions in British colonial Africa promoted ideals of domesticity, through their proselytising and through formal education. Missionaries preached the virtues of monogamous marriage, and a division of labour between male providers and female homemakers [*Gaitskell, 1990; Bowie, Kirkwood and Ardener, 1993*].

This preaching was reinforced by explicit state ideology, as well as by the encounter with contemporary Western models of the nuclear family. Bound up with these changes in ideology was the fact that avoiding poverty depended so greatly on a resource – paid employment – to which men dominated access. People who described themselves as 'modern' and 'educated' prided themselves on this arrangement, which sat uneasily with other self-consciously 'modern' ideals of gender equality. The 'breadwinner' model gave women a claim on men's resources, and men a justification for male control and female dependence. They were claims that were difficult to reconcile with the pressures undermining men's ability to play breadwinner.

In order to understand how these changes came about, we need to go back to the period when large numbers of Luo men began to migrate for work on European farms and plantations and in the towns of colonial Kenya. In the 1920s, most migrants were unmarried men, who played a minor role in agriculture. In the 1930s, as many of these early migrants continued to work outside after they got married, their labour began to be missed. There were many jobs on the farm and around the home that could not wait for their return.

Most importantly, somebody had to hold the rural household together and protect and manage the land. Women took on the roles of occupants of household land, validating and protecting men's rights in land, and *de facto* farm managers.[5] The kinds of responsibilities that women took on made it unlikely that labour migration would lead to agricultural growth. They became guardians of the land, rather than managers of a farm enterprise. Their control over resources was strictly limited. A woman was relied on to guard the land and livestock, but she would not be able to acquire or dispose of these resources. Nor would she have the money needed to intensify farm production. It was a recipe for stagnation.

Until real-wages in the urban economy began to rise in the 1950s, most Luo migrants did low paid work, first mainly on the European farms and plantations and later in the urban areas. A few men found better-paid work as teachers, clerks and other jobs in the administration, but they did not invest their wages in raising the productivity of their farms. Nor was there much difference in gender relations between these better-off households and the rest.

Most migrants' wives stayed at home, growing crops to feed their children, perhaps doing some seasonal trading to earn some cash. Men were too far away, for too long, to play much of a role in day-to-day household decision-making. I found no evidence that wives of better-off migrants were able to use remittances to expand farm production. Migrants had other priorities. The first migrants spent their wages on taxes, clothing and bridewealth. Migrants in better-paid work bought cattle and paid school fees. Most migrants would not have been able to afford to use their wages to expand farm production, but better-paid migrants were also reluctant to do so. Low prices, poor infrastructure and distance from markets limited the returns to farm investment, but the fact that there were some men living locally in the 1930s who expanded production on their farms suggests that these were not overriding problems.

Few migrants were willing to delegate financial responsibility and decision-making power to their wives. This reluctance stemmed from a deep-seated distrust of women's reliability. Nor could migrants easily ask their male kin living in Koguta to supervise their investments. The growing importance of the conjugal unit at the expense of relationships beyond the household made it difficult for relatives to intervene. Men's reluctance to send money to their wives for them to buy farm inputs could probably also be explained by their concern to put their earnings into investments, like cattle, that could not easily be converted into money when food was short.[6]

For migrants who thought they might be able to improve their position in life, money from outside became more important than farming. In the past, it was men who made investments. They acquired cattle and used them for bridewealth. More wives meant more land, more granaries and more children. Now that it was money and education that meant the difference between poverty and achieving a degree of upward mobility, men dominated access to these resources. So, despite the differences in wages earned by migrants, divisions of labour between migrant husbands and their wives were fairly uniform. Furthermore, men's reluctance to delegate financial responsibility to their wives was one of the factors that weakened the impact of differences in wage income on the rural economy and slowed down the growth of inequality.

After the Second World War, the loss of male labour began to be felt in farm production. Additionally, women began to withdraw labour from agriculture and spend more time earning the money they needed more and more to provision their households on a day-to-day basis. Output began to decline and Nyanza Province became a net importer of food crops. People now needed cash to buy the food they needed to live. Alongside this, new household goods – clothing, furniture, cooking pots – appeared in the markets of western Kenya. More and more of the essentials of daily life could only be found in the market.

The transformation of the basis of the household economy from the farm to cash income changed expectations about who was responsible for what in the household. It also intensified conflicts over the authority that this responsibility should confer. Who was responsible for making sure that people had enough to eat? Could a woman demand money from her husband to buy food, or was it her duty to find the money? Were clothing and school fees the man's responsibility? If so, did this mean that he should decide how much to spend, and when?

From the 1970s, these issues became even more contentious. Growing urban unemployment, and falling real wages, meant that many migrants could not afford to send back adequate remittances. When I carried out fieldwork in Koguta, in the late 1980s, I found that in some households, the growing need for cash was still met largely from remittances. Some of these households consisted of the wives and children of migrant men doing clerical or supervisory work. Others contained men who had retired from this kind of work with a pension.

In both types of household, the bulk of remittances tended to come from a single source and be received by one household member, the woman in the former case and the man in the latter. Either arrangement left the wife almost entirely financially dependent upon her husband and responsible for only the details of budgetary management. There was less pressure on her than there was on other women to engage in independent economic activity and they tended to play a very passive role in their household's financial affairs, simply receiving a regular allowance to cover food purchases. Household reproduction was fundamentally dependent on male earnings and women's role in reproduction was limited to providing domestic labour and a security function through their farm production.

Claims and Responsibilities

In households where men were the main source of money, women's growing financial dependence on their husbands meshed with a 'breadwinner' model of domestic relations, modifying the ideal of a good husband and proper division of responsibilities. In the years before the beginning of mass migrancy, women expected to have authority in their own spheres – to decide what to plant in their fields, how much time to spend working in them, whether to exchange some of the crop for sheep or goats, in other words, to be *wuon puodho* and *wuon agulu* (the person in charge of the cooking pot). When the cooking pot needed money to fill it, women became more dependent on their husbands. This dependence engendered a more unified model of the household, one that gave men ultimate responsibility for feeding their families and the authority that came with this responsibility. Trading carried a stigma of poverty and women who could avoid it prided themselves on not having to 'sit in the market'.

Claims about responsibilities are claims about authority, but they are also claims about duties. To acknowledge a man's authority and his financial responsibility was to demand that he fulfil his responsibilities. Recognising that statements about who had *teko* [the power to decide] over what involved making claims about responsibilities, as well as authority, problematises the descriptions people gave. My questions about *teko* could be taken to be an enquiry about what usually happened in the homes of JoKoguta, what should be happening in that particular home, or what was actually happening. Carrying out a household budget survey helped me to navigate through these uncertainties, by providing information on decisions about specific flows of money as they were made. These could be compared with more stereotyped descriptions given at other times.

However, the stereotypes were also revealing, because they showed discontinuities as well as continuities with (no doubt equally stereotyped) descriptions of the past. Women, it was said, continued to have *teko* over matters do with cooking and bringing up the children. Men still had *teko* over the acquisition and disposal of land and stock, over building and repairing the house, over children's marriages and bridewealth, over the organisation of funerals and over women's travel. They were attributed *teko* over the new issues posed by the cash economy. These included decisions about children's schooling or other major outgoings like furniture or medical fees. Male *teko* in farming, at least 'where the husband is interested in farming' also became the norm. In the stereotypical pattern, then, men took on new powers of decision making in a more unified household.

Whether the strategies of household members did conform to common goals was an issue lying just below the surface of discourse in Koguta. Women complained about husbands who did not support them and their children. Parents complained about uncaring children.

> My children stopped helping me somewhere between one and two years ago and my sons haven't visited for a year and a half. My daughter is working. She sometimes sends money, when she remembers, but my sons don't send anything ... It's not because they don't have enough money, it's because they don't want to. One of my sons is a driver, so he gets a good wage. Children in town despise their parents. They want to drink and smoke and they have their wives. Nowadays, children don't love their parents [Martha Odhiambo].

The ideal of an economically unified household was a claim on men's, and children's, resources, by other household members.

But the ideal could also justify restricting women's access to money. Many men felt ambivalent about their wives getting involved in any independent economic activity. While many women were turning to off-farm activities, men who were just about able to sustain their households' cash needs preferred not to give their wives scope for gaining an independent income. Although the wife of a migrant almost inevitably played a greater managerial role in the household than the wives of most non-migrants, a greater decision-making role for women was considered to pose a threat to the authority of men. This threatened the unity of the household and ultimately the whole social order.[7] It was a topic men, and women, quickly warmed to, using a discourse that combined fear of the supposedly chaotic potential of women's sexuality with a stress on the divided loyalties of a woman who has always married in from another clan.

> Luo men do not like their wives to trade, because they think that they will walk around (Judith Achieng).

> Women don't know how to look after money properly. They take the money, leave the house and wander around the country – to Mombasa, Nairobi – and they want to show off, for example, by buying clothes, but a man will want to use the money properly, for example, by paying school fees ...

> Very few Luo women trade because they are weak (compared with Kikuyu women). Their husbands are not willing for them to trade, because of what they might do when they are away from home, like going with other men. Some women are trusted and they do trade like this, but it is better for the woman to be older (Philip Ojwang).

> Luo men take their wives' trading income ... a Luo woman who travels around trading is called a prostitute (Mary Anyango).

> There are not many ways for a woman to get money around here. So when a man sees his wife with money, he gets suspicious (John Obala).

These comments convey a basic distrust of women – their loyalties and their sexuality. A woman was an outsider who had married in from another clan and she could rarely be completely trusted. She had a rampant sexuality that needed to be closely controlled. The best way to do this was to restrict her movements. A mobile woman was suspect, because movement and sexual laxity were practically synonymous[8] and both threatened the cohesiveness of her marital home. A woman with her own resources might leave her husband for another man. But as well as being based on fears of women's latent sexuality and unreliability, the wish to control the movement of women had its origins in the reorganisation of the sexual division of labour on which labour migration depended. For the rural household to be maintained, it was essential that someone remain to hold it together. Regular trading, with the continual travelling it required, threatened this pivotal role. The disquiet felt by many men at the thought of allowing women to get economic resources independently also stemmed from a fear of power struggles between a man and a 'strong woman' (*dhako ratego*). Relationships within households were sometimes described as a zero-sum game: 'When the man is up, the woman is down and when the man is down, the woman is up' (Margaret Ojwang). And the key to who was up or down was relative economic power: 'It is income that makes a woman strong. The thing that makes a man strong is that he does not want to be conquered in terms of getting income for the family' (Peter Olal).

As in any collection of beliefs, Luo gender ideologies are not all congruent and people voiced contrasting attitudes to domestic relationships in different contexts. When describing ideal domestic relationships, both sexes drew on the concept of *winjruok*. In a home where there was *winjruok*, men and women co-operated according to their expected roles. In the case of men this amounted to using their authority benignly. People often used the word 'co-ordination' when they spoke about this ideal in English. It could be achieved only if women accepted the authority of men. An overly assertive woman [*jalelo*] could undermine it. However, the ideal pattern of male 'breadwinner' and dependent wife was far from the necessities of survival in most households. Increasingly, what mattered was whether people could earn money locally, through trading, or farm labouring, or whether they could get access to food or cash from other people. All this meant that economic roles were becoming more variable. In some cases this amounted to a transformation of gender relations and household structures that challenged received gender stereotypes.

Where the husband kept up active contact, or even was resident, he found it extremely difficult to play the role of breadwinner. If a migrant, he often could not send remittances, or, if he was resident, there were few opportunities to earn a regular income. Some women had altogether lost access to their husbands' incomes, taking on full financial responsibility for themselves and their children. Where the man was a migrant, this de-coupling of the rural and urban components of households left the woman as the effective head of the household. It was a very vulnerable position. Unless she was a widow, the authority of a woman in this position was only provisional. Her husband might turn up at any time and intervene in her running of the household. She lacked the ability to acquire or dispose of the household's assets as she saw fit. It was a frustrating position to be in – responsibility without power. Most women put up with these frustrations because the alternative looked even worse.

The rate of divorce in Luoland has usually been thought of as low compared with some other ethnic groups in Kenya.[9] The main reason was believed to be the consequences of divorce for Luo women. These reflected the strongly patrilineal nature of rules governing descent, marriage and the inheritance of property. A woman married into the patrilineage. Bridewealth secured rights to her labour and over the children of the marriage. Women who left their husbands would expect to lose their children. They might also not get a warm welcome in their natal homes. A divorced woman was a burden to her family, both because they might be required to repay her bridewealth and because they would need to provide her with land. Nevertheless, marriages did break down. I was told that many women had left their husbands and 'gone to town' because they were not getting any support. There were a few such women in Koguta, as well as young women with children who had not married. In Kombewa, in the north of Kisumu

District, Odaga found women who had earned the epithet '*Odhi, oduogo*' ['she leaves and comes back again'], as they oscillated between an unsupportive husband and their already overstretched parents.[10]

If a returned migrant did take his responsibilities seriously, his options were very limited. Many older men had hoped to get support from their children when they retired, but not many did. Other returnees were younger men who had lost their jobs, or never found work, in town. The pressing need to find money led some men to try to intensify farm production and sell some of their crops. The effects of this strategy on gender relations resembled the changes that had been played out in better off households in the 1930s and 1940s.

The idea that it was right for a man who took his family's welfare seriously to take charge reflected the ideological legacy of labour migration, as well as the shrinking resource bases of rural households. A man living at home who tried to feed and clothe the household was a good husband and his involvement in farming was seen as a help to his wife, not an unjustified takeover of her sphere. Men who were involved in farm work described themselves, and were described by women, as 'helping' (*konyo*). *Konyo* gave entitlement to a role in farm decision-making and a share of crop income. It was then only a short step to full appropriation, which could be justified by the man's greater financial responsibilities and his ultimate ownership of the land. An older woman had more authority to resist full appropriation and work out a compromise. Her husband and she might share the crop income and the financial responsibilities. Younger women who were still seen as newcomers to the community, could not easily adopt that position. Yet even a joint strategy was often not sustainable.

If a man was not prepared to pull his weight, either by running the farm or by trying to find a steady income, the woman had to do so instead. When this happened, she took on more of the decision-making and the financial responsibilities.

When a man fell short of expectations about a 'good husband', his wife took on most day-to-day financial responsibilities by default. The choices open to a woman who took on these responsibilities were very narrow and the threat of a fall into extreme poverty was always in the background. It was difficult to build up capital for large-scale trading or sinking money into purchased inputs for the farm, because any profits needed to be used straight away to buy food. Even if she did manage to earn money, a woman became more vulnerable to extreme poverty as she got older and her health deteriorated.

The fact that most households could not hope to satisfy their need for food from farming threw up a contradiction. Many men hoped to provide their wives with enough money to allow them to remain at home, but this hope was becoming unrealistic for most people. Women needed to find money themselves. Although many men disliked the idea of their wives having their own money, they often changed their minds. Many women who traded commented that their husbands had not at first liked the idea, but then they saw that they could bring home money and they no longer objected. Women who traded regularly often had much more authority. Their command of a cash income gave them a greater voice (*duol*).

A *dhako ratego* played a much greater role in making strategic decisions (about buying and selling assets, about what crops to plant, about the children's schooling). Her voice carried most weight when her money financed these activities. This greater authority seemed to come both from sheer financial clout, and from the assertiveness that came along with an independent income:

> What the strong women have in common is that each has been in a position where she several times asked her husband for money to buy food and he replied that he didn't have any; that she should start making baskets. There aren't any women with husbands who don't help who have done nothing to get money. You will work hard only if you don't have money. Women who are like this are stronger than other women, but they can't be equal to their husbands – the husband should still be over his wife [Martha Odhiambo].[11]

Whether or not a woman could hope to make her own living depended very much on her age. It was difficult for younger women to spend most of their time trading or doing paid farm labour, because of their responsibilities for childcare. Younger women also had less land, because their husbands had inherited a subdivision of an already small piece of land. Older women might be freer to trade or do farm labouring, but their need for money was often greater, especially if they were paying school fees. Trading was a tiring and frustrating way to make a living and only a few women managed to become regular traders. Far more put a livelihood together by juggling several different activities.

To summarise, the growing gap between expectations of men and their ability to deliver led to tension and, sometimes, open conflict. It raised urgent questions about domestic responsibilities and authority. People responded to these questions in quite different ways. If the husband was a migrant, or if he was living at home without a regular income, the weakening of financial links between husband and wife raised difficult issues concerning the wife's response and her husband's right to control how she responded. Men were often reluctant for their wives to begin trading, seeing women's greater financial independence as a threat to their authority and to the unity of the household. The conflict might go in several different directions – the husband might acquiesce; or he might himself appropriate his wife's labour in order to grow crops for sale.

These outcomes were sustainable only through acknowledging interdependence and a willingness to negotiate. Whether they would be sustained could not be predicted from material conditions alone. The outcome involved questions of personality and agency. Where neither of these outcomes could be reached, the husband might disengage, leaving his wife responsible for supporting the household. Even then her authority was provisional and subject to challenge, either from him, or, more unusually, from close male kin in the patrilineage. Changes in the regional political economy, particularly the decline of the remittance economy, were making gender relations based on simple dependence unsustainable and were increasing pressures for negotiation and bargaining. Where this failed, the centrifugal pressures on the household as an economic unit were immense. What could hold it together was women's need for marriage to get access to land and to retain custody of their children.

Adhiambo Odaga provides an insightful analysis of similar processes in Kombewa sub-location, which is also in Kisumu District. Like Koguta, Kombewa is an impoverished area where low agricultural yields and land shortage make access to off-farm income critically important for survival. Odaga had some unexpected findings which revealed recent processes of agrarian change in the region. In an area of acute land shortage, she found that 47 per cent of the women in her sample did not cultivate their own plots in the short rains of 1986–87, or reduced their labour into them.[12] She also found that 42 per cent of her sample were not receiving remittances of any kind.

Taken together, these figures offer clues to the strains facing women and men and the strategies open to them. Odaga argues that women tend to invest their labour where they are likely to receive most return. The household head does not automatically control women's labour. In households where the husband is living at home, there are circumstances where this calculation will encourage women to co-operate with their husbands in a 'household strategy'. This may involve the woman working with her husband on the farm to produce crops for sale (over which he has decision-making power), or he may work the land while she engages in paid agricultural labour or trading in order to bring in a cash income. This is a risky strategy for the woman, because she cannot be sure that the crop income will be used for the benefit of the whole household. Where it fails, the woman may withdraw her co-operation and follow an individualised strategy of labouring or trading, rather than working on the household plot.

Women's ability to engage in income-earning activities depends on the access of other members of the household or compound to her labour, but this, in turn, is contingent on their providing her with some security. Because this part of the bargain is becoming increasingly difficult for men to fulfil, the material basis of household co-operation is being undermined. As in Koguta, interdependence is only one approach to constructing household livelihoods. Fragmentation is becoming increasingly common. In many respects, the pressures rural households were experiencing in western Kenya resembled the predicaments of households in Lesotho and the former 'homelands' of South Africa which have been losing access to urban employment.

Migrancy and Retrenchment in Lesotho

For the last century, life in Lesotho has been dominated by labour migration to the South African mines. Under pressure from shortages of labour and other resources for agriculture, Lesotho moved from being a prosperous, commercialised farming economy to an impoverished labour reserve. Murray in the 1970s and Ferguson in the 1980s studied the heavy dependence of Lesotho households on mine labour incomes.[13] Murray and Ferguson looked at the conflicts that arose between migrant husbands and their wives in Lesotho over the uses to which mine wages were put. Husbands and wives had different priorities. Male migrants were concerned to make sure that their incomes were used for long-term investments that could be used to support them and their households on their retirement ('building the house'). They assumed that women could finance day-to-day household reproduction from farming and occasional, small-scale income generating activities. They were opposed to their wages being used to pay for short-term needs. Because they were working so far from home, however, men found it difficult to control the ways in which women used cash.

Ferguson showed that men dealt with this problem by investing in cattle. Far from clinging irrationally to a 'bovine mystique', Lesotho men were following a rational investment strategy. It was generally accepted that cattle should not be sold off merely to meet day-to-day needs for money. The barrier between cash and cattle could be crossed readily only in one direction – from cash to cattle. So men's investments in cattle were relatively insulated from demands from the rest of the household for cash. They were a retirement fund. At the same time, men resisted the idea of their wives' earning money outside the household. According to the prevailing gender ideology, 'Sesotho tradition' dictated that a husband should provide for his wife. Men should control cash.[14] This ideology arose in response to centrality of migrant incomes to household economies in Lesotho.

More recently, families in Lesotho have had to deal with the impact of retrenchment in the mining sector. The numbers of Basotho mine workers in South Africa peaked in 1987, at 126, 000. Since then their numbers have fallen substantially.[15]

Sweetman [*1995*] looked at the impact of retrenchment on gender relations in the households of ex-miners. She found that ideologies of gender were resistant to people's changed circumstances. Before retrenchment, the dominant gender ideology constructed the household as a unit. People's behaviour often conformed to this model. Women who did not have access to land for farming had time on their hands that they could have used to earn an income. Instead, many conformed to a 'patriarchal bargain' in which wives got cash from their husbands, rather than earning a separate income. The activities which women did undertake (such as beer brewing) were ideologically constructed as an extension to 'reproductive' subsistence agriculture.

Sweetman found that people often held on to this division of responsibilities after retrenchment, even though the economic rationale for it had disappeared. Ex-miners' wives were more likely to be unemployed than to migrate for domestic work, for example. Where they did earn an income, they were restricted to low-paying informal sector activities. This ideological resistance sometimes masked tacit acceptance of changes to domestic divisions of labour. Women negotiated a delicate balance between increasing their contribution to the household's income without challenging prevaling gender norms.

This balancing act made it possible for women to take more responsibility for the houshold economy, while systematically devaluing their contributions. If the income-earning activities women took up were ideologically constructed as 'female', the money they brought in would also be ideologically constructed as limited to subsistence functions (rather than contributing to 'building the house'). This devalued it. The tendency for women's contributions to household income to be devalued has been found in other contexts.[16]

There were other changes. When men were in work, they tended to make decisions about how the wage was used. Now joint decision-making was becoming more common. Women were taking on more managerial involvement in household finances. However, joint decision-making did not necessarily imply greater equality. Women might devalue their own welfare and there might be conflict over priorities. Women's greater responsibilities might well amount only to 'stretching' the households' limited finances to meet subsistence needs. Equally important: 'As income goes down, the residue which remains may be viewed as more valuable than before and this, together with time to kill and the need for self-assertion, may lead to male input into previously "female" gendered areas of responsibility.'[17] Men had clung to the ideology of male headship and, ironically, were now much more able to make it a reality, because they were around to enforce it. It was too early to tell whether this state of affairs could persist in the face of the fact that many Basotho women were making a much greater financial contribution to their households. It is a good illustration of why domestic power relations are not a simple reflection of members' contributions to household finances.

Wright's research [1993] shows the strains this divergence between material contributions and domestic power relations can set up. Women were the main contributors to household finances in 38 per cent of her rural sample and 35 per cent of her urban sample. Yet men tended to monopolise available income, even when their wives had generated it. There were also strains because men and women had quite different priorities. Women wanted to spend more of the household's income in the household domain (on food, clothing, education, house-building), while men wanted to spend it in the public domain, such as drinking. They often demonstrated that they were still head of the family through violence. All this opens the question of whether marriage remains women's best option.

Wright does not want to overstate this. Non-marriage may be an outcome, more than a choice. Growing numbers of Basotho women were not marrying, but this can also be explained by a demographic deficit of young men and women's superior educational attainments. An explanation in terms of the undermining of the material basis of the household is plausible, however. It would suggest that the strains being experienced by men and women in Basotho households are similar to the processes undermining households in other parts of southern Africa.

Poverty and Household Instability in South Africa

South African research on household poverty emphasises how material insecurity can undermine people's ability to sustain domestic relations. Research carried out in QwaQwa in the 1980s explored the impact of relocation on the formation and composition of households and the stresses that often led households to fragment and reconfigure. John Sharp shows how a division opened up within QwaQwa between households with a reliable source of income (usually from wage employment in common South Africa) and those without [Sharp, 1994].

In the 1980s, the distinction between workers with stable employment and the marginalised majority hardened, partly due to state policy and partly due to the changing labour needs of employers. In the latter group (by far the larger), the relationship between men and women was 'turned on its head'. Previously, men in regular employment had taken on a breadwinner role, with gender relations governed by an ideology of female domesticity.

This is commonly found in African households whose livelihood depends on circulatory labour migration.

Just as Sweetman found in Lesotho, women with unemployed husbands took on more and more responsibility for finding money and it was activities open to women that became crucial. Many took up shebeening and street trading. Others were able to find work in the factories that were set up in QwaQwa at this time, mainly offering work to women. In Lesotho, women took on greater responsibility for household reproduction without challenging prevailing gender norms. In QwaQwa, these changes were much more explicit and men contested them. In 1984, unemployed men rioted and attacked women factory workers, chasing them away and protesting that the jobs should be given to men [*Bank, 1994*].

Marriage was becoming an unattractive option, for both men and women. Men were delaying marriage until they felt they could support a family. Masculinity was being redefined and played out in street gangs, rather than through taking on the role of provider. Women's growing reluctance to marry reflected their seeming inability to control resources within marriage. Marriage undermined their security [*Moore, 1994*].

When this happens, households do not necessarily fragment, but the form they take may change. Isak Niehaus's research in QwaQwa focused on the role of kinship in household formation in Phuthaditjhaba, the only town in QwaQwa [*Niehaus, 1994*]. Niehaus challenges the assumption that the erosion of marriage inevitably leads to the formation of matrifocal households. He found, instead, that sibling relations had become the key principle underlying the formation of households. There seemed to be material reasons for this development. Many women and men in Phuthaditjhaba were commuting long distances to work in the town of Harrismith, while we have also seen that many women worked in local factories. Long-distance migrancy, more often by men, was common.

Niehaus confirms Bank's findings about marital conflict over women's employment and men's inability to act as providers. He found a high rate of divorce and growing reluctance to marry. Instead, a significant number of households were formed around sibling relationships. Gender relations seemed more flexible in these households, making it easier for men to take on childcare for their working sisters. Sibling relationships, being more informal and flexible than marital relations, were more compatible with the demands of wage labour than the roles of husband and wife. Nuclear families were often worse off than extended-family based households. They had higher dependency ratios and often dispersed their dependent to other households. In other words, they could not maintain themselves independently of wider networks.

In QwaQwa, sibling-based households could be sustained by access to waged work or trading income for men and women. In the remote settlement of Dixie in Gazankulu (now Mpumalanga) in the eastern Transvaal, options were much more restricted and the consquences for household relations were profound. In this area, the only significant employers are nearby game reserves. Competition for these jobs is intense, and this is carried over into conflict between individuals and families within Dixie. Men compete for work on the game farms; women compete for access to men's wages through sexual liaisons.

This competition puts a strain on domestic life and makes marriages fragile. Households and household membership are unstable. All this threatens women's ability to support their children. Neglected wives may leave and return to their parents, or they may be 'chased away'. Even then, a woman's parental household may be unwilling to provide much support, unless she herself can earn a wage. In order to do so, she will have to leave her children in the care of relatives or older children, and these carers may neglect them. Children's insecurity is reinforced by their 'social invisibility'. Adults tend to give priority to their own needs [*Kotzé, 1992*]. They are also unreliable, because their own positions are so precarious. For many children, deprivation and insecurity are the norm.

Kotzé's research in Dixie concentrated on children's responses to this extreme insecurity. Because they could not count on any one adult to provide food and shelter, they had to find these for themselves. Toddlers were particularly vulnerable, but once children passed the age of four or five they developed long- and short-term strategies, building networks to replace their dependence on mothers and other relatives. Children worked at other homes in return for cash, food or accommodation. They also foraged in the veld. But the world of children in Dixie was not a Hobbesian nightmare. Children put a great deal of effort into building social bonds with other children. In contrast, children's allegiances to their families tended to be pragmatic and mobile. Their relationships with adults were shaped by high levels of mistrust. Here, then, households were unable to sustain the reproduction of children, who had to reproduce themselves through social co-operation.

Kotzé stresses that the reasons why households in Dixie were so unstable, particularly the competition for access to wages from the game reserves, were location-specific. However, it is worth thinking about why these conditions should have such devastating consequences. Kotzé suggests that the crucial factors were men's access to higher wages, coupled with women's ability to find employment (which made it possible for them to establish homesteads independently of men and to enter relationships with other women's husbands). Women needed access to men's wages in order to subsist, but they were free enough from male control to be able to compete for them with other women. So, if women were even more dependent on their husbands, they would not have the option of infidelity and households would perhaps be more stable.

In other contexts where men dominate access to wages, women redistribute these wages through selling them commodities. One reason why this did not happen in Dixie may be that there was not much scope for diversifying women's livelihoods. Villagers were resettled in Dixie from the game reserves in the early 1960s. Kotzé relates that they had access to grazing land (for stock which are, presumably, owned by men), but does not mention any agricultural activity. Dixie was also an isolated settlement, remote from markets, so there is not much scope for trading. So women's options were either to compete for men's wages, or to go off to work themselves.

CONCLUSION

In migrant labour economies, women who are dependent on migrants' earnings seem to have less domestic power than women who have to find money for themselves. This dependence chimes with 'breadwinner' ideologies of household relations that emerged in the colonial period. As fewer and fewer men can provide this kind of support, issues of responsibility for finding an income come to the fore. Husbands and wives may acknowledge interdependencies and negotiate, or they may disengage, as the household fragments.

Where men cannot deliver in terms of access to land or wage income, the material basis of the household may be undermined. When unemployed men appropriate their wives' incomes, marriage starts to look like a more unattractive option than some of the alternatives. Marriages break down, or women become reluctant to marry at all. These outcomes do not represent social breakdown. As in South Africa, women-centred households may become more common, as multi-generational groups share resources and domestic labour. However, residential instability is likely to become more common. The migrant labour economies of Kenya are likely to grow more similar to these regions, as agricultural land becomes scarcer and job prospects in urban areas diminish.

NOTES

1. *Mail and Guardian,* Johannesburg, 'No End to Miners' Pain', 9 June 1999.
2. See Reardon [*1997*]. Reardon defines non-farm income as income from non-farm wage employment, local non-farm self-employment and migration income. Farm income is income in cash and kind from cropping and livestock husbandry.
3. See Sen [*1992*], cited in de Haan's article on Bihar, in this volume.
4. See Hay [*1972, 1976, 1982*].
5. See Hay [*1982*]; also Hay [*1976*].
6. See Ferguson [*1992*].
7. See Parkin [*1978*].
8. Literally – *bayo,* to wander or walk around, also has sexual connations.
9. See Potash [*1978*].
10. See Odaga [*1990*].
11. All names are pseudonyms.
12. Rainfall in the region is bi-modal, with two growing seasons in the short rains (October to November) and long rains (March/April to May/June). Odaga found that cultivation was more intensive during the long rains.
13. See Murray [*1981*]; Ferguson [*1992*].
14. See Sweetman [*1995*].
15. See Crush and James [*1995*], Sweetman [*1995*], and Wright [*1993*], carried out studies of gender relations in the context of this retrenchment.
16. See Whitehead [*1984*].
17. See Sweetman [*1995: 36*].

REFERENCES

Baker, J. and P. Pedersen (eds.), 1997, *Rural–Urban Dynamics in Francophone Africa,* Uppsala: Nordiska Afrikainstitutet.
Bank, L., 1994, 'Angry Men and Working Women', *African Studies,* Vol.53, No.1, pp.89–113.
Becker, C, Hamer, A. and A. Morrison, 1994, *Beyond Urban Bias: African Urbanisation in an Era of Structural Adjustment,* London: James Currey.
Bowie, F., Kirkwood, D. and S. Ardener, 1993, *Women and Missions: Past and Present,* London: Berg.
Bozzoli, B., 1983, 'Marxism, Feminism and South African Studies', *Journal of Southern African Studies,* Vol.9, No.2, pp.139–71.
Bryceson, D., 1999, 'Sub-Saharan Africa Betwixt and Between: Rural Livelihood Practices and Policies', Leiden, African Studies Centre, Working Paper No.34.
Crush, J., 1995, 'Mine Migrancy in the Contemporary Era', in Crush and James (eds.) [*1995*].
Crush, J. and W. James (eds.), 1995, *Crossing Boundaries: Mine Migrancy in a Democratic South Africa,* Cape Town: IDASA/IDRC.
Eades, J., 1987, 'Anthropologists and Migrants: Changing Models and Realities', in J. Eades (ed.), *Migrants, Workers and the Social Order,* London and New York: Tavistock Publications.
Ellis, F., 2000, *Rural Livelihood Diversity in Developing Countries: Analysis, Policy, Methods,* London: Department for International Development.
Ferguson, J., 1992, 'The Cultural Topography of Wealth – Commodity Paths and the Structure of Property in Rural Lesotho', *American Anthropologist,* Vol.94, No.1, pp.55–73.
Ferguson, J., 1999, *Expectations of Modernity: Myths and Meanings of Urban Life on the Zambian Copperbelt,* Berkeley, CA: University of California Press.
Francis, E., 2000, *Making a Living: Changing Livelihoods in Rural Africa,* London and New York, Routledge.
Gaitskell, D., 1990, 'Devout Domesticity? A Century of African Women's Christianity in South Africa', in C. Walker (ed.), *Women and Gender in Southern Africa to 1945,* Cape Town: David Philip.

Gluckman, M., 1950, 'Kinship and marriage among the Lozi of Northern Rhodesia and the Zulu of Natal', in A.R. Radcliffe-Brown and D. Forde (eds.), *African Systems of Kinship and Marriage*, London: Oxford University Press for the International African Institute (reprinted London: Kegan Paul International, 1987).

Hay, M., 1972, 'Economic Change in Luoland: Kowe, 1890–1945', Ph.D. dissertation, Department of History, University of Wisconsin, Madison.

Hay, M., 1976, 'Luo Women and Economic Change During the Colonial Period', in N. Hafkin and E. Bay (eds.), *Women in Africa: Studies in Social and Economic Change*, Stanford, CA: Stanford University Press.

Hay, M., 1982, 'Women as Owners, Occupants and Managers of Property in Colonial Western Kenya', in M. Hay and M. Wright (eds.), *African Women and the Law: Historical Perspectives*, Boston, MA: Boston University African Studies Center.

Heyer, J., 1996, 'The Complexities of Rural Poverty in Sub-Saharan Africa', *Oxford Development Studies*, Vol.24, No.3, pp.281–97.

Jamal, V. and J. Weeks, 1993, *Africa Misunderstood, or Whatever Happened to the Rural–Urban Gap?* London: Macmillan.

Kotzé, J., 1992, 'Children and Family in Rural Settlement in Gazankulu', *African Studies*, Vol.51, No.2, pp.143–66.

Loxley, J., 1990, 'Structural Adjustment in Africa: Reflections on Ghana and Zambia', *Review of African Political Economy*, Vol.47, pp.8–27.

Moore, H., 1994, 'Households and Gender in a South African Bantustan', *African Studies*, Vol.53, No.1, pp.137–42.

Moore, H. and M. Vaughan, 1994, *Cutting Down Trees: Gender, Nutrition and Agricultural Change in the Northern Province of Zambia, 1890–1990*, Portsmouth, NH: Heinemann; London: James Currey; Lusaka: University of Zambia Press.

Moore, S.F., 1994, *Anthropology and Africa: Changing Perspectives on a Changing Scene*, Charlottesville, VA and London: University Press of Virginia.

Murray, C., 1981, *Families Divided: The Impact of Migrant Labour in Lesotho*, Cambridge: Cambridge University Press.

Niehaus, I., 1994, 'Disharmonious Spouses and Harmonious Siblings', *African Studies*, Vol.53, No.1, pp.115–35.

Oboler, R.S., 1994, 'The House-Property Complex and African Social Organisation, *Africa*, Vol.64, No.3, pp.342–58.

Odaga, A., 1990, '"Kech en Mar Pesa": Gender and Livelihood in a Western Kenya Sub-Location', D.Phil. thesis, University of Oxford.

Parkin, D., 1978, *The Cultural Definition of Political Response: Lineal Destiny among the Luo*, London: Academic Press.

Potash, B., 1978, 'Some Aspects of Marital Stability in Rural Luo Community', *Africa*, Vol.48, No.4, pp.380–96.

Potts, D., 1995, 'Shall We Go Home? Increasing Urban Poverty in African Cities and Migration Processes', *Geographical Journal*, Vol.161, No.3, pp.676–98.

Potts, D., 1997, 'Urban Lives: Adopting New Strategies and Adapting Rural Links', in C. Rakodi (ed.), *The Urban Challenge in Africa: Growth and Management of its Large Cities*, Tokyo: United Nations University Press.

Reardon, T., 1997, 'Using Evidence of Household Income Diversification to Inform Study of the Rural Nonfarm Labor Market in Africa', *World Development*, Vol.25, No.5, pp.735–47.

Satterthwaite, D.,1996, *The Scale and Nature of Urban Change in the South*, London: IIED.

Sen, S., 1992, 'Women Workers in the Bengal Jute Industry, 1980–1940: Migration, Motherhood and Militancy', Ph.D. thesis, University of Cambridge.

Sharp, J., 1994, 'A World Turned Upside Down: Households and Differentiation in a South African Bantustan in the 1980s', *African Studies*, Vol.53, No.1, pp.71–88.

Sharp, J. and A. Spiegel, 1990, 'Women and Wages: Gender and Control of Income in Farm and Bantustan Households', *Journal of Southern African Studies*, Vol.16, No.3, pp.527–49.

Sweetman, G., 1995, *The Miners Return: Changing Gender Relations in Lesotho's Ex-Migrants' Families*, Norwich: University of East Anglia, GAID, 9.

Tripp, A., 1997, *Changing the Rules: The Politics of Liberalization and the Urban Informal Economy in Tanzania*, Berkeley, CA: University of California Press.

Wright, C., 1993, 'Unemployment, Migration and Changing Gender Relations in Lesotho', Ph.D. thesis, University of Leeds.

Whitehead, A., 1984, '"I'm Hungry, Mum": The Politics of Domestic Budgeting', in K. Young *et al.* (eds.), *Of Marriage and the Market: Women's Subordination Internationally and its Lessons*, London: Routledge.

Abstracts

Introduction: Migrant Workers and their Role in Rural Change
ARJAN DE HAAN and BEN ROGALY

This introductory essay and collection concern the social processes within which migration for manual work is located and which are influenced by that same migration. Writing from detailed empirical studies of migration in South and South-east Asia and Africa, the contributors provide illustrations of the importance and normality of migration in rural life. The studies show that the relationship between migration and rural change is complex and context-specific. Migration has often increased inequality, but in many cases also supported vulnerable livelihoods. Much depends on the social processes at work, the ways in which identities shift through migration and how gendered ideologies of work are deployed and change. Labour mobility usually serves the interests of capital, not only in ensuring labour supply, but also, often, in dividing workers; however, the power of capital relative to labour is contingent. We conclude this essay by exploring ways in which public policies can support migrants by making migration less costly and more secure, through reducing discrimination and enhancing access to health care and other services.

Fulani on the Move: Seasonal Economic Migration in the Sahel as a Social Process
KATE HAMPSHIRE

Most research on short-term rural to urban migration and its impacts takes an economic approach and often emphasises negative aspects of migration, linking it synergistically with rural poverty in sending areas. Data from Fulani migrants in Northern Burkina Faso challenge this pessimistic view of short-term labour migration. Rather than a response to destitution, migration seems to be a useful way in which reasonably prosperous households can further enhance livelihood security. Moreover, factors not easily incorporated into a standard economic analysis, identity and village networks, emerge as being essential to the understanding of migration in this population. Finally, migration emerges as a highly dynamic process, which an ahistorical, static framework of analysis fails to capture.

Migration, Livelihoods and Institutions: Contrasting Patterns of Migration in Mali
ARJAN DE HAAN, KAREN BROCK and NGOLO COULIBALY

Migration is a common and essential livelihood strategy in the risk-prone environment of Sahelian West Africa. But migration is not a passive reaction to economic and environmental forces. Patterns of movement are determined by context-specific and complex dynamics, mediated by social networks, gender relations and household structures. IDS-based research on sustainable livelihoods illustrated this in two locations in Mali: in a village in the Sahelian dryland with different and gendered migration patterns of various ethnic groups; and exceptional patterns in the Sudano-Sahelian cotton region with extensive and long-lasting engagement in small cocoa and coffee plantations in Côte d'Ivoire.

Brokered Livelihoods: Debt, Labour Migration and Development in Tribal Western India
DAVID MOSSE, SANJEEV GUPTA, MONA MEHTA, VIDYA SHAH, JULIA REES and the KRIBP PROJECT TEAM

Seasonal labour migration is an increasingly important aspect of rural livelihoods in tribal areas of Western India. Such migration can no longer be viewed merely as an adjunct to an essentially agrarian way of life, but has to be seen as integral to the coping, survival and livelihood strategies of tribal farming families. Rural to urban migration is often viewed as a consequence of environmental crisis in which migrants are 'ecological refugees' [*Gadgil and Guha, 1995*] are forcibly displaced by processes of deforestation, soil erosion, water scarcity, land fragmentation, declining agricultural productivity and population increase. While increasing pressure on a fragile resource base has indeed contributed to widespread failure to meet subsistence needs among tribal households, the research discussed in this study shows that the forces leading to migration are as much to do with the *social* relations of dependency and indebtedness which subsistence failure entails, as with ecological decline. The problem is not so much one of declining production, as of systems of usurious moneylending, labour contracting and exploitation. The social experience and consequences of migration are far from uniform, but shaped by class and gender. For a minority of Bhil households migration offers positive opportunities for saving, investment and meeting contingencies. For the poorer majority, migration is a defensive coping strategy covering existing debts and extreme economic vulnerability. In combining unequal and individualised income accrual with the need for joint livelihood strategies, migration has a major impact on intra-household relations.

Seasonal Migration and Welfare/Illfare in Eastern India: A Social Analysis
BEN ROGALY, DANIEL COPPARD, ABDUR RAFIQUE, KUMAR RANA, AMRITA SENGUPTA and JHUMA BISWAS
Over 500,000 people are regularly engaged in seasonal migration for rice work into southern West Bengal. This study analyses social processes at work in the interactions between employers and workers, and the welfare/illfare outcomes. Group identities based on religion and ethnicity are strengthened through the experience of migration and deployed by some migrants to make this form of employment less degrading. In West Bengal seasonal migration can involve practical welfare gains. Importantly, an informal wage floor has been put into place and managed by the peasant union allied to the largest party in the Left Front regime. However, the costs and risks of migration remain high.

Migration and Livelihoods in Historical Perspective: A Case Study of Bihar, India
ARJAN DE HAAN
Whereas other contributions in this volume focus on contemporary migration, this study explores the role migration has played over a long period of time, in western Bihar, India. By doing so, it reinforces one of the central themes in this volume, regarding the importance of migration for livelihoods: this case study challenges the assumption that migration would be a recent phenomenon, and argues that to understand the history of this area one needs to take account of the complex interaction between migration and development. Migration has been a livelihood strategy for many groups within the area, and the study explores how migration has been caused by and in turn influences poverty and livelihoods for men and women, and how these relationships have changed over time.

Daughters and Displacement: Migration Dynamics in an Indonesian Transmigration Area
REBECCA ELMHIRST
This study considers the ways 'indigenous' people have responded to the constraints and opportunities posed by the Indonesian government's transmigration programme in North Lampung, Sumatra. Migration is of increasing importance to the livelihoods of this group; particularly that involving the employment-related movement of young, unmarried women to the export-oriented factory zones of West Java. Female migration is notable in the context of customs confining unmarried women to the house, and negating their working in agriculture. The study explores how factory migration has developed, drawing on fieldwork conducted in 1994 and during the economic crisis in 1998, and focusing on the shifting terrain of intrahousehold power relations and decision-making in the community. The key to understanding migration dynamics in this area is the emergence of a culturally-conditioned social network linking village and city. This network has altered the terms upon which migration decisions and remittance practices are made, and may have cushioned.

Gender, Migration and Multiple Livelihoods: Cases from Eastern and Southern Africa
ELIZABETH FRANCIS
Focusing on Kenya, Lesotho and South Africa, this study examines the social impact in migrant-labour source areas of dramatically reduced employment prospects in urban areas. It considers the implications for rural livelihoods and the role which gender relations play in making possible, or impeding, people's ability to construct diversified livelihoods. When livelihoods change, gendered rights, responsibilities and power must be renegotiated. Husbands and wives may acknowledge interdependencies and negotiate, or they may disengage. Marriages may break down, or women become reluctant to marry at all, as the material basis of the household is undermined. These outcomes do not represent social breakdown, but residential instability is likely to become more common.

Index

Printed in the United States
by Baker & Taylor Publisher Services